DECISION MAKING IN THE WORKPLACE

A UNIFIED PERSPECTIVE

DECISION MAKING IN THE WORKPLACE

A UNIFIED PERSPECTIVE

Edited by

LEE ROY BEACH
UNIVERSITY OF ARIZONA

LEA LAWRENCE ERLBAUM ASSOCIATES, PUBLISHERS
1996   Mahwah, New Jersey

Lawrence Erlbaum Associates, Inc., Publishers
10 Industrial Avenue
Mahwah, NJ 07430

Cover design by Gail Silverman

Library of Congress Cataloging-in-Publication Data

Decision making in the workplace : a unified perspective / edited
    by Lee Roy Beach
            p. cm.
    Includes bibliographical references and index.
    ISBN 0-8058-1992-4 (cloth : alk. paper).-- ISBN 0-8058-1993-2
(pbk. : alk. paper)
    1. Decision-making. 2. Corporate culture. 3. Decision-making
(Ethics) 4. Imagery (Psychology) I. Beach, Lee Roy.
HD30.23.D3825   1996
658.4'03--dc20   96-5263
                                                                    CIP

Books published by Lawrence Erlbaum Associates are printed on acid-free paper, and their bindings are chosen for strength and durability.

Printed in the United States of America
10 9 8 7 6 5 4 3 2 1

CONTENTS

Preface   vii

1 **Image Theory, the Unifying Perspective**
   Lee Roy Beach and Terence R. Mitchell   1

2 **Why a New Perspective on Decision Making is Needed**
   Lee Roy Beach and Raanan Lipshitz   21

3 **Job Search and Job Selection**
   Cynthia Kay Stevens and Lee Roy Beach   33

4 **Career Decisions**
   Cynthia Kay Stevens   49

5 **Supervision and Job Satisfaction**
   Byron L. Bissell and Lee Roy Beach   63

6 **Why Employees Quit**
   Thomas W. Lee   73

7 **Audit Decisions**
   Lee Roy Beach and James R. Frederickson   91

8 **Screening of Clients by Audit Firms**
   Stephen K. Asare   101

9 **Organizational Culture and Decision Making**
   Kristopher A. Weatherly and Lee Roy Beach   117

10 Mitigating Cultural Constraints
on Group Decisions
Kenneth R. Walsh   **133**

11 Imagination and Planning
Lee Roy Beach, Helmut Jungermann,
and Eric E. J. De Bruyn   **143**

12 Designing Marketing Plans and
Communication Strategies
Christopher P. Puto and Susan E. Heckler   **155**

13 Consumer Decisions Involving
Social Responsibility
Kim A. Nelson   **165**

14 Image Compatibility and Framing
Kenneth J. Dunegan   **181**

15 Image Theory and
Workplace Decisions: Challenges
Terry Connolly   **197**

Author Index   **209**

Subject Index   **215**

PREFACE

This collection of essays reflects two important truths about decision making. First, many of any decision maker's most important decisions are made in the context of his or her work. Second, it is difficult to appreciate the commonalties in these decisions without a unifying perspective with which to examine them. Therefore, all of the chapters in this book examine workplace decisions using the same perspective, a descriptive theory of decision making called image theory.

The plan is quite straightforward. To avoid repeating it in every chapter, chapter 1 contains a description of image theory. Because this perspective and its vocabulary is assumed in everything that follows, the reader is advised to become familiar with it before going on to the chapters that use it to examine workplace decisions.

Readers familiar with the expected value perspective on decision making may find chapter 1 a bit startling—because it describes a very different way of thinking about decisions. Chapter 2 explains why the status of expected value has decreased so markedly in applied decision research, and why alternative views such as image theory are replacing it.

The analysis of workplace decision making begins with chapter 3, which examines decisions about job search and job choice. Then, because at the beginning of one's worklife anyway, jobs often dictate career decisions rather than the other way around, chapter 4 builds on chapter 3 to examine career choice.

It is one thing to decide to take a particular job; it is another thing to decide to stay in that job. Chapter 5 examines how the discrepancy between what one expects from one's supervisor and what one actually gets from that supervisor influences satisfaction with one's job, satisfaction with the organization, and intentions to leave the organization. Chapter 6 carries the theme further to examine a wide range of conditions that lead employees to quit their jobs and begin searching for new ones.

The next two chapters examine a specific kind of workplace decision as an illustration of the kind of analysis and research afforded by the image theory perspective. Chapter 7 looks at the way an agent of an auditing firm goes about deciding whether the firm should accept business from a particular client, and then about whether there is material error in that client's financial statements. Chapter 8 presents empirical evidence supporting part of the analysis in chapter 7, that is, how an audit firm makes a decision about whether to accept a potential client's business.

Chapters 9 and 10 examine the effects of organizational culture on decisions. Chapter 9 describes the problems that arise when managers try to make changes that are counter to the culture. It also provides a way of measuring culture and describes some studies that support the central theses. Chapter 10 examines how cultural constraints may prevent suggestions of new and original solutions to problems and argues that a technology exists that can mitigate these constraints.

Chapter 11 introduces a new topic. It looks at planning, in particular the role of scenarios in designing workable plans. It also examines what happens when plans begin to go awry—when it becomes clear that the plan will not produce the desired results.

Chapters 12 and 13 look at consumer decision making. The idea is that by understanding how consumers make decisions, the organization and its employees can better anticipate customer needs. Chapter 12 describes marketing plans and communication strategies from the viewpoint of the person who designs them. Chapter 13 focuses on decisions made by individual consumers, in this case by consumers concerned about environmental issues (so-called "green decisions"), and then shows how this concern influences their product choices.

Chapter 14 examines a persistent problem for managers, the problem of framing decisions properly, and then explains how those frames influence subsequent decisions. The discussion is perhaps more theoretical than those that precede it, but the problem is so important that it warrants the rigorous treatment it is given. This analysis also bears upon the broader usefulness of the image theory perspective for understanding workplace decisions, and thereby provides an appropriate introduction to the final chapter in the book.

The final chapter, chapter 15, is a critique of image theory and its usefulness in thinking about human decision making. Although the critique is generally sympathetic, it is nonetheless insightful, pointing out that there is much to be done if the theory is to fulfill the promise implied by the earlier chapters. It is an appropriate ending to the book, lest we think that the successful application of the theory in the earlier chapters signifies that the battle is won in trying to understand decision making in the workplace.

ACKNOWLEDGEMENT

I would like to thank Todd Marble for his assistance with preparation of this volume.

— Lee Roy Beach

IMAGE THEORY,
THE UNIFYING PERSPECTIVE[1]

Lee Roy Beach
University of Arizona

Terence R. Mitchell
University of Washington

The purpose of this chapter is to describe the conceptual foundation, image theory, on which subsequent chapters are built. We begin with an informal description of image theory, followed by a more formal presentation. Finally, we describe the main themes and findings of research on image theory.

BACKGROUND

It seems to us that in the 40 years of behavioral decision research there have been four major changes in how unaided decision making is viewed (Beach, 1993). The early view, which still prevails in some quarters, was that all decisions were properly regarded as (usually risky) choices that, after extensive evaluation of the available options, resulted from maximization of expected utility or some normative variation thereof.

The first change came from recognition that evaluation seldom is extensive and virtually never is exhaustive (e.g., Simon, 1955; Tversky & Kahneman, 1974). This means that maximization in any strict sense does not occur and that two courses are open to decision theorists. One is to insist that decision makers are flawed, that they should be trying to maximize

---

[1]Portions of this chapter are from "Broadening the Definition of Decision Making: The Role of Pre-Choice Screening of Options," by L. R. Beach, 1993, *Psychological Science, 4*, pp. 215–220. Copyright Cambridge University Press, 1993. Reprinted with the permission of Cambridge University Press.

expected utility in the manner prescribed by the normative model (Pratt, 1986), and that they need help to do it properly (Humphreys, Svenson, & Vari, 1983). The other is to attempt to understand what decision makers are trying to do rather than presuming that maximization is the sole aim and then prescribing how it should be done.

The second change came from recognition that decision makers possess a variety of strategies for making choices, many of which have aims quite different from maximization of expected utility (e.g., Beach & Mitchell, 1978; Payne, 1976). This finding reinforces the second of the two options just cited —namely, that there may be more value in attempting to understand what decision makers are trying to do and how they are trying to do it, than in prescribing what they should be trying to do and how they should be trying to do it.

The third change, which is still happening, comes from recognition that choices occur relatively rarely and that past experience usually provides ways (policies, habits) of dealing with problems. Decisions are required primarily when failure of these solutions occurs or is anticipated, and even then the decision may not be merely a choice of the best option from some delineated set of options (e.g., Beach & Mitchell, 1987, 1990; Klein, 1996). This places decision making squarely within the broader context of cognitive science, suggesting that it is a backup for the times when experience fails to provide adequate guidance for how to behave. Because people are conscious of much of their decision making, and perhaps less conscious of their use of past experience, they tend to overestimate the role that decision making plays in guiding their moment-to-moment activity.

The fourth change, which is an extension and consolidation of the previous three, comes from recognition that when decisions occur they occur in steps. The first step consists of *screening out unacceptable options,* and the second step consists of *choosing the best option* from among the survivors of screening (Beach, 1990; Beach & Mitchell, 1987; Beach & van Zee, 1992; van Zee, Paluchowski, & Beach, 1992). That is, the first step focuses on what is wrong with options, and the second step focuses on what is right—and the two steps are accomplished in quite different ways. It is here that image theory enters the picture: Choice, and the many strategies by which it can be accomplished, is a familiar topic in the decision literature, but screening is less so. Moreover, the standards used in screening, as well as the factors that give utility to the outcomes of options in choice, have received very little attention in the behavioral decision literature. Image theory is an attempt to address both screening and the origins of standards, and choice and the origins of utility within the same theoretical framework.

IMAGE THEORY

The Informal Version

The decision maker is seen as an individual working either alone or as a member of a group. Most decisions are, in fact, made in concert with others, be it a spouse, a friend, a business colleague, or whomever. In all cases the decision maker has to make up his or her own mind, and then differences of opinion are resolved in some manner that depends upon the dynamic of the group. That is, groups are not seen as decision makers per se; they are merely the contexts within which individual members' decisions become consolidated to form a group product (Beach, 1990; Beach & Mitchell, 1990: Davis, 1992).

Each decision maker possesses values, morals, ethics and so on that define how things should be and how people ought to behave. Collectively, these are called *principles,* "self-evident truths" about what he or she (or the group) stands for, about the goals that are therefore worthy of pursuit, and about what are and what are not acceptable ways of pursuing those goals. Often these principles cannot be clearly articulated, but they are powerful influences on decisions. They run the gamut from the general ("One should tell the truth") to the specific ("We should focus on our customers") to the compelling ("I must always set a good example for my employees"), and, as Freud tried to tell us, they are not all especially admirable or rational. Whatever one's principles, they are the foundation of one's decisions: Potential goals and actions must not contradict them, or those goals and actions will be deemed unacceptable. Moreover, the utility of decision outcomes derives from the degree to which they conform to and enhance the decision maker's values.

In addition to principles, the decision maker has an agenda of goals to achieve—some are dictated by his or her principles ("Because I believe in salvation through acceptance of Jesus Christ, and because I am my brother's keeper, I must seek to convert unbelievers and thereby save their souls") and some are dictated by problems encountered in the environment, although principles still influence how these problems are addressed ("Because my boss refuses to promote me, I must find a new job—but I still wouldn't feel right about leaving without giving proper notice"). Each goal has an accompanying plan for its accomplishment, either formulated at the time the goal is adopted or soon afterward. The various plans for the various goals must be interleaved in time, and it must be possible to coordinate them so that they do not interfere with one another.

Decisions are about the adoption of goals and plans (and, more rarely, principles). Adoption of a potential goal or plan is based, first of all, on whether it is reasonable. That is, does it cause trouble for other goals or plans; is it counter to relevant principles? If the answer is "yes", how unreasonable is it? If it is not too unreasonable, it might work out all right, but there is some point at which it simply is too unreasonable and must be rejected.

If this initial screening process involves only one potential goal, and if it is judged to be not unreasonable, it is adopted, and the decision maker moves on to considering a plan for accomplishing it. If the process involves multiple potential goals, and only one survives screening, the situation is similar to starting with only one option and having it survive screening—it is adopted and a plan is sought. However, if more than one potential goal is involved, and if more than one survives screening, something must be done to break the tie. This may involve raising the standard and rescreening until there is only a single survivor, or it may involve comparing the relative merits of the multiple survivors and choosing the best of them.

Adoption of a plan is similar to goal adoption except that it also involves imagining (forecasting) what might result if the plan were implemented; in particular, would it attain its goal? The ability to imagine what will happen as a result of plan implementation also serves to monitor the progress of implementation once the plan is adopted ("If I continue with this plan do I foresee goal attainment?"). If progress is not foreseen, the plan must be rejected and either revised or replaced. If a failing plan cannot be revised sufficiently, or if a promising replacement cannot be found, the goal itself must be reviewed and revised or replaced.

Of course, this all assumes that a decision actually must be made. In familiar situations the decision maker may be able to call on past experience to deal with whatever is demanded. That is, if he or she has encountered this situation (or one very like it), successful behavior used then can be used now; it becomes a policy for this sort of situation. If the past behavior was unsuccessful, it at least provides information about what not to do this time and may even suggest alternatives that can then be considered for adoption through the decision process outlined earlier.

The existence of policies reminds us that decisions are not made in a vacuum; they occur as points in an ongoing flow of experience. The decision maker usually knows about the events that led up to the present and has some grasp of the constraints upon what can be done. Without such historical knowledge in which to embed decisions, they would not make sense at all. Moreover, this knowledge helps simplify the decision process by defining a subset of the decision maker's principles, goals, and plans as relevant to the current decision, thus reducing the cognitive effort that would be involved if they all were used as criteria for decision making

The Formal Version

Having informally outlined the thinking behind image theory, we turn now to a more formal presentation:

Images.   Image theory assumes that decision makers use three different schematic knowledge structures to organize their thinking about decisions. These structures are called *images*, in deference to Miller, Galanter, and Pribram (1960), whose work inspired image theory. The first of the three is the *value image*, the constituents of which are the decision maker's principles. These are the imperatives for his or her behavior and the behavior of the organization to which he or she belongs; they serve as rigid criteria for the rightness or wrongness of any particular decision about a goal or plan. Principles serve to internally generate candidate goals and plans for possible adoption, and they serve as criteria for decisions about adoption of externally generated candidates.

The second image is the *trajectory image*, the constituents of which are previously adopted goals. This image represents what the decision maker hopes he, she, or the organization will become or achieve. Goals can be concrete, specific events (getting a particular job), or abstract states (being successful). The goal agenda is called the trajectory image to convey the idea of extension, the decision maker's vision of the ideal future.

The third image is the *strategic image*, the constituents of which are the various plans that have been adopted for achieving the goals on the trajectory image. Each plan is an abstract sequence of potential activities, beginning with goal adoption and ending with goal attainment. The concrete behavioral components of plans are called *tactics*. Tactics are specific, palpable actions intended to facilitate implementation of an abstract plan to further progress toward a goal. A second aspect of plans is *forecasts*. A plan is inherently an anticipation of the future, a forecast about what will happen if certain classes of tactics are executed in the course of plan implementation. However, it need not be inflexible; it can change in light of information about the changing environment in which implementation is (or might be) taking place. Therefore, it serves both to guide behavior and to forecast the results of that behavior. By monitoring these forecasts in relation to the goals on the trajectory image, the decision maker can evaluate his or her progress toward realization of those goals. Realization of goals realizes the decision maker's principles—how things should be and how people ought to behave—which are the driving force behind the whole process.

Decision Framing.   A frame is that portion of the decision maker's knowledge that he or she brings to bear on a particular situation in order to endow that situation with meaning. As such it involves using information about the present situation to probe memory. If the probe locates a contextual memory that has features virtually the same as those of the current situation, the situation is said to be *recognized.* Recognition serves two ends: First, it defines the image constituents that are relevant to the situation at hand; second, it provides information about goals that previously have been pursued in this situation and about the plans, both successes and failures, that have been used to pursue them.That is, not all of the image constituents are relevant to the present situation, and in order to reduce cognitive load, it is prudent to limit decision deliberation to those that are relevant. The relevant constituents of each of the three images constitute the working images for the decision at hand. (Of course, if for some reason the situation is misrecognized or misframed, the decision maker may later find that the working images did not contain the appropriate subsets of constituents. Thus, for example, principles that were deemed irrelevant to the decision may, in retrospect, turn out to have been relevant; therefore, the goals and plans that seemed acceptable at the time should not in fact have been adopted.)

In addition, part of the recognized contextual memory is the goal(s) that was pursued before, as well as the plan(s) that was used to pursue it; if the same or a similar goal is being pursued this time, the previously used plan may either be used again (in which case it constitutes a policy) or form the foundation for a new plan (which then must pass through the adoption process described next).

Two Kinds of Decisions, Two Decision Tests.   There are two kinds of decisions, *adoption decisions* and *progress decisions.* Both kinds of decisions are made by using either or both of two kinds of decision tests, the *compatibility test* or the *profitability test.*

Adoption decisions also can be divided into two kinds: *screening* decisions and *choice* decisions. Adoption decisions are about adoption or rejection of candidate goals or plans as constituents of the trajectory or strategic images. (Principles also are adopted, but this is infrequent for adults.) Screening consists of eliminating unacceptable candidates. Choice consists of selecting the most promising candidate from among the survivors of screening.

Progress decisions consist of assaying the fit between the forecasted future if implementation of a given plan is continued (or if a particular candidate plan were to be adopted and implemented) and the ideal future, as defined by the trajectory image. Incompatibility triggers rejection of the plan and the adoption of a substitute (often merely a revision of the old plan that takes into consideration feedback about the environment). Failure to find a promising substitute plan prompts reconsideration of the plan's goal.

The compatibility test screens adoption candidates on the basis of the compatibility between the candidate and the three images. Actually, the focus is on lack of compatibility in that the candidate's incompatibility (I) decreases as a function of the weighted sum of the number of its violations of the images, where the weights reflect the importance of the violation.

Violations are defined as negations, contradictions, contraventions, preventions, retardations, or any similar form of interference with the realization of one of the image's constituents. Each violation is all-or-none. The decision rule is that if the weighted sum of the violations exceeds some absolute rejection threshold, the candidate must be rejected; otherwise it must be adopted. The rejection threshold is that weighted sum beyond which the decision maker regards the candidate as incompatible with his or her or the organization's principles, existing goals, and ongoing plans.

The compatibility test can be formally stated as follows:

$$I = \sum_{t=1}^{n} \sum_{c=1}^{m} W_c V_{tc}; \; V_{tc} = -1 \text{ or } 0, \tag{1}$$

where incompatibility, I, is zero when a candidate has no violations, and decreases (i.e., is more and more negative) as the number of violations increases; t is a relevant attribute of the candidate; c is a relevant image constituent; V is a violation of image constituent c by attribute t of the candidate; and W is the importance weight for each of the relevant image constituents.

Thus, whereas the violations are all-or-none (-1 or 0), violations of some constituents may count more than others (W_c) and incompatibility is a continuous scale between 0 and $-mn$, where m is the number of relevant image constituents and n is the number of the candidate's relevant attributes (an attribute may violate more than one image constituent).

When more than one adoption candidate survives screening, the decision maker must choose the best from among them. This is accomplished using the profitability test, which is actually not a single decision mechanism but a collective term for the individual decision maker's repertory of strategies for making choices and the mechanism for selecting one of those strategies for use in a particular choice.

The profitability test is the Beach and Mitchell (1978) strategy selection model as formalized by Christensen-Szalanski (1978, 1980). The underlying assumption is that each decision maker possesses a repertory of choice strategies and that the strategy that is selected for the task at hand depends upon three categories of variables: characteristics of the choice, characteristics of the environment in which that choice is embedded, and characteristics of the decision maker.

Characteristics of the choice include choice unfamiliarity, ambiguity, complexity, and instability (the goal of the choice changes over time). Characteristics of the environment involve irreversibility of the choice, whether the choice can be made iteratively (a little bit at a time with feedback about how things are going), the significance of the choice, accountability for a choice that fails to yield acceptable outcomes, and the time and money constraints on the choice process. Characteristics of the decision maker consist of knowledge of different choice strategies (the breadth of his or her repertory), ability to actually use the strategies, and motivation to expend the least possible time, effort, and money on the choice while still doing a satisfactory job.

The decision maker's repertory contains strategies that range from the aided analytic (e.g., decision analysis) to unaided analytic (e.g., balancing pros and cons in one's head) to unanalytic strategies (e.g., imagining possible scenarios if one were to choose this or that option, coin tossing, asking others for advice).

As formulated by Christensen-Szalanski (1978, 1980), the metalogic of the selection process is cost–benefit, with benefit in terms of subjective expected utility (SEU). Where the utility of choosing a strategy that will produce what ultimately will prove to be a correct choice is designated U_c, the utility of a correct choice is U_i, the cost of using a given strategy is $\bar{U}_e$, the subjective probability of a given strategy yielding a correct choice is P_c, and the subjective probability of that strategy yielding an incorrect choice is $1 - P_c$.

Assume that the decision maker believes that, in general, the more analytic a strategy, the higher the probability that it will yield a correct choice (an assumption for which there is evidence). Also assume that the decision maker believes that more analytic strategies cost more time, effort, and money to use. It follows then that the subjective expected utility for any strategy in the decision maker's repertory is:

$$SEU = P_c\,U_c + (1 - P_c)\,U_i$$
$$= P_c\,(U_c - U_i) + U_i, \tag{2}$$

which is the equation for the straight line in Fig. 1.1. The abscissa is a probability scale, and the ordinate is a utility scale. The straight line indicates the range from the utility of an incorrect adoption choice, U_i, which is seen by the decision maker to be virtually assured at $P_c = 0$, to the utility of a correct choice, U_c, which is seen as virtually assured at $P_c = 1.00$. (U_i is a positive number in the figure, but it could be negative if an incorrect choice would result in a loss.) The slope of the line is U_c minus U_i, the difference between the utility of a correct choice and the utility of an incorrect choice.

The decision maker's repertory of choice strategies can be arrayed along the abscissa of the figure according to the decision maker's subjective probabilities, P_c, that they will yield a correct adoption choice in the present situation. On the left will be the simple, nonanalytic, strategies, perceived to have low P_c, and on the right will be the aided analytic strategies, perceived to have high P_c. The unaided–analytic strategies will be somewhere in the middle. Of course, which strategies are in the array and where they lie on the P_c scale depends on the individual decision maker's repertory and his or her beliefs about the efficacy of each strategy.

Assuming that the strategies are arrayed from nonanalytic to aided–analytic, and assuming that the perceived cost of using them varies from quite low for the nonanalytic strategies to quite high for aided–analytic strategies results in the increasing cost curve, $\bar{U}_e$, in the figure. (The cost curve could be illustrated as a negative utility, but doing so complicates the rather simple picture that this method permits.)

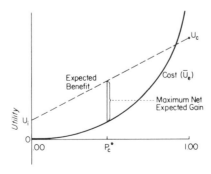

FIG. 1.1. The relationship between cost and benefits in determining the optimal probabilty level (P_c*) for the strategy to be selected for a decision. From Christensen-Szalanaski, Copyright 1978 by Academic Press Inc., reproduced by permission of the author and the publisher.

The straight line in the figure represents the expected utility (benefit) of each strategy on the probability scale. The cost curve represents the cost of using each of those strategies. The difference between the expected benefit line and the cost curve represents the net expected gain of using each strategy. The optimal strategy to use on the adoption choice at hand is the one for which the net expected gain is maximal—which is the strategy that lies closest to the point at which the difference between the line and the curve is largest. This point, called P_c^*, is the optimal probability level for the choice strategy to be used. That is, using a strategy with a higher P_c would increase the expected benefit, but it would increase the cost more, thereby reducing the expected benefit. Using a strategy with a lower P_c would decrease the cost, but it would decrease the expected benefit more, thereby reducing the net expected benefit. Of course, the decision maker may not have a strategy in his or her repertoire with a P_c that corresponds to P_c^*, in which case he or she should select the strategy whose P_c most nearly corresponds to P_c^*.

At the moment the strategy is selected, the decision maker need not take into account anything about the individual adoption candidates that have survived screening by the compatibility test. The utilities of making a correct (U_c) or incorrect (U_i) choice derive from the decision environment rather than from the adoption candidates themselves. Thus, irreversibility, significance, accountability, and constraints on time and money induce a high utility for making a correct choice and a low (or negative) utility for making an incorrect choice. The decision maker's job is to balance these perceived utilities against the probabilities and costs associated with each of the choice strategies in his or her repertoire in order to select the strategy that offers the best hope of success at the lowest cost in resource expenditure.

RESEARCH ON IMAGE THEORY

Until very recently image theory research has focused almost exclusively on screening and choice. Because the more recent developments are featured in subsequent chapters of this book, the following discussion will describe the earlier work.

Studies of Screening

The research on screening has used decision options (entry level jobs, rental rooms, or condominia) that are easily understood and evaluated by the college students who generally have served as research subjects. The strategy has been to present an array of options to the subjects with instructions to examine the options' characteristics and form a short list of options (i.e., to screen and to form a choice set). Then they are instructed to choose the best option from the short list. Depending on the experiment, the dependent variables are the way in which information is examined, ratings of the options' attractiveness before or after screening but before choice, the computed incompatibility (sum of weighted violations, sometimes with unit weights) of the options that do or do not survive screening, or subjects' choices of the best options.

Violations. Beach and Strom (1989) asked subjects to assume the role of a newly graduated student looking for a job. The job seeker's preferences about 16 job characteristics were provided so that all subjects were using the same standards. Then each subject was presented with an array of jobs. The 16 characteristics of each job were presented on 16 successive pages of a small booklet, one booklet for each job. Each characteristic violated or did not violate one of the job seeker's 16 standards. The characteristics violated different standards for different jobs, and each job had a different number of violations. The subject read the information on the successive pages in a booklet until he or she decided either to reject the job or to save it for his or her short list. By noting where the subject stopped looking through a particular booklet, the experimenters were able to calculate the numbers of violations and nonviolations that had been observed before the subject made the decision to reject the option or to place it in the choice set.

The results showed that rejection of options regularly occurred after observation of roughly 4 violations; this is the rejection threshold. There was no comparably constant number of nonviolations for the decision to place options on the short list. In fact, nonviolations played virtually no role at all in screening except to stop information search when no violations were observed (or else a perfect option never would be accepted because the search for violations would never stop).

The Beach and Strom (1989) study supported the image theory position that screening relies almost exclusively on on violations of standards. It also demonstrated the existence of a rejection threshold and suggested that for a specific decision task the rejection threshold may remain fairly constant.

The relationship between violations and acceptability also has been tested in a different context (Rediker, Mitchell, Beach, & Beard, 1993). Here MBA students role-played a business executive who was seeking to diversify his or her company's services by acquiring a computer firm. The students read detailed descriptions both of the acquiring company and of a number of different computer firms that were options for acquisition. Then they rated each computer firm in terms of its acceptability for further consideration for acquisition (i.e., for its acceptability for inclusion in the choice set). A correlation of $r = -.95$ was obtained between rated acceptability and the number of violations by each computer firm of the acquiring company's stated acquisition criteria (standards).

This relationship between violations and rated acceptability, and between either or both of them and rejection or retention of options, has been found in all of the studies we have done, thus supporting the primacy of violations in screening and revealing the existence of a rejection threshold (Beach, Smith, Lundell, & Mitchell, 1988; Beach & Strom, 1989; Potter & Beach, 1994a, 1994b; Rediker, et al., 1993).

Screening Versus Choice. In a series of experiments, van Zee, Paluchowski, and Beach (1992) examined what happens to the information used in screening when the time comes to choose the best from among the survivors on the short list. Here the options were rooms to rent. The subjects were told that a friend was moving to town to attend the university and wanted the subject to find a room for him or her. A list of the friend's criteria for a room (standards) was provided.

For each of 5 rooms, subjects were given the kind of information one might find in a newspaper classified advertisement. They screened out the unacceptable rooms on the basis of this information and formed a short list. Then they were given additional information about the survivors, information that normally would be obtained by actually visiting the short-listed rooms. Then they chose a room for their friend.

Depending on the experimental or control condition in which they were placed, subjects made ratings of the acceptability of the options either before screening or after screening but before choosing a room. As expected on the basis of the Beach and Strom (1989) results, the ratings made prior to screening precisely reflected the sums of the options' violations of the friend's standards, and both the rated acceptability and the sums of the violations (incompatibility) precisely predicted which options were rejected and which were retained for the short list. However, when ratings were made after screening but before a choice was made, something quite unexpected was found. These prechoice ratings reflected only the information obtained about the surviving options after they had been screened. That is, the information used to screen the options did not have much impact on the evaluations that preceded choice (correlations between .02 and .07), whereas information received after screening and prior to choice had a major impact on prechoice evaluations (correlations between .67 and .86). As one subject remarked, it was as though the information used in screening had been "used up" and had nothing to contribute to the choice.

At first this result might not seem strange. All of the options that survive screening must be fairly similar because they all violated few enough standards to make it into the choice set. However, recall that violations (and nonviolations) are defined as all-or-none; an option's characteristics fail or do not fail to meet the standards; how much they fall short of (or exceed) those standards is not part of the equation. However, some characteristics fall short of or exceed the standards more than others. Thus, if the screening information were carried forward and used with what is learned later, some other option might be chosen. In short, by not carrying the screening information forward, and by basing their choices exclusively on the new information, subjects might end up making suboptimal choices. Indeed, van Zee (1989, Experiment 7) showed that this can happen.

As might be expected, this screening effect was not obtained if subjects did not screen the options prior to choice (i.e., if they were given five options and all of the information about them and merely asked to make a choice). However, when they screened, the effect was very robust. Repeating the old information along with the new information during the choice made no difference. Reminders to use all available information also made no difference. Directing the subject to evaluate the options for screening but having the actual screening done by "the friend" made no difference. Even changing the task to one in which the options are potential acquisitions by a business firm (using the task from Rediker, et al., 1993), made no difference. Indeed, interviews of subjects revealed that they simply regarded the screening information as having little further interest when it came time to evaluate the rooms in order to make a choice.

The results of these experiments, together with the results described previously, make an important point. Subjects apparently regard screening and choice as distinctly different tasks, and because they do so, they regard the information requirements as different. Information used in screening is regarded as uniquely relevant to that task. Then when the survivors are considered prior to choice, they all are regarded as roughly equal in attractiveness until the new information shows them to be otherwise. In fact, about 95% of the subjects choose as the best option the one that is most attractive in light of the new information alone.

That screening and choice are regarded as quite different tasks is even more clearly shown by the results of a study by Potter and Beach (1994a). Here some of the subjects were given descriptions of time-share condos and asked to rate their attractiveness, and then to screen them to create a choice set. Other subjects were given the descriptions of the condos and asked to rate their attractiveness and then to choose the best from among them—omitting the screening step. The unique feature of the experiment was that in both cases each description contained information about the probability (.75 or .25) that the time-share condo would be available when the decision maker wanted to use it.

For the screening group, the image theory prediction was that the availability information would be used as a standard, with .25 being regarded as a violation and .75 being regarded as a nonviolation. This means that when the probability is .25, the result is simply an increase in the number of violations. In the data, this increase would be evidenced as an additive combination of the violation of the availability standard and the violations of other standards when attractiveness ratings are subjected to an analysis of variance: significant main effects for availability and number of other violations, but no interaction.

For the choice group, the image theory prediction was that availability would be used as a probability in the manner prescribed by the expected utility choice model (Raiffa, 1968). That is, the utility of the options' attributes would be discounted by the probability (.25 or .75,) that the condo would be available. Discounting would be evidenced as a multiplicative combination of availability and the options' utilities when attractiveness ratings are subjected to an analysis of variance: significant main effects for availability and utility and a significant interaction.

The results showed that the availability information was used differently in the two tasks and in the ways predicted by image theory. In screening, availability was treated as simply another standard and violation of it by an option counted as merely an additional violation. In choice, however, availability was treated as a probability and used to multiplicatively discount the attractiveness of the options. As with the results reported above, these results suggest that screening and choice involve distinctly different processes and that image theory appears to describe these processes rather well.

Having established that uncertainty about future events is used differently in screening than in choice, Potter and Beach (1994a) went on to examine the implications for screening of other forms of imperfect information for screening. Given the task of finding a rental room for a friend, subjects in one experiment were familiarized with 8 standards for selecting a room. Then they were presented with descriptions, some of which obviously had missing information relevant to some of the 8 standards. It was found that subjects treated each piece of missing information as though it were a violation, simply adding it to the other violations in evaluating the incompatibility of the option.

In a second experiment, subjects were not familiarized with a common set of standards. Instead, descriptions of options contained information relevant to 4 to 10 standards, and there was great variety among those standards. It was found that the greater the paucity of information, the more inclined subjects were to reject options, but paucity counted only about half as much as actual violations of standards in determining whether an option would be screened out. A possible interpretation of this result is that paucity of information may lower subjects' rejection thresholds.

Together, these last two studies underscore the image theory contention that screening is a conservative process that serves to prevent options of dubious or unknown quality from entering the choice set. By holding violations constant, options for which expected information is absent or options for which little is known in general are less likely to be admitted to the choice set than are options for which more complete information is available.

Having gathered evidence for violations as the focal point for screening, for the existence of a rejection threshold, for screening and choice being different processes, and for the conservative nature of screening, our attention turned in another direction. This time the question asked concerned what happens when the prototypical chain of events does not occur. That is, the picture presented earlier is of an array of options being screened and a choice made from among the survivors. But what if this is not the sequence?

The Empty Choice Set.   Potter and Beach (1994b) investigated what happens when subjects screen and then move on to make a choice only to find that the options in the choice set have become unavailable. For example, suppose that the job applicants on an employer's short list all have taken other jobs, or that all of the condos one was going to examine before choosing have already been sold.

In the first experiment, 35 subjects screened and chose rooms to rent for a friend. When they were ready to choose the best room from among the survivors of screening, subjects were told that all of the rooms already had been rented. Then they were asked whether they would prefer to search for new rooms or to go back and reconsider the rooms they had previously rejected. Of the 35 subjects, 31 (89%) said that they would prefer to start all over with a new set of options.

Other subjects were presented with the same task except that they were told that there were no new rooms to be had. Because the friend needed a room, they would have to rescreen the rooms that they had rejected in order to arrive at a new short list. The subjects rated the importance of the various standards for selecting a room, both before performing the first screening and before rescreening.

Results revealed that two things happened. On the one hand, subjects rated the standards a little lower when they rescreened. On the other hand, subjects also raised their rejection thresholds a little when they rescreened. That is, they both lowered their standards and became more tolerant of violations of those standards. Apparently, by making these two small compromises, subjects were able to avoid having to make a large compromise in either their standards or in their tolerance of imperfection. A control group that rated the standards before and after screening, with nothing being said about unavailability of the surviving options, gave nearly identical ratings both times, implying that the lowering of standards by the first group was in response to the request to rescreen the rejected options. In fact, the standards remained lowered even the next day. In a related study, Potter (1991) found that the degree to which standards get lowered is contingent upon the circumstances. When the standards are dictated by the decision maker's job, they are lowered less than when they are the decision maker's own private standards.

Implications.   The major implication of these results is that screening plays a far more important role in decision making than previously has been appreciated. It is not just a way for the decision maker to reduce the work of decision making, nor is it merely preliminary to the real business of decision making—choice. Note that choice, at least as it is modeled in decision theory (e.g., Payne, Bettman & Johnson, 1994; Raiffa, 1968; Svenson, 1979), always selects something, albeit the best of whatever is in the choice set. Screening ensures the quality of choice by admitting to the choice set only those options that meet the decision maker's standards. In fact, it may screen out all options, leaving an empty choice set, thus preventing the choice of a bad option.

The evidence suggests that screening and choice differ, not only in their focus, but also in the cognitive processes involved. Not only does screening turn solely on violations of decision standards (Beach, Smith, Lundell, & Mitchell, 1988; Beach & Strom, 1989; Potter & Beach, 1994a, 1994b; Rediker, et al., 1993; van Zee, et al., 1992), but decision makers regard screening and choice as so different that they may not carry information forward from the one to the other (van Zee, et al., 1992). Moreover, they may use the same information in different ways in the two tasks: Information about an option's availability, used additively in screening, was used multiplicatively in choice (Potter & Beach, 1994b).

If screening were simply a method of cutting down the number of options that must be evaluated prior to choice, subjects should be relatively indifferent about returning to the previously rejected options when the options in the choice set turn out to be unavailable. Instead, subjects overwhelmingly prefer to start all over with a new set of options rather than rescreen the rejected options. When forced to rescreen, subjects both raise their rejection thresholds and lower their standards. These adjustments of the threshold and the standards during rescreening may serve to reduce the distastefulness of having to form a choice set from previously rejected options and of having to choose the "best" from among these low-quality options.

Recall that in addition to differentiating between screening decisions and choice decisions, and describing mechanisms for them, image theory differentiates between decisions about options and decisions about progress toward goal achievement, again describing the mechanisms. In contrast to choice theories, which have nothing to say about what happens after an option has been chosen, image theory's inclusion of progress decisions within the same theoretical framework as decisions about screening and choice serves to link the latter with decision implementation and the process by which progress toward goal attainment is monitored and kept on track. That is, image theory encompasses prechoice screening decisions, choice decisions, and postchoice implementation and progress decisions. In doing so, both the theory and the research it has generated suggest a broader, more inclusive view of decision making than is afforded by a narrow focus on choice alone.

Studies of Choice

Because these studies are relatively old and have been discussed in detail elsewhere (Beach, 1990), we will present a rather bare-bones account aimed mostly at showing that the strategy selection model has been empirically tested and found to be a fairly satisfactory description of the choice process (i.e., the profitability test).

McCallister, Mitchell, and Beach (1979) examined the effects of decision environment characteristics on strategy selection. In a series of experiments using both practicing managers and business students, they found that increases in irreversibility, significance, and accountability resulted in increases in subjects' willingness to use more costly, analytic strategies.

Huffman (1978) had students read scenarios of business decisions and indicate how much time, effort, and analysis was appropriate for each choice. Both decision environment variables (irreversibility, significance, and accountability) and decision task variables (familiarity and complexity) influenced strategy selection. As environment and task stringency increased, subjects' willingness to expend resources increased.

Christensen-Szalanski (1978) manipulated the payoffs for correct choices and the costs for executing various strategies and found that strategy selection changed in the manner predicted by the profitability test. That is, as the payoffs for correct choices increased, subjects used more analytic strategies. In a second series of studies, Christensen-Szalanski (1980) examined the effects of time limits on choice, thus extending the theory. In addition, he studied the effects of individual differences in decision makers' ability to execute strategies and found profound effects on strategy selection and choice accuracy.

Smith, Mitchell, and Beach (1982) extended Christensen-Szalanski's work on time limits, showing that sometimes limits can lead to selection of more analytic strategies for less important decisions. This result had not been anticipated by the theory; it expanded Christensen-Szalanski's (1980) treatment of time limits. The most important result, however, was that time constraints affect decision makers' confidence in their ability to execute strategies properly, and thereby influence strategy selection. In addition, it was found that decision makers have a range of implementation times and subjective probabilities associated with each strategy in their repertoires rather than the specific (point) times and probabilities assumed in the original model. This means that decision makers have more latitude in strategy selection than we originally thought.

Finally, using accounting students as subjects, Waller and Mitchell (1984) examined the significance of the decision for both the decision maker and the organization, as well as the effects of the decision maker's uncertainty about whether an accounting process was or was not in control. The independent variables were high and low ambiguity about whether the process is out of control as well as high and low significance of the decision in terms of how its results will affect the subject's compensation and the financial status of the organization. The dependent variable consisted of five accounting information systems that varied in the amount of analysis required, their accuracy, and their cost. Results showed that greater ambiguity about the process and greater significance of the choice resulted in selection of more analytic information systems (strategies). These results are congruent with the model as originally proposed.

CURRENT STATUS OF IMAGE THEORY

The foregoing discussion brings us up to date on image theory as it stood when planning for this book began. The purpose of succeeding chapters is to strengthen the described empirical support, to identify changes that must be made, and to move the theory in new and interesting directions. Moreover, these chapters are aimed at trying to generalize the theory to an ever broader range of real-world decision situations, testing its adequacy at each point. The goal is twofold: to use the theory to gain insight into how decisions are made in the workplace and to use the workplace as a laboratory for testing, revising, and extending the theory.

REFERENCES

Beach, L. R. (1990). *Image theory: Decision making in personal and organizational contexts*. Chichester, UK: Wiley.

Beach, L. R. (1993). Four revolutions in behavioral decision theory. In M. Chemers & R. Ayman (Eds.), *Leadership theory and research: Perspectives and directions* (pp. 271–292). New York: Academic Press.

Beach, L. R., & Mitchell, T. R. (1978). A contingency model for the selection of decision strategies. *Academy of Management Review, 3*, 439–449.

Beach, L. R., & Mitchell, T. R. (1987). Image theory: Principles, goals and plans in decision making. *Acta Psychologica, 66*, 201–220.

Beach, L. R., & Mitchell, T. R. (1990). Image theory: A behavioral theory of decisions in organizations. In B. M. Staw & L. L. Cummings (Eds.), *Research in organizational behavior* (Vol. 12, pp. 1–41), Greenwich, CT: JAI Press.

Beach, L. R., Smith, B., Lundell, J., & Mitchell, T. R. (1988). Image theory: Descriptive sufficiency of a simple rule for the compatibility test. *Journal of Behavioral Decision Making, 1*, 17–28.

Beach, L. R., & Strom, E. (1989). A toadstool among the mushrooms: Screening decisions and image theory's compatibility test. *Acta Psychologica, 72*, 1–12.

Beach, L. R., & van Zee, E. H. (1992). Close, but no cigar: A reply to Pitz. *Journal of Behavioral Decision Making, 5*, 22–23.

Christensen-Szalanski, J. J. J. (1978). Problem-solving strategies: A selection mechanism, some implications, and some data. *Organizational Behavior and Human Performance, 22*, 307–323.

Christensen-Szalanski, J. J. J. (1980). A further examination of the selection of problem-solving strategies: The effects of deadlines and analytic aptitudes. *Organizational Behavior and Human Performance, 25*, 107–122.

Davis, J. H. (1992). Some compelling intuitions about group consensus decisions, theoretical and empirical research, and interpersonal aggregation phenomena: Selected examples, 1950–1990. *Organizational Behavior and Human Decision Processes, 52*, 3–38.

Huffman, M. D. (1978). *The effect of decision task characteristics on decision behavior* (Tech. Rep. No. 78-16). Seattle, WA: University of Washington, Department of Psychology.

Humphreys, P., Svenson, O., & Vari, A. (Eds.). (1983). *Analysing and aiding decision processes*. Budapest: Akademiai Kiado.

Klein, G. (1996). *Sources of power: The study of naturalistic decision making*. Manuscript submitted for publication.

McAllister, D., Mitchell, T. R., & Beach, L. R. (1979). The contingency model for selection of decision strategies: An empirical test of the effects of significance, accountability, and reversibility. *Organizational Behavior and Human Performance, 24*, 228–244.

Miller, G. A., Galanter, E., & Pribram, K. H. (1960). *Plans and the structure of behavior.* New York: Holt, Rinehart & Winston.

Payne, J. W. (1976). Task complexity and contingent processing in decision making: An information search and protocol analysis. *Organizational Behavior and Human Performance, 16,* 366–387.

Payne, J. W., Bettman, J. R., & Johnson, E. J. (1994). *The adaptive decision maker.* Cambridge, UK: Cambridge University Press.

Potter, R. E. (1991). *When unacceptable options become unavailable: The effects of job role and organizational compromise.* (Tech. Rep. No. 91-5). Tucson: University of Arizona, Department of Management and Policy.

Potter, R. E., & Beach, L. R. (1994a). Decision making when the acceptable options become unavailable. *Organizational Behavior and Human Decision Processes, 57,* 468–483.

Potter, R. E., & Beach, L. R. (1994b). Imperfect information in pre-choice screening of options. *Organizational Behavior and Human Decision Processes, 59,* 313–329.

Pratt, J. W. (1986). Comment. *Statistical Science, 1,* 498–499.

Raiffa, H. (1968). *Decision analysis: Introductory lectures on choices under uncertainty.* New York: Addison-Wesley.

Rediker, K. J., Mitchell, T. R., Beach, L. R., & Beard, D. W. (1993). The effects of strong belief structures on information processing evaluations and choice. *Journal of Behavioral Decision Making, 6,* 113–132.

Simon, H. A. (1955). A behavioral model of rational choice. *Quarterly Journal of Economics, 69,* 99–118.

Smith, J. F., Mitchell, T. R., & Beach, L. R. (1982). A cost-benefit mechanism for selecting problem solving strategies: Some extensions and empirical tests. *Organizational Behavior and Human Performance, 29,* 370–396.

Svenson, O. (1979). Process descriptions in decision making. *Organizational Behavior and Human Performance, 23,* 86–112.

Tversky, A., & Kahneman, D. (1974). Judgment under uncertainty: Heuristics and biases. *Science, 185,* 453–458.

van Zee, E. H. (1989). *Use of information in decision deliberation.* Unpublished doctoral dissertation, University of Washington, Seattle.

van Zee, E. H., Paluchowski, T. F., & Beach, L. R. (1992). The effects of screening and task partitioning upon evaluations of decision options. *Journal of Behavioral Decision Making, 5,* 1–23.

Waller, W. S., & Mitchell, T. R. (1984). The effects of context on the selection of decision strategies for the cost variance investigation. *Organizational Behavior and Human Performance, 33,* 397–413.

2

WHY A NEW PERSPECTIVE ON DECISION MAKING IS NEEDED[1]

Lee Roy Beach
University of Arizona

Raanan Lipshitz
University of Haifa

It is customary to attribute two roles to the formal, axiomatic, rational actor theory of decision evaluation and choice: a normative role and a prescriptive role. For brevity, we will call the formal theory *classical decision theory*, by which we mean the collection of axiomatic models of uncertainty and risk (probability theory, including Bayesian theory) and utility (utility theory, including multiattribute utility theory), that prescribe the optimal choice of an option from an array of options, in which optimality is defined by the underlying models and the choice is dictated by an explicit rule, usually some variant of maximization of (subjective) expected utility.

In its normative role, classical decision theory is an abstract system of propositions designed to describe the choices of an ideal hypothetical decision maker—omniscient, computationally omnipotent Economic Man—given the theory's very specific assumptions about the nature of the decision task. In this role the theory actually has little relevance to real-world decisions. It is merely an internally consistent, logical system that, perhaps unfortunately, reflects its origins as an attempt to rationalize

[1]Revised from "Why Classical Decision Theory is an Inappropriate Standard for Evaluating Most Human Decision Making," 1993. In G. Klein, J. Orasanu, R. Calderwood, & C. Zsambok (Eds.), *Decision Making in Action*. Norwood, NJ: Ablex. Reproduced by permission of the editors and the publisher.

observed decisions (Bentham, 1789/1970) by couching itself in terms that also are commonly used to describe the behavior of human beings.

Since the publication of the theory of games by von Neumann and Morgenstern (1947), followed by Edwards' (1954) introduction of classical decision theory to psychology, it has become common to attribute a prescriptive role to classical decision theory. Prescriptive means that the way that Economic Man would make decisions is assumed to be the uniquely appropriate way, the only "rational" way. Indeed, the optimality of humans' decisions usually is judged by whether the decisions conform to the prescriptions of the theory. The assumption that classical theory is prescriptively appropriate has motivated nearly 40 years of empirical behavioral research: Every study that has evaluated the quality of human decision making using the prescriptions of classical theory as the standard of comparison has been a reaffirmation of this assumption.

Implicit in the prescriptivity assumption is the further assumption that if decision makers behaved as they should, classical decision theory would not only be normative and prescriptive, it also would be descriptive of human decision behavior; thus the assumption comes full circle from Bentham (1789/1970) and the Utilitarians. Starting with the work of Allais (1953) and Ellsberg (1961) and following on through the work of Tversky and Kahneman (1974) and up to the present, it has been repeatedly demonstrated that decision makers only infrequently behave as they "should." That is, decision behavior does not appear to conform consistently, or even often, to the logic of classical theory or to the operations implied by that logic. Of course, classical theory is mathematically precise, and it is unreasonable to expect the same precision in the behavior compared to it. Quite beyond this understandable lack of conformity, however, it doubtless is the case that human decision making cannot be described adequately by using classical theory as a descriptive theory.

This lack of conformity, this inability to use classical theory as a descriptive theory has prompted four responses from decision researchers. One response is merely to damn the behavior: "If your procedures or decisions or feelings are intransitive or otherwise discordant with subjective expected utility, they are incoherent, irrational, or whatever you want to call it, and trying to justify them as coherent or find other rationalities is a waste of time" (Pratt, 1986, p. 498). This view saves the theory and rejects the behavior. Some scholars hold this view because they prize the theory and simply are uninterested in the behavior—a position to which they certainly are entitled.

Others who hold this view prize the theory but are interested in the behavior strive to reduce the gap between theory and behavior by changing the behavior. This is the second response to the nonconformity of behavior to theory, and it has given rise to decision analysis as an art and profession, as well as to a sizable array of decision aids designed to help people make their decision processes conform to classical theory.

The third response has been to retain the general logic and structure of classical theory but to modify some of the theory's components and operations in light of the research findings. Scholars adopting this response prize the theory but are far more interested in the behavior—hence, their willingness to compromise the theory in order to better understand decision behavior. This is the position taken by behavioral economics (Bell, 1982; Loomis & Sugden, 1982; Machina, 1982), of which prospect theory (Kahneman & Tversky, 1979) is perhaps the most famous example. As pointed out by Beach and Mitchell (1990; Beach, 1990), although this response follows a time-honored tradition in science (i.e., modifying theory in the light of evidence), it also runs the risk of retaining a point of view (in this case the logic and structure of classical theory) that may not be as valuable as it once appeared. To be sure, history provides examples of theories being improved by modification in the light of evidence. It also provides examples of theories being repaired and shored up until all but the "true believers" lose interest in the increasingly pedantic arguments that signal the theory's impending death. One example is the overlong extension of the Ptolemaic theory of the solar system; stimulus–response theories of learning are another example. (One sign of theoretical moribundity may be that "true believers" begin to talk almost exclusively to each other.)

The fourth response is represented by attempts to describe more accurately the process involved in real-world decision making by individuals acting alone or in groups. The underlying notion is that if decision makers know what they actually are attempting to do, perhaps they can be helped to do it better. Scholars committed to this response are almost wholly interested in understanding behavior. Because classical decision theory has been found to give only limited help in achieving such understanding, it has been either completely replaced or relegated to the back of the stage. Of course, many of these scholars retain a great deal of respect for classical theory; they acknowledge that it is appropriate for some decision tasks and that human decisions sometimes conform to its prescriptions. However, they are unconvinced (or more often have lost the conviction) that classical theory always is the standard against which decision behavior should be judged. Rather, they have come to believe that it is misdirected to force every or even most decision tasks into the rather limited mold that classical theory provides.

Herbert Simon (1955) led the way in the formulation of this fourth response, and organizational theorists of various stripes were the first to carry it forward (e.g., Cohen, March, & Olsen, 1972; Cyert & March, 1963; Gore, 1964; Janis & Mann, 1977; Lindblom, 1959; March & Simon, 1958; Weick, 1983). Most of these earlier efforts focused heavily on group processes, and it is only recently that theories formulated as part of this fourth response have widened their focus to include individuals, image theory being the most thoroughly developed example.

WHEN BEHAVIOR AND CLASSICAL THEORY DIFFER

Even the most casual reader of the decision literature is aware of the research on decision heuristics and biases. This work, started in large part by Ward Edwards, Daniel Kahneman, and Amos Tversky, and subsequently carried on both by them and by many other researchers, focuses primarily on judgment rather than decision making. However, insofar as it has examined decision making per se, it suggests or documents discrepancies between decision behavior and classical theory. Add to this the more pertinent literature on choices among bets, in which decision makers' choices between gambles often are found to be governed by factors irrelevant to the theory's prescriptions, and the picture looks pretty dismal. Of course, that picture is framed, if you will, by classical theory.

Because the heuristics and biases research has been examined in detail in many other places, there is no need to discuss it here. Instead, let us consider the results of another literature often overlooked by the decision research establishment that the causal reader might not know exists, a literature that has important implications for the results of choices between gambles as a source of insight into decision behavior. This second literature does more than merely document the lack of conformity of decision behavior to theoretical prescriptions. It suggests that human decision making consists of many tasks quite different from the gambling task for which classical theory peculiarly was designed. In short, this literature demands that the unthinkable be thought; classical theory frequently may be an inappropriate standard for evaluating and aiding human decision making.

Most of this second literature does not come from laboratory experiments. Rather, it comes from observation of decision makers engaging in routine, on-the-job decisions. As a result, each study is perhaps less compelling than an experiment would be, but the consistency of the results across studies argues for their overall credibility. For example, Mintzberg

(1975), observing business managers, found that most decisions involved only one option rather than multiple options, and that the decision was whether to go with that option rather than a choice from an array of competing options. Moreover, few decisions required or received the careful balancing of losses and gains, let alone explicit use of probability, that are central to classical theory.

Peters's (1979) observations of managers yielded the same conclusions, and, in addition, showed that most decisions are elements of a larger endeavor directed toward achieving some desired state of affairs, with each decision providing a small step in the appropriate direction. That is, decisions are not determined solely by the relative attractiveness of their potential outcomes; they are determined in large part by how these potential outcomes fit into a larger scheme of things. It is compatibility with and contribution to this larger scheme that is the chief criterion for decisions. Findings by Donaldson and Lorsch (1983) in an extensive study of the executives of 12 major corporations corroborate these conclusions. In addition, numerous observers noted that the decision process consists more of generating and clarifying actions and goals than of choosing among prespecified alternative actions (options). Moreover, the research consistently suggests that the decision making manager acts primarily as a promoter and protector of the organization's values rather than as a relentless seeker of maximal payoffs (Donaldson & Lorsch, 1983; Peters, 1979; Selznik, 1957).

It is illuminating that, even when managers have been trained to use classical decision theory (and even with decision aids available to help them apply it), managers rarely use it. When they do use it, they seldom follow prescriptions that disagree with their own subjective intuitions (Isenberg, 1984, 1985). This suggests, by the way, that intuition, not cognition, is the primary engine for decision making, if only because intuition holds veto power (Mitchell & Beach, 1990). These are competent, intelligent, successful executives, not college students who have been dragooned into laboratory studies. Their unwillingness to use classical theory suggests that something is wrong. The usual view is that they are what is wrong—that they ought to be using the theory. Actually, they know how, they have aids available, and yet they resist. To use the theory's own terms, the executives appear to regard the costs of using the theory to be greater than the benefits. One must wonder why.

Certainly, one reason why decision makers resist using classical theory is that its prescribed operations are cumbersome and time consuming, and the decision maker's time and resources (and patience) simply are insufficient. Phillips (1985, 1986,) suggested an additional reason. Like Isenberg (1984, 1985), Phillips observed that corporate decision makers usually rely on their "subjective mode" to make decisions, even when extensive, computerized technology is available. His discussions with executives suggested that because the databases for deriving probabilities and projecting trends consist of records of past events, the probabilities and trends are "backward looking" and therefore of questionable pertinence to decisions that often concern time frames projecting 20 years or more into the future. In a rapidly changing world the relative frequencies of past events may provide little guidance for decisions about such an extended future, and decision makers rely on their own vision of what the future holds. By the same token, reliance upon data about the past assumes that the world is static; the data are useful only for predicting what will happen if the future looks a great deal like the past, or if identified trends continue.

Strategic decisions are made in order to act upon the world, to make sure that the future does not look like the past. Decision makers go to great lengths to insure that they have the ability to control key future events, and controllability is factored into their decisions. As it turns out, the issue of control is an important key to understanding why classical theory frequently is neither an appropriate standard by which to evaluate decision behavior nor a relevant model for decision aiding.

CONTROL IN DECISION BEHAVIOR

To understand why control is important, let us turn to an incisive critique of classical theory by Shafer (1986). Shafer directed his analysis at Savage's (1954) conclusion that it is optimal to make choices that maximize subjective expected utility (i.e., the version of classical theory that uses subjective probabilities and utilities), and that to do otherwise is to behave irrationally.

The vehicle used by Savage (1954) and many others is the gamble. That is, decisions under uncertainty are regarded as gambles, and the analysis of the decisions is the same as that which would be appropriate for gambles. For example, a familiar decision dilemma (Behn & Vaupel, 1982) pits the status quo (the certain alternative) against an alternative that could, with some uncertainty, result either in an outcome that is better than the status quo or in one that is worse. Classical theory views the latter as a gamble that should be preferred to the status quo if its subjective expected utility is greater than the utility of the status quo.

Shafer argued that analysis of a decision in terms of subjective expected utility is an argument by analogy between what the decision maker must do to decide and what a gambler must do to bet on a comparable game of chance. He pointed out that sometimes such an analogy is cogent, but at other times it is not.

It is worth noting that in most games of chance, the gambler does not influence events: He or she must assay the circumstances, make a bet, and then wait for some external process to determine whether the bet is won or lost. In short, the gambler exerts little or no control over the events of interest. This is in marked contrast to the control that is so much a part of most human decisions, and insofar as such control exists, the analogy between those decisions and gambling is not cogent. The analogy is vulnerable on at least two additional points. First, in real-life decisions, subjective probabilities and utilities seldom are independent (Slovic, 1966). This is intuitively reasonable because "the process of formulating and adopting goals creates a dependence of value on belief, simply because goals are more attractive when they are feasible" (Shafer, 1986, p. 479). Second, basing decisions on the expected values of the alternatives may not be appropriate for unique decisions (Lopes, 1981).

The expectation for a gamble is a weighted mean of the gains and losses that may result from choosing it, where the weights are the probabilities of the gains and the losses occurring. As such, the expectation is wholly imaginary for any single gamble: The gambler will receive either the gain or the loss, but not their weighted mean. In contrast, for a series of similar gambles, the expectation is the amount that the gambler is likely to lose or gain in the long run. It therefore has meaning for each gamble as part of the series.

If a decision is not one of a series of highly similar gambles, it is not in the least clear that it is rational to decide by maximizing expectation, and decision makers appear to realize this. Research shows that even when decisions are explicitly about gambles, bets on unique gambles tend not to be based upon their expected values. Keren and Wagenaar (1987) had participants choose between pairs of gambles (e.g., $100 with 99% certainty, or $250 with 50% certainty). In one condition the chosen gamble would be played only once (unique), and in the other condition the chosen gamble would be played 10 times (repeated). The gambles were designed so that the one with the highest expected value had the lowest probability of winning. If the participants' decisions conformed to the prescriptions of classical theory, they would choose the higher expected value gamble whether or not it was unique or repeated (e.g., $250 with 50% certainty, which has an expectation of $125 but also has the lower probability of winning, rather than $100 with 99% certainty, which has an expectation of

$99). However, the data showed that, across study conditions, 71% of the participants chose the higher expected value gamble when it was to be repeated, but only about 57% chose it when it was unique. In further studies it was found that neither students nor casino gamblers rely very heavily upon expected value in making wagers (Keren & Wagenaar, 1985; Wagenaar & Keren, 1988; Wagenaar, Keren, & Lichtenstein, 1988; Wagenaar, Keren, & Pleit-Kuiper, 1984). As Wagenaar (1988; Beach, Vlek, & Wagenaar, 1988) emphasized, if even real gamblers fail to conceive of real gambles in the way that classical decision theory prescribes, it is a bit far-fetched to assume that ordinary decision makers conceive of common-place decisions according to those prescriptions. All told, it is difficult to sustain much belief in the gambling analogy as a universal characterization of risky decision making—at least from the point of view of human decision makers. Whether or not their views count is, of course, a question.

DO DECISION MAKERS' VIEWS COUNT?

The preceding conclusions rely heavily upon the differences between how decision makers and classical theory view the demands and structure of various decision tasks. It can be argued that the very reason for using classical theory as a prescriptive model is that human decision makers' views of their decision tasks are flawed, so their views do not count for much. But what is the evidence for this "flawed view" argument? The major evidence is its subjective appeal. Most of us feel uneasy about our decisions, primarily because we have made decisions that did not turn out well, and we live with the clear understanding that someday we will regret decisions that we have not even made yet. Classical decision theory, however, does not address the question of making correct decisions; it merely addresses the question of making decisions correctly—which is not the same thing. That is, classical theory is about making the best bet given conditions at the moment; it is specifically about process and only indirectly about outcome. As in casino gambling, "you bet your money and take your chances," and some failures are the price of playing. Certainly, it is an article of faith that, in the long run, proper process (i.e., classical theory) will result in a greater number of satisfactory decisions than will any other process, but this is merely faith until it has been empirically demonstrated. Actually, it has not been empirically demonstrated; Research (Paquette & Kida, 1988; Payne, Bettman, & Johnson, 1988; Thorngate, 1980) shows, both in computer simulations and in solid laboratory experiments, that a variety of alternative decision methods yield results comparable to or, under short deadlines, even superior to classical theory.

The second reason why decision makers' views often are not considered to count derives from the literature on flawed judgment and decision making. However, flawed is defined as a deviation from classical theory, and the possibility that the theory is inappropriate is seldom entertained. With the possible exception of sociobiology, it is difficult to think of any discipline that has made its central theoretical viewpoint so unassailable.

Make no mistake; in its normative role of prescribing decisions for hypothetical Economic Man, classical theory is not subject to these criticisms. It is when behavioral scientists assume that these prescriptions apply to any and all human decisions that the mischief is done. Because the theory's prescriptive role is assumed to have the same status as its normative role, the legitimacy of the theory is not questioned when behavior does not conform to its prescriptions. Instead, it is concluded that the behavior, and thus the decision maker, is wrong or irrational and must be made to conform to the theory. If the rules that hold in other branches of science were applied here, the possibility that the theory is not universally appropriate as a standard for evaluating and aiding decision behavior at least would have to be considered.

In summary, our point and the point made by the preceding literature is that it is not sufficient to conclude that real decision makers lack the superhuman cognitive powers of omniscient, computationally omnipotent Economic Man, and that they therefore fall short of the classical decision theory's perfection. Although human frailties must be duly noted, the difficulty is not wholly attributable to human shortcomings. Clearly, classical theory does not provide the conceptual depth needed to deal with real-world complexity; in some ways people seem far more capable than the theory. Newer theories, such as image theory, are attempts to break the stranglehold of classical theory on both the scientific analysis and the real-world practice of decision making. This is in contrast to behavioral economics, which appears satisfied to tinker with classical theory to make it fit laboratory data. However unsystematic, the development of newer, post-classical theory has been marked by attempts to be more sensitive to the constraints imposed by the environments in which decisions arise. In the effort to do this, it has become increasingly clear that the decision maker's way of perceiving or framing (Minsky, 1968) those environmental constraints is central to understanding decision making, and that different decision strategies follow from those perceptions. Because it is cumbersome, perhaps impossible, to adequately include those constraints and perceptions within the confines of classical theory, the theory often fails to be useful when the time comes to apply it in real-world decision settings, particularly, as we have seen, in the workplace. Therefore, its prescriptions often are inappropriate either as guides for action or as standards for the evaluation or aiding of human decision behavior. In light of these shortcomings, there is no real alternative to replacing classical theory with new, more realistic theories and to looking at decision making in new ways.

REFERENCES

Allais, M. (1953). Le comportment de l'homme rationnel devant le risque: Critique des postulates et axioms de l'écol américaine [The behavior of rational man in the face of risk: Critiques of the postulates and axioms of the American school]. *Econometrica, 21*, 503–546.

Beach, L. R. (1990). *Image theory: Decision making in personal and organizational contexts.* Chichester, UK: Wiley.

Beach, L. R., & Lipshitz, R. (1993). Why classical decision theory is an inappropriate standard for evaluating and aiding most decision making. In G. A. Klein, J. Orasanu, R. Calderwood, & C. E. Zsambok (Eds.), *Decision making in action: Models and methods* (pp. 21–35). New York: Ablex.

Beach, L. R., & Mitchell, T. R. (1990). Image theory: A behavioral theory of decisions in organizations. In B. M. Staw & L. L. Cummings (Eds.), *Research in organizational behavior* (Vol. 12, pp. 1–41). Greenwich, CT: JAI Press.

Beach, L. R., Vlek, C., & Wagenaar, W. A. (1988). *Models and methods for unique versus repeated decision making* (Leiden Psychological Reports: Experimental Psychology, EP04–88). Leiden, The Netherlands: Leiden University, Psychology Department.

Behn, R. D., & Vaupel, J. W. (1982). *Quick analysis for busy decision makers.* New York: Basic Books.

Bell, D. E. (1982). Regret in decision making under uncertainty. *Operations Research, 30*, 961–981.

Bentham, J. (1970). *An introduction to the principles of morals and legislation.* London: Athlone. (Original work published 1789)

Cohen, M. D., March, J. G., & Olsen, J. P. (1972). A garbage can model of organizational choice. *Administrative Science Quarterly, 17*, 1–25.

Cyert, R. M., & March, J. G. (1963). *A behavioral theory of the firm.* Englewood Cliffs, NJ: Prentice-Hall.

Donaldson, G., & Lorsch, J. W. (1983). *Decision making at the top.* New York: Basic Books.

Edwards, W. (1954). The theory of decision making. *Psychological Bulletin, 51*, 380–417.

Ellsberg, D. (1961). Risk, ambiguity, and the Savage axioms. *Quarterly Journal of Economics, 75*, 643–669.

Gore, W. J. (1964). *Administrative decision making: A heuristic model.* New York: Wiley.

Isenberg, D. J. (1984, November/December). How senior managers think. *Harvard Business Review*, 81–90.

Isenberg, D. J. (1985). Some hows and whats of managerial thinking: Implications for future army leaders. In J. G. Hunt & J. Blair (Eds.), *Military Leadership in the Future Battlefield* (pp. 27–41). New York: Pergamon.

Janis, I. L., & Mann, L. (1977). *Decision making: A psychological analysis of conflict, choice, and commitment.* New York: Free Press.

Kahneman, D., & Tversky, A. (1979). Prospect theory: An analysis of decision under risk. *Econometrica, 47*, 263–291.

Keren, G. B., & Wagenaar, W. A. (1985). On the psychology of playing blackjack: Normative and descriptive considerations with implications for decision theory. *Journal of Experimental Psychology:General, 114*, 133–158.

Keren, G. B., & Wagenaar, W. A. (1987). Violation of utility theory in unique and repeated gambles. *Journal of Experimental Psychology: Learning, Memory and Cognition, 13*, 387–396.

Lindblom, C. E. (1959). The science of "muddling through." *Public Administration Review, 19*, 79–88.

Loomis, G., & Sugden, R. (1982). Regret theory: An alternative theory of rational choice under uncertainty. *Economic Journal, 92*, 805–824.

Lopes, L. L. (1981). Decision making in the shortrun. *Journal of Experimental Psychology: Human Learning and Memory, 1*, 377–385.

Machina, M. J. (1982). "Expected utility" analysis without the independence axiom. *Econometrica, 50*, 277–332.

March, J. G., & Simon, H. A. (1958). *Organizations.* New York: Wiley.

Minsky, M. (1968). *Semantic information processing.* Cambridge, MA: MIT Press.

Mintzberg, H. (1975). The manager's job: Folklore and fact. *Harvard Business Review, 53*, 49–61.

Mitchell, T. R., & Beach, L. R. (1990). ". . . Do I love thee? Let me count. . ." Toward an understanding of intuitive and automatic decision making. *Organizational Behavior and Human Decision Processes, 47*, 1–20.

Paquette, L., & Kida, T. (1988). The effect of decision strategy and task complexity on decision performance. *Organizational Behavior and Human Decision Processes, 41*, 128–142.

Payne, J. W., Bettman, J. R., & Johnson, E. J. (1988). Adaptive strategy selection in decision making. *Journal of Experimental Psychology: Learning, Memory and Cognition, 14*, 534–552.

Peters, T. J. (1979). Leadership: Sad facts and silver linings. *Harvard Business Review, 57*, 164–172.

Phillips, L. D. (1985, April). Systems for solutions. *Datamation*, 26–29.

Phillips, L. D. (1986, October). Computing to consensus. *Datamation*, 2–6.

Pratt, J. W. (1986). Comment. *Statistical Science, 1*, 498–499.

Savage, L. J. (1954). *The foundations of statistics.* New York: Wiley.

Selznick, P. (1957). *Leadership in administration: A sociological interpretation.* Evanston, IL: Row, Peterson.

Shafer, G. (1986). Savage revisited. *Stastical Science, 1*, 463–501.

Simon, H. A. (1955). A behavioral model of rational choice. *Quarterly Journal of Economics, 69*, 99–118.

Slovic, P. (1966). Value as a determiner of subjective probability. *IEEE Transactions on Human Factors in Electronics, HFE–7*, 22–28.

Thorngate, W. (1980). Efficient decision heuristics. *Behavioral Science, 25*, 219–225.

Tversky, A., & Kahneman, D. (1974). Judgment under uncertainty: Heuristics and biases. *Science, 185*, 1124–1131.

von Neumann, J., & Morgenstern, O. (1947). *Theory of games and economic behavior.* Princeton, NJ: Princeton University Press.

Wagenaar, W. A. (1988). *Paradoxes of gambling behavior.* Hillsdale, NJ: Lawrence Erlbaum Associates.

Wagenaar, W. A., & Keren, G. B. (1988). Chance and luck are not the same. *Journal of Behavioral Decision Making, 1*, 65–75.

Wagenaar, W. A., Keren, G. B., & Lichtenstein, S. (1988). Islanders and hostages: Deep and surface structures of decision problems. *Acta Psychologica, 68*, 175–189.

Wagenaar, W. A., Keren, G. B., & Pleit-Kuiper, A. (1984). The multiple objectives of gamblers. *Acta Psychologica, 56*, 167–178.

Weick, K. E. (1983). Managerial thought in the context of action. In S. Srivastva (Ed.), *The Executive Mind* (pp. 221–242). San Francisco: Jossey-Bass.

JOB SEARCH
AND JOB SELECTION

Cynthia Kay Stevens
University of Maryland

Lee Roy Beach
University of Arizona

Robert looked down the list of job descriptions. All but two were out of the question. Either he had no training, or they involved work that definitely was beneath him (not that he would ever admit to having such feelings). The two survivors were not terrific, but they might turn out to be okay. He dialed the phone number for the first one. The person who answered did not sound enthused, and as she talked it became clear to Robert that the job simply was not for him. He would feel awful in a week and the job clearly was not going to lead anywhere. He called the other job with much the same result. The rent might need paying, but he would keep on looking until something more promising came along—perhaps in tonight's paper.

People's decisions about how to search for and evaluate job opportunities have far-reaching implications for their own career progress. Often overlooked, however, are the organizational consequences of these decisions. Organizations benefit when they hire people who "fit in" with the job, work group, and culture. When employees do not fit in, their job satisfaction and performance suffer (Caldwell & O'Reilly, 1990). This can lead to turnover or termination, yielding a poor return on the money invested in recruiting, screening, and training these employees. Managers who understand how people look for and select jobs can protect their human resource investments by encouraging applicants to make the right decisions during recruitment and selection.

Several theories help us to understand how people search for and choose jobs; these include Vroom's (1966) expectancy theory, Tom's (1971) vocational choice approach, and Soelberg's (1967) generalized decision process model. Unfortunately, these theories give incomplete and contradictory accounts of job seekers' decision processes (e.g., Schwab, Rynes, & Aldag, 1987; Wanous & Colella, 1989), thereby limiting their usefulness as guides for management practice. We believe that image theory provides the basis for a unified theory of how people look for and evaluate jobs. As such, it enables managers to tailor their recruitment and selection practices to meet applicants' needs, increasing the chances that organizations and applicants will make the right decisions.

This chapter describes in image theory terms how people search for and select job opportunities. We begin by briefly reviewing three existing theories. Then we present an image theory account, emphasizing its similarities to other theories. Finally, we highlight the implications of this unified image theory approach for improved recruitment and selection practices. In what follows we refer to job opportunities as *job options* and choices among these options as *job selection*. In addition, we limit our discussion to circumstances in which job seekers have already made conscious decisions to look for jobs. Lee (chapter 6, this volume) applied image theory to an analysis of the processes leading up to the decision to leave one's current job.

CURRENT THEORIES OF
JOB SEEKERS' DECISION PROCESSES

Vroom's (1966) Expectancy Theory

In 1966, Vroom proposed that expectancy theory (a theory of motivation) may explain how job seekers evaluate and choose from among several job options. Specifically, expectancy theory suggests that people examine how likely it is that different jobs will offer attractive features (e.g., high pay, preferred geographic location, pleasant work conditions). It assumes that people consider the desirability (the *valence*) of each job feature as well as the ability of each job option to provide these features (the *instrumentality*). Expectancy theory predicts that people will choose the most attractive job option, and attractiveness, in turn, depends on the number of desirable features associated with each job. Mathematically, the option with the largest sum of valences × instrumentalities across all features is the most attractive. This means that many minor attractive features (e.g., a short commute, nice office, pleasant lunchroom) should offset one major unattractive feature (e.g., a very low salary). Finally, expectancy theory predicts that the motivation to pursue a job will be greatest when the job is attractive (i.e., has a large sum of valences × instrumentalities) and when the *expectancy* (i.e., perceived chances) for receiving a job offer is high.

Research.   Expectancy theory has been studied extensively in many contexts. The typical experiment involves measuring people's valence (V) and instrumentality (I) estimates and comparing predictions from these estimates (i.e., the sum of $V \times I$) with their actual preferences and choices. Research findings comparing expectancy theory predictions with chance or with I or V alone show that expectancy theory does a better job (Connolly & Vines, 1977; Wanous, Keon, & Latack, 1983). In contrast, other mathematical combinations (e.g., $I + V$) and noncompensatory models (in which attractive and unattractive features do not balance each other out) often prove superior in predicting job seekers' intentions and decisions (e.g., Arnold, 1981; Baker, Ravichandran & Randall, 1989; Osborn, 1990).

Evaluation.   Expectancy theory has been useful in predicting how job seekers weigh and combine information when evaluating several job options. However, empirical research indicates that people sometimes weigh and combine information in ways not suggested by expectancy theory. In addition, expectancy theory incorporates some important deliberations into its valence, instrumentality, and expectancy components. This means that expectancy theory does not tell us very much about how people react to external constraints, such as labor market conditions, or how they consider internal constraints, such as long-term career objectives. Finally, although expectancy theory addresses job seekers' motivation for pursuing jobs, it does not provide insight into how they select and implement job search strategies.

Tom's (1971) Vocational Choice Approach

Tom's (1971) account of job seekers' decision processes represented an extension of Super's (1953) vocational choice theory. Super had proposed that people select vocations that match their self-concepts—their self-perceived abilities, characteristics, goals and values. Tom (1971) extended this reasoning to job selection processes, suggesting that people may select jobs in organizations for which their image of the organization matches their own self-concept. Keon, Latack, and Wanous (1982) furthered this logic, arguing that the tendency to match self- and organizational images should be stronger among high than among low self-esteem job seekers.

Research.   Research that has explored the predictions of this approach is sparse. Tom (1971) reported that subjects' self-descriptions more closely matched descriptions of their most preferred organizations than they did descriptions of their least preferred organizations. Bretz, Ash and Dreher (1989) found some support for the related idea that people would be most attracted to organizations with reward systems that fit their personalities. Finally, Keon et al. (1982) found a greater tendency to match organizational images and self-images among applicants with positive (as opposed to negative) self-images.

Evaluation.   Tom's (1971) approach proposed that people evaluate and select jobs in much the same way that they evaluate and select occupations. However, it does not tell us much about what these decision processes are—how job seekers compare their self- and organizational images, which features are used to make comparisons, or whether some minimal degree of matching is necessary. As with expectancy theory, the vocational choice approach does not help us understand how people react to external constraints or how they select and use job search strategies.

Soelberg's (1967) Generalized Decision Process Model

Soelberg (1967) developed the generalized decision process (GDP) model from observations of students who were seeking jobs. This model is complex and can best be summarized as four overlapping activity phases: identifying the ideal job, planning the job search, searching for and selecting a job, and confirming and committing to the decision (Power & Aldag, 1985).

According to Soelberg (1967), job seekers begin phase 1 by identifying their ideal jobs and the criteria they will use to evaluate job options. These criteria are assumed to vary in importance from essential to supplemental (i.e., "tie-breaking" standards). As job seekers solidify their criteria, they also consider ways to search for information about jobs that might meet their criteria (phase 2). Soelberg (1967) predicted that job seekers will choose the easiest search methods that they think will be effective in leading to information and job offers.

The GDP model proposes that job seekers enter phase 3 when they implement their search strategies from phase 2. As they generate information about job options, job seekers are predicted to compare it with their ideal job criteria to screen out unacceptable options. Soelberg (1967) suggested that screening may become more or less stringent over time, depending on how scarce jobs are, whether time and money permit a longer search, and other unpredictable events (e.g., being rejected by an employer). He predicted that the first job option that meets all important criteria will become the implicitly favored—and eventually chosen—option. Job seekers are assumed to stop searching when they receive offers from the implicitly favored and at least one other alternative. According to Soelberg, job seekers compare the implicit favorite with one other option in an attempt to rationalize their selection of the implicit favorite (phase 4). The GDP model predicts eventual selection of the implicitly favored job.

Research.   Research on the GDP model does not provide clear-cut support for its predictions. Studies have found that job seekers use ideal-comparison processes (Herriot & Rothwell, 1981) and that the GDP model provides more accurate predictions than does expectancy theory (Hill, 1974). However, Glueck (1974) reported that only 25% of the students he surveyed showed evidence of using ideal-comparison processes, as predicted by the GDP model. Fully 50% of these students followed a strategy more similar to expectancy theory than to the GDP model.

Evaluation.   The GDP model offers a more extensive picture of job seekers' decision processes than either expectancy theory or the vocational choice approach. It also predicts how job seekers may respond to both external constraints, such as a tight labor market or rejection by an employer, and internal constraints, such as career goals. However, it does not tell us much about how job options are compared to the ideal or how this information is used to determine which option is the favorite.

Summary

Each of the theories provides unique insights into job seekers' decision processes. Expectancy theory specifies how people weigh and combine information when evaluating several job options. The vocational choice approach highlights the importance of job seekers' self-concepts and career choices. Finally, the GDP model suggests how internal and external constraints and job search activities affect job seekers' decisions.

Nevertheless, there are also problems with these theories. None of them provides a complete picture of how job seekers look for and evaluate jobs. Moreover, they make conflicting predictions about how people select job offers. Because existing research does not clearly support any of the theories, we cannot use it as a basis for recommending one over the others.

An alternative strategy for resolving these problems is to integrate the theories by building on their strengths. We believe that image theory provides a useful framework for integrating the strengths of these different approaches.

IMAGE THEORY AND JOB SEEKERS' DECISION PROCESSES

An image theory analysis of job seekers' decision processes begins when a person decides to find a job. In image theory terms, when the status quo ceases to exist (due to completion of one's education, being laid off, or needing additional income), the person will seek options that will remedy the situation.

The process begins with adoption of a goal. The search for options may produce many interesting goals that are unacceptable or impractical—bum around Europe, win the lottery, go back to school in the fine arts. However, assuming that self-sufficiency is a basic principle, the goal probably will be to find a suitable job. This may proceed in either of two ways. The decision maker may have in mind a clear idea of the desired job (the goal), in which case the decision standards and appropriate search strategies have obvious constraints. Alternatively, the decision maker may have only a fuzzy idea of the desired job (i.e., getting "a job"), which produces ill-defined standards and a haphazard search strategy.

Whether the desired job is clear or fuzzy, the final result may be the same. However, variations in goal clarity bring about different plans for goal achievement. For a clearly defined goal, the job search will be more focused on sources that are likely to offer desired job features. For example, if the preferred job is in a local financial consulting firm, the job seeker may canvass such companies in person, relying less on employment services or ads. In contrast, if the goal is diffuse (a job in management), the job seeker is more likely to use state and private employment agencies or want ads to learn about a broad range of options.

The first step in a plan to find employment is to generate job options; the second step is to screen those options according to their compatibility with relevant standards (see Fig. 3.1). If no option survives screening, more options must be sought. If only one option survives screening, it is retained. If two or more options survive, all of which meet minimum standards (and thus are roughly equivalent in acceptability), additional information will be sought for choosing the best option. If no additional information is available, the job seeker will reconsider the information used in screening, only this time it will be used to determine the best option, rather than to eliminate unacceptable options (see Fig. 3.2).

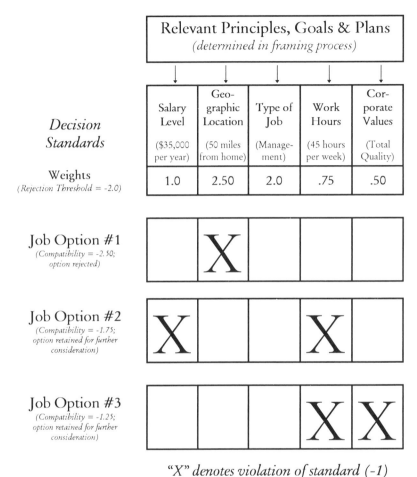

	Salary Level	Geo-graphic Location	Type of Job	Work Hours	Cor-porate Values
Decision Standards	($35,000 per year)	(50 miles from home)	(Manage-ment)	(45 hours per week)	(Total Quality)
Weights *(Rejection Threshold = -2.0)*	1.0	2.50	2.0	.75	.50

Relevant Principles, Goals & Plans
(determined in framing process)

Job Option #1
(Compatibility = -2.50; option rejected)

Job Option #2
(Compatibility = -1.75; option retained for further consideration)

Job Option #3
(Compatibility = -1.25; option retained for further consideration)

"X" denotes violation of standard (-1)

FIG. 3.1. Compatibility test for a hypothetical job seeker.

A job option can be either a possibility or an actual offer. A possibility is a job opening that meets the job seeker's standards. He or she now replaces the old goal of getting a job with the new, more specific goal of turning *this* job possibility into an offer. An offer is a job option that can be accepted or rejected by the job seeker. In other words, the original goal is to find a job and it is served by a strategy for obtaining information about job options. If the search is successful, the original goal will be replaced by the new goal of being offered the preferred job option(s); this is served by a strategy for obtaining job offers. The revised goal is achieved if the job possibility becomes a job offer, at which point the decision sequence ends. If no offer is forthcoming, the original goal of getting a job is reinstated and the process begins again.

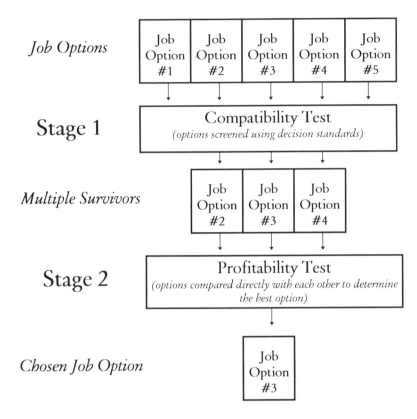

FIG. 3.2. Two-stage decision process.

Once a job option becomes an offer, it assumes the status of a possible goal that must be considered for acceptance as part of one's trajectory image. If the job option previously passed the compatibility test, acceptance is usually automatic (unless negative information relevant to one's standards emerges). If it has been an unsolicited offer, it must be subjected to screening, and perhaps weighed against the present job, before it is accepted or rejected. If multiple offers are received, all of which pass the compatibility test, they will be subjected to the profitability test in an attempt to choose the "best" offer.

Image Theory Research

As described in the introductory chapter to this volume, image theory research has focused primarily on screening (the compatibility test; Beach, 1993), and secondarily on choice (the profitability test; Beach, 1990). It is sufficient for our purposes to summarize the relevant results before describing their implications for job search and job selection. Results show the following:

1. Rejections are based solely on the number and importance of rejected options' violations (Beach, Smith, Lundell & Mitchell, 1988; Potter & Beach, 1994a, 1994b; van Zee, Paluchowski, & Beach, 1992).
2. The rejection threshold remains fairly constant across screened options (van Zee et al., 1992).
3. Information use is always noncompensatory in screening and sometimes compensatory in choice, indicating that these are two very different cognitive processes (Potter & Beach, 1994b).
4. Information used in screening has little impact on choice if additional postscreening information about the survivors is available—it is as though the information is "used up" in the screening process (van Zee et al., 1992).
5. If the survivors of screening become unavailable before a choice can be made, subjects resist having to rescreen rejected options and prefer to start with a fresh set of options (Potter & Beach, 1994a).
6. If forced to rescreen rejected options, subjects both lower their standards and raise their rejection thresholds in an effort to make formerly unacceptable options acceptable (Potter & Beach, 1994a).

These findings suggest that job options will be screened according to whether they violate the job seeker's standards and that a consistent rejection threshold will be maintained as long as job options are plentiful. Further, information used for screening will not affect the final choice if more information can be obtained before a choice is made. However, if no additional information is forthcoming, a choice will be made using the old information, but it will be used differently. Finally, if job options that have survived screening become unavailable, job seekers will resist having to reconsider previously rejected options and will strive to find new options. If no new options can be found, job seekers will both lower their standards and become more tolerant of violations (raise their rejection threshold) when reconsidering the options that they previously had rejected as unacceptable.

Research on Job Seekers' Decision Processes. Two studies provide evidence supporting these predictions. In the first study, Beach and Strom (1989) asked 16 college students to assume the role of a graduating MBA student looking for a job. To control for differences in their preferences, all students used the same standards to evaluate job options. The students screened a list of 14 jobs to determine which ones they would retain for or reject from further consideration. The features (e.g., pay level, geographic location, etc.) of these jobs were printed on successive pages in individual booklets. These features were designed to fit or violate job seekers' standards. All jobs had the same number of features, but some jobs violated more standards than other jobs. Students read through each job booklet until they reached a decision about whether to reject or retain that job.

Results showed that subjects rejected job options based solely on the number of features that violated their standards; nonviolations had no effect on their decisions. The rejection threshold seemed to be about four violations. When 4 features violated subjects' standards (no matter how many features matched their standards), the job was rejected. If there were fewer than 4 violations, the job was retained. The results made it very clear that nonviolations did not balance out violations.

The second study (Osborn, 1990) was conducted independently of image theory, but provides data relevant to its predictions. Graduating students who were seeking jobs completed several surveys during the time they interviewed for jobs. Initially, they indicated what their minimum standards were and how important these would be in evaluating jobs. For each of their interviews, the students reported whether the job met each of their standards (yes–no), whether the job was acceptable (yes–no), and how acceptable it was on a scale from 1 (*not acceptable*) to 7 (*acceptable*). One month later, students were asked to rank order and choose one of the jobs they had rated on their earlier questionnaires as being acceptable.

The 96 students had 544 interviews and rated the jobs as acceptable in 344 interviews (i.e., these jobs survived screening). Of these acceptable job options, 88% did not violate any of the students' minimum standards. Conversely, 100% of the 200 jobs that did not survive screening violated one or more minimum standards. This pattern is consistent with image theory's predictions that screening is based on violations of job seekers' standards, and that nonviolations do not balance out violations.

Next, Osborn (1990) explored whether expectancy theory could explain the students' decisions. For each student, he added up the products of their importance ratings (V) and their ratings of how well the job met the standard (I) across all standards. These product sums were then used to predict students' choices on the final questionnaire. He found that for 31 students, jobs that expectancy theory predicted would be attractive were rated as unacceptable. All of these unacceptable jobs violated one or more of the students' standards, a finding consistent with image theory.

Finally, Osborn (1990) examined whether students used information differently as they progressed through their searches. We recall that image theory predicts that information used in screening will have little impact on the choice of multiple survivors of the screening process. Consistent with this prediction, Osborn found that the standards that were most important during screening were unrelated to students' final choices. In fact, choices were most strongly correlated with the information that had played the smallest role during screening.

INTEGRATING THE THEORIES

We believe that image theory provides a useful framework for integrating the insights of existing theories of job seekers' decision processes. To recap briefly, the major features of these theories are the following:

1. *Expectancy theory*: balancing out of valences and instrumentalities to select the "best" job option; strong motivation to pursue attractive jobs for which the chances of a job offer are high.
2. *Vocational choice approach*: comparisons between one's self-image and the images of different organizations; selection of the organization with the image most similar to the self-concept.
3. *GDP model*: comparisons between features of job options and ideal job standards; identification of an implicitly favored option; biased comparisons between the implicit favorite and one other option to justify selection of the implicitly favored.

By interpreting these features broadly, we can see several correspondences with image theory.

Expectancy theory suggests that job seekers prefer options that are likely to provide features they value. It assumes that positive and negative features can offset each other and that job seekers are looking for the "best" job given two or more options. As such, it is a theory of choice and can be subsumed under image theory's profitability test. Recall that the profitability test represents a repertory of decision strategies for choosing the best option from two or more survivors of the screening process. Balancing out the positive and negative features of each option is one of several decision rules that can be used at this stage (see Svenson, 1979).

The vocational choice approach emphasizes the importance of job seekers' self-concepts in evaluating job options. Its similarity to image theory is readily apparent in that both highlight the need for important decisions to promote the decision maker's integrity and existing goal agenda. Image theory extends the vocational choice predictions in two ways. First, it suggests that factors beyond the organizational image (e.g., perceptions of job characteristics, other relevant goals and plans) will affect job seekers' decisions. Second, it provides an explicit decision rule, the compatibility test, for evaluating whether options "fit" with job seekers' standards.

Finally, the GDP model bears many similarities to image theory in that both approaches recognize the reciprocal relationship between job search activities and screening processes. Like image theory, the GDP model specifies that an ideal job determines the standards used to screen options. The GDP model also predicts that an implicit favorite and one other option will be subjected to different evaluation processes at later stages. These predictions are consistent with the two-stage decision process proposed by image theory. Again, image theory is more precise in specifying how job options will be screened. It also makes predictions about job seekers' decisions when they must decide whether to accept a single offer or continue searching, a situation not considered by the GDP model.

MANAGEMENT IMPLICATIONS

At the beginning of this chapter, we suggested that understanding job seekers' decision processes could help managers improve their recruitment and selection practices. Our review of existing theories and the way these fit an image theory framework helped to explain how job seekers look for and evaluate job options. We now consider how this explanation can be used in designing more effective recruitment and selection procedures.

All of the theories we examined pointed to the importance of different job features—pay, organizational values and culture, working conditions—in affecting job seekers' decisions. Accordingly, an important first step for managers concerned about recruitment and selection would be to collect information on their own and their competitors' job features. This information can be obtained from several sources: government surveys (by region) of pay and benefits for benchmark jobs, in-house surveys of organizational values and culture, or even direct inquiries of competitors about their job openings. Knowledge of where one's jobs stand relative to those in the labor market provides useful information for improving recruitment outcomes. It permits recruiters to highlight favorable job information when interacting with applicants. It also provides a sound basis for determining when jobs and benefits should be modified to increase their attractiveness. Finally, concrete information about one's organizational culture and values can aid in screening applicants because it permits early identification of applicants who have compatible values and goals.

Both image theory and the GDP model predict that applicants who have clear ideas about their desired jobs will engage in more focused job searches. Therefore, one strategy for increasing the cost-effectiveness of recruitment would be to target carefully the desired applicant pool. Managers who spend time up front determining knowledge, skill, and ability requirements can use this information to determine which advertising outlets are best suited for reaching people who meet their requirements. For example, organizations could set up cooperative arrangements with trade schools, colleges, and universities for recruiting graduates to fill designated job openings. Some public accounting firms use this strategy to reduce substantially the time and money they spend on recruitment and screening. An added benefit is that available jobs should meet the minimum standards of most applicants. For organizations that must rely on less targeted sources (e.g., want ads), an alternative strategy is to write ads that clearly specify what the minimum requirements for applying are and what the key features of the job will be. This can help applicants screen out options quickly, reducing the time that must be spent on applicants who are likely to be a poor fit.

A general recommendation that derives from all the theories is for employers to provide information relevant to important standards early in the recruitment process. Jurgensen (1978) suggested that applicants generally are interested in information about the type of work, pay and benefits, advancement potential, hours, coworkers, and supervisors. Organizations should consider collecting and disseminating this information prior to or during their first contact with applicants. Image theory research (Potter & Beach, 1994b) suggests that the absence of information about important screening standards can increase the chances that an option will be rejected out of hand. Applicants may assume that missing information about important standards will translate into violations of those standards. In contrast, early rejection by applicants whose standards are violated can be cost-effective; these applicants need not be interviewed or subjected to other selection procedures.

Another promising strategy would be to modify job interviews. For example, interviewers can be trained to provide specific, positive information about the job and organization, including its culture, values, and work relationships. Interviewers can also ask applicants what standards they will use to evaluate job offers. If the applicant looks promising, interviewers can make sure that information relevant to those standards is conveyed at later stages in the selection process (e.g., the site visit). Even if the applicant does not look promising, collection of this information can be used strategically to determine whether the job or benefits should be redesigned to adapt to trends in applicants' preferences. For example, if applicants consistently mention that they are interested in jobs that help them build their skills, entry-level jobs can be redesigned to include rotation or training programs.

Finally, the unified approach to understanding job selection processes has several implications for the way organizations extend job offers to applicants. If an applicant appears to fit the job, and the job appears to "fit" the applicant, organizations should extend the job offer quickly. If the job option meets the applicant's standards and the applicant has no other offers pending, an early offer can increase the chances that the applicant will accept it. In contrast, if the applicant has several offers that meet her or his minimum standards, the final choice is likely to be idiosyncratic. Applicants will rely on information other than that used to screen job options. In this case, the organization should provide a variety of other kinds of positive information about the job to increase the odds that it will be accepted.

Conclusions

Managers often fail to consider job seekers' decision processes when developing recruitment and selection procedures. Tailoring these procedures to meet applicants' needs can be cost-effective and reduce the disruption of unnecessary turnover. Given the contradictions in existing theories, this oversight is perhaps understandable. Our hope is that by using an image theory framework, managers can gain insight into the way people look for and evaluate job opportunities. In an era of increased competition for skilled labor and shrinking budgets, this knowledge can lead to improved management of organizations' human resources.

REFERENCES

Arnold, H. J. (1981). A test of the validity of the multiplicative hypothesis of expectancy-valence theories of work motivation. *Academy of Management Journal, 24,* 128–141.

Baker, D. D., Ravichandran, R., & Randall, D. M. (1989). Exploring contrasting formulations of expectancy theory. *Decision Sciences, 20,* 1–13.

Beach, L. R. (1990). *Image theory: Decision making in personal and organizational contexts.* Chichester, UK: Wiley.

Beach, L. R. (1993). Broadening the definition of decision making: The role of prechoice screening of options. *Psychological Science, 4,* 215–220.

Beach, L. R., & Mitchell, T. R. (1987). Image theory: Principles, goals, and plans in decision making. *Acta Psychologica, 66,* 201–220.

Beach, L. R., Smith, B., Lundell, J., & Mitchell, T. R. (1988). Image theory: Descriptive sufficiency of a simple rule for the compatibility test. *Journal of Behavioral Decision Making, 1,* 17–28.

Beach, L. R., & Strom, E. (1989). A toadstool among the mushrooms: Screening decisions and image theory's compatibility test. *Acta Psychologica, 72,* 1–12.

Bretz, R. D., Jr., Ash, R. A., & Dreher, G. F. (1989). Do people make the place? An examination of the attraction-selection-attrition hypothesis. *Personnel Psychology, 42,* 561–581.

Caldwell, D. F., & O'Reilly, C. A. (1990). Measuring person-job fit with a profile-comparison process. *Journal of Applied Psychology, 75,* 648–657.

Connolly, T., & Vines, C. V. (1977). Some instrumentality-valence models of undergraduate college choice. *Decision Sciences, 8,* 311–317.

Glueck, W. F. (1974). Decision making: Organization choice. *Personnel Psychology, 27,* 77–93.

Herriot, P., & Rothwell, C. (1981). Organizational choice and decision theory: Effects of employers' literature and selection interview. *Journal of Occupational Psychology, 54,* 17–31.

Hill, R. E. (1974). An empirical comparison of two models for predicting preferences for standard employment offers. *Decision Sciences, 5,* 243–254.

Jurgenson, C. E. (1978). Job preferences (What makes a job good or bad?). *Journal of Applied Psychology, 63,* 267–276.

Keon, T. L., Latack, J. C., & Wanous, J. P. (1982). Image congruence and the treatment of difference scores in organizational choice research. *Human Relations, 35,* 155–166.

Osborn, D. P. (1990). A reexamination of the organizational choice process. *Journal of Vocational Behavior, 36,* 45–60.

Potter, R. E., & Beach, L. R. (1994a). Decision making when the acceptable options become unavailable. *Organizational Behavior and Human Decision Processes, 57,* 468–483.

Potter R. E., & Beach, L. R. (1994b). Imperfect information in pre-choice screening of options. *Organizational Behavior and Human Decision Processes, 59,* 313–329.

Power, D. J., & Aldag, R. J. (1985). Soelberg's job search and choice model: A clarification, review, and critique. *Academy of Management Review, 10,* 48–58.

Schwab, D. P., Rynes, S. L., & Aldag, R. J. (1987). Theories and research on job search and choice. In K. M. Rowland & G. R. Ferris (Eds.), *Research in personnel and human resources management,* (Vol. 5, pp. 129–166). Greenwich, CT: JAI Press.

Soelberg, P. O. (1967). Unprogrammed decision making. *Industrial Management Review, 8,* 19–29.

Super, D. E. (1953). A theory of vocational development. *American Psychologist, 8,* 185–190.

Svenson, O. (1979). Process descriptions in decision making. *Organizational Behavior and Human Performance, 23,* 86–112.

Tom, V. R. (1971). The role of personality and organizational images in the recruiting process. *Organizational Behavior and Human Performance. 6,* 573–592.

van Zee, E. H., Paluchowski, T. F., & Beach, L. R. (1992). Information use in screening and choice. *Journal of Behavioral Decision Making, 5,* 1–23.

Vroom, V. H. (1966). Organizational choice: A study of pre and post decision processes. *Organizational Behavior and Human Performance, 1,* 212–225.

Wanous, J. P., & Colella, A. (1989). Organizational entry research: Current status and future directions. *Research in personnel and human resources management* (Vol. 7). Greenwich, CT: JAI Press.

Wanous, J. P., Keon, T. L., & Latack, J. C. (1983). Expectancy theory and occupational/organizational choices: A review and test. *Organizational Behavior and Human Performance, 32,* 66–86.

4

CAREER DECISIONS

Cynthia Kay Stevens
University of Maryland

You are almost finished with your degree and are unsure of what you want to do next. Initially, you thought about going into consulting, but an internship convinced you that the long hours, travel, and continual "wooing" of clients were not for you. Your focus then shifted to management, but your résumé's career objective ("interested in management position with opportunities to utilize my diverse talents") has not exactly sent interviewers stampeding to your door. Should you try a different degree program? (You have often thought about becoming a counselor.) Or should you keep your part-time bartending job until a management position turns up?

One of your subordinates, Chris, comes to you for advice. Chris has been a solid, productive performer in your division for 15 years. When a project manager position opened up two months ago, Chris lobbied hard for the promotion. However, the job ultimately went to another person. Because of the glut of talented employees at Chris's level, Chris probably will never be promoted into management. Yet you would hate to lose Chris's practical and technical expertise. What advice or recommendations can you offer Chris?

Your uncle has worked for 30 years on the assembly line at a midsize manufacturing company. In the past few years, however, his company has been losing money. It recently announced that it will close its U.S. plants, putting hundreds of employees (including your uncle) out of work. Your uncle is unlikely to find a comparable job unless he moves to an area with a stronger economy. Yet he and your aunt cannot bear to leave their family and friends. The company has provided funds to retrain displaced workers, but your uncle (who is depressed and apathetic) has not participated in this program. Your aunt finally calls you for advice. What kind of training should he get? What should she do to get him "moving" before the retraining funds run out?

These situations illustrate some of the problems people may confront during their careers. A career refers to the pattern of work-related experiences that span the course of one's life (Greenhaus, 1987). The work opportunities available at any point in one's career depend heavily on the outcome of previous decisions concerning what occupation to pursue, what training to obtain, which job offer to accept, and what work assignments to seek. Therefore, understanding how these decisions are made is essential for resolving problems and effectively managing one's career.

The objectives of this chapter are to explain, in image theory terms, how people make career-related decisions and to explore image theory's implications for helping people effectively manage their careers. Toward these ends, the chapter begins with a brief summary of the career-decision-making literature. Then an image theory explanation of career-related decision processes is introduced. The chapter closes with several recommendations for helping people resolve common career-related dilemmas.

OVERVIEW OF THE
CAREER DECISION MAKING LITERATURE

Research into how people make career-related decisions has progressed in three distinct streams (see Taylor & Giannantonio, 1990). The earliest work focused on occupational choice, or how people select occupational groupings (e.g., Holland, 1959; Super, 1953). Most of this work pointed to the central role of the self-concept, which encompasses one's interests, goals, abilities, values, and other self-beliefs (Super, 1953). A general prediction in this literature is that people will gravitate toward occupational groupings that "fit" with their self-concepts. For example, Holland (1959) classified individual personalities and work environments into six categories: realistic, investigative, artistic, social, enterprising, and conventional. He predicted that people will experience the greatest success (i.e., satisfaction, achievement, stability) when their occupational work environments match their personalities.

A second, related research stream has concentrated on vocational development, or how predictable stages in people's lives affect their career decisions. This work assumes that people's identities and roles change throughout the course of their lives. As a consequence, their career directions and decisions are also predicted to change. As one example, Super (1980) proposed that people progress through five sequential career stages: growth, exploration, establishment, maintenance, and decline. He argued that the time devoted to work and nonwork roles will vary at each stage, shifting the pattern of career decisions.

Both the occupational choice and vocational development approaches help us to understand what issues people may consider when making career-related decisions. However, they do not explain how people weigh and combine information when considering these issues. A third research stream, the vocational decision making literature, has attempted to fill this gap. Although several decision models have been proposed (see Brown, 1990, for a summary), most studies have investigated subjective expected utility (SEU) theory or its counterpart, expectancy theory (e.g., Bartol, 1976; Brooks & Betz, 1990). These conceptually similar theories assume that decision makers evaluate the desirability (termed the *utility* or *valence*) of various career-related outcomes (e.g., major work activities, salary potential) and the ability of different careers to provide those outcomes (called the *subjective probability* or *instrumentality*). The career option that maximizes people's chances of obtaining their most desired outcomes should be selected.

Empirical studies have compared SEU–expectancy theory predictions to students' attitudes toward different occupations and choice of college majors. Summarizing this research, Mitchell and Beach (1976) found that both theories yielded fairly accurate predictions. In contrast, Pitz and Harren (1980) argued that people lack the information processing capacity to make the mental calculations suggested by SEU and expectancy theory. Other evidence indicates that when students are instructed to evaluate career options using whatever method they wish, their choices more closely resemble the results of simple decision rules (e.g., elimination by aspects) than of SEU decision rules (Lichtenberg, Shaffer, & Arachtingi, 1993).

In summary, current theories emphasize matching the work environment to one's self-concept as a basic principle in career decision making. Moreover, they also highlight the central role played by the self-concept as it develops and changes during one's lifetime. Less well understood are the ways that the self-concept and preferences for matching it to the work environment affect people's decision processes (i.e., how they weigh and combine information when making career decisions). Expectancy and SEU theory do not consider the person's self-concept, nor do they propose matching as a decision rule. Image theory provides an alternative explanation that postulates that people will compare career options with standards derived from their self-concepts to find an appropriate match. Therefore, it may help to integrate the different streams of research. A fuller image theory account of career decision processes follows.

AN IMAGE THEORY PERSPECTIVE ON CAREER DECISION MAKING

Image theory proposes that people's images of themselves (i.e., value images) and plans and visions for their futures (i.e., strategic and trajectory images) affect their career decision making. It predicts that people will strive to make career decisions that are consistent with the way they see themselves and their futures. Over time, people are predicted to develop particular interpretations and understandings of career-related events (e.g., getting a promotion, failing a certification exam). These interpretations and understandings (called the decision frame) require judgments about what knowledge is and is not relevant (e.g., one's desire to help others may be seen as relevant to choosing an occupation, whereas one's health and fitness goals may be seen as irrelevant). They also codify people's standards for evaluating different occupations and evaluating their career progress. The following sections describe in greater detail how these processes operate when people are confronted with career-related decisions.

The Images and Decision Types

The Value Image.   The value image includes a person's principles, morals, and values—essentially, the person's beliefs about how things should be and how people, including oneself, ought to behave. However, the value image is more than simply the sum of one's values; it encompasses self-beliefs about one's place or status in the world, what one is entitled to expect or receive from others, and assessments of one's capabilities and interests. In this sense, it is consistent with the self-concept as defined by occupational choice and vocational development theorists (e.g., Super, 1953). The value image is heavily influenced by childhood experiences, particularly one's family life, upbringing, and socioeconomic status. Acceptance of the family's world views should lead to decisions consistent with those views (e.g., following the occupational and lifestyle choices of one's parents). Conversely, rejection of the family's world views should lead to dissimilar decisions (e.g., selecting an occupation at a different socioeconomic level).

The Trajectory Image and Career Adoption Decisions.   The trajectory image reflects decision makers' visions of their desired futures, including near- and long-term outcomes they want to achieve (i.e., goals). Goals that comprise the trajectory image may be well-defined or indistinct and may refer to events (e.g., completing a graduate degree) or states of being (e.g., being happy in one's work). The major requirement for all goals is that they must be consistent with the way decision makers see themselves (i.e., the value image). For example, a person might think it would be nice to be wealthy but will only adopt becoming wealthy as a goal if that outcome is compatible with his or her value image (i.e., if being wealthy does not violate self-beliefs about one's place or status in the world) and with other preexisting goals and plans (e.g., goals for one's family life or community service).

Selecting an occupation, in image theory terms, entails adopting a goal for the trajectory image. Settling on a particular occupation is a central, defining decision that substantially affects many other future goals (e.g., whether time or money will be available for other activities or purchases, such as travel to exotic locations or a nice house in the suburbs). Therefore, people will consider these other goals and plans, in addition to their values, interests, or self-perceived abilities when adopting occupational goals.

Image theory predicts that people will use the compatibility test to narrow down their range of acceptable options (i.e., they will screen out occupations that deviate significantly from how they envision themselves in the future). Different occupational groups differ dramatically from one another in their implications for the future (e.g., consider differences in the task demands and lifestyles associated with medical versus manual labor occupations). Therefore, people often discard entire groupings without much thought. This process may not conform to rational choice prescriptions, but it does provide a simple mechanism for quickly eliminating unsuitable occupations.

Although the screening process is simple and quick, it does not necessarily yield a single occupational goal as its end result. Several incompatible career options may emerge as interesting candidates: consultant, manager or counseling psychologist. Fortunately, career decisions evolve over time, and educational prerequisites permit decision makers to gain needed information, as illustrated in the scenario at the beginning of the chapter. If decision makers still find several different occupations to be compatible when they begin their job searches, they often seek hybrid or interim career goals. For example, they may simultaneously look for jobs in different occupations (e.g., both marketing and human resource management jobs) and take the first option that presents itself. Alternatively, they may search for unique openings that involve aspects of multiple occupations (e.g., a small firm manager who handles both marketing and human resource duties) or pursue different occupations sequentially (e.g., begin in a marketing position and later seek opportunities in human resources). In the image theory analysis, people rarely use maximizing of decision rules to choose a single, "best" occupational goal.

The Strategic Image and Progress Decisions. Image theory predicts that as career goals come into clearer focus, decision makers will develop plans and tactics for goal attainment. These plans and tactics (part of the strategic image) may derive from several sources: They may be constructed from prior experience (e.g., study habits developed in youth may be applied when undertaking job training); they may be "borrowed" from successful models (e.g., mentors); or they may be explicitly taught in career development courses. To be viable, plans and tactics must be consistent with the way decision makers see themselves (i.e., the value image). For example, decision makers who value honesty would not seriously consider career plans that involve cheating on employment tests or sabotaging others' career advancement by spreading rumors. In addition to matching their compatibility with the value image, career plans and tactics are selected by forecasting their probable outcomes and comparing these with desired goals. When forecasted and desired outcomes are compatible, the plan or tactic will be adopted and implemented.

Note that for overarching goals, such as career goals, decision makers often begin with only hazy goals and plans. This is appropriate when decisions unfold over extended time periods. New information helps to clarify which goals and plans are most suitable. Moreover, unexpected opportunities sometimes arise during plan implementation; these can facilitate goal achievement in unforeseen ways. Thus, the absence of a fully developed career goal or plan need not pose an absolute barrier to action.

Once an occupational goal and the plan for attaining it have been adopted, decision makers will periodically evaluate their progress. In image theory terms, this evaluation is called a *progress decision*: People compare how far they have come with where they had expected to be. This is illustrated in the example at the beginning of the chapter: Chris compared her promotion progress to date with what she needed to achieve her career goals. If the outcomes forecasted under the current plan are sufficiently similar to desired outcomes, decision makers should continue with their current plans. Conversely, if the forecasted and desired outcomes diverge substantially, this discrepancy will trigger a search for better plans and tactics (e.g., Chris might get an MBA or tackle more challenging projects). If no plans or tactics can reasonably be expected to lead to goal attainment, decision makers eventually will revise their goals (e.g., Chris might seek a management job in another company or abandon the goal of moving into management).

The Decision Frame

According to image theory, decision makers develop standards to evaluate career options and current or expected career progress. These standards derive from the knowledge (principles, goals, plans) seen as relevant to the current situation. *Framing*, the process of determining what knowledge is relevant, helps decision makers to structure or organize their understanding and interpretation of the situation. This reduces the cognitive demands involved in making decisions by restricting the range of issues that must be considered. Typically, past experience in similar situations provides guidance in framing situations. Without prior experiences, decision makers must consider a large array of issues to evaluative standards and derive an appropriate interpretation. This process can be time-consuming, cognitively taxing, and anxiety-provoking, thereby delaying decisions and action.

In cases of overarching decisions, such as selecting an occupation, the framing process may be particularly difficult if decision makers have few experiences on which to draw. Contributing to this difficulty is the fact that young decision makers may find that their sense of themselves (i.e., the value image) is in flux. Thus, the array of issues that must be considered is both broad and unstable. Part of the challenge in selecting an occupation at this life stage is clarifying the value image through exploration and feedback.

Once a career decision frame has been established, it provides a basis for assimilating new information. Although it tends to be stable, the decision frame will shift over time as new information and experiences enrich the person's knowledge base. For example, a person may initially regard office politics with distaste and avoid becoming involved. Later, after observing the career consequences of involvement, the same person may come to view political behavior as necessary and desirable for career advancement.

Occasionally, new information can shatter one's understanding of the situation, triggering abrupt and dramatic revision of the career decision frame. Generally, the information must be extreme or discordant to prompt such upheaval. Examples include sudden loss of the status quo (e.g., due to a plant closure, as in the example at the beginning of this chapter) or midlife events that significantly alter one's self-beliefs or view of the world (e.g., a life-threatening illness, a divorce). In these situations, decision makers may not realize that the old frame and decision standards are no longer viable. Effort should be devoted to construction of a revised frame, even if this delays decision making and action. Without a coherent new frame, decision makers run the risk of making suboptimal career decisions (e.g., losing the opportunity for retraining assistance).

Summary

In comparison with SEU or expectancy theory, image theory provides a very different picture of the way people weigh and combine career information to make decisions. It suggests that decision makers' images of themselves, their futures, and their plans will be used to develop standards for evaluating career options and progress. Rather than weighing pros and cons to select the "best" occupation, decision makers are predicted to develop one or more hazy career goals that may influence career decisions throughout their lives. Image theory also specifies the decision processes people use to evaluate their progress once they have embarked on a course of action. Because it is consistent with theorizing in the occupational choice and vocational development literatures, it holds promise for integrating these research streams. Image theory also has a number of practical implications for helping people resolve career-related dilemmas. These are now explored more fully.

PRACTICAL IMPLICATIONS
OF AN IMAGE THEORY PERSPECTIVE
ON CAREER DECISION MAKING

As the situations at the beginning of the chapter suggest, people often experience difficulty making and implementing career-related decisions. The vocational guidance literature suggests that people experience difficulty at three points: when deciding a career or occupation, when implementing career decisions, and when making career transitions (i.e., from one occupation to another or when progressing within the same occupation). An image theory analysis of career decision processes helps to explain where difficulties are rooted and why some standard recommendations can be helpful. It also suggests some unique strategies for resolving career decision difficulties.

Deciding on a Career or Occupation

According to image theory, people typically do not select occupations by carefully and rationally weighing the pros and cons of each option. Rather, occupational goals most often emerge by default—by seeing what remains after unsuitable options have been eliminated. As a result, occupational goals may be fuzzy, perhaps including multiple options that point only in a general direction. One implication of this analysis is that it may be inappropriate to encourage the use of rational choice decision aids (e.g., multiattribute utility analyses) as a way to narrow down or clarify career goals. Decision makers frequently have unstable preferences and incomplete information about their options (Pitz & Harren, 1980); therefore, analytic methods that focus on choosing the "best" option may yield misleading recommendations or force premature closure. A simpler strategy that more closely mirrors decision makers' thought processes would involve helping them to clarify their preferences, explore options, and eliminate unsuitable alternatives.

Many vocational guidance interventions help decision makers clarify their preferences by identifying their interests or abilities (e.g., the Strong–Campbell Vocational Interest Inventory, Hansen & Campbell, 1985). Although this strategy is beneficial, it is incomplete. Image theory suggests that judgments of occupational suitability will also be based on holistic appraisals of larger lifestyle issues ("Can I see myself having the lifestyle associated with this occupation?"). Therefore, it may be more effective in the long run to help decision makers clarify this gestalt (i.e., their current understanding of themselves and what they can envision for their futures). One method for doing this involves helping them to develop mental pictures of themselves in the future, not in particular occupations, but rather in terms of what they see themselves doing. Bolles (1995) provided several exercises useful in this regard; another possibility is provided in Table 4.1. Getting decision makers to envision themselves in the future can open them to a wider array of employment possibilities. As the labor market shifts from job-based to project-based employment (Bridges, 1994), these visions can help steer people into worthwhile non-traditional opportunities such as temporary or part-time jobs, project-based employment contracts, and so forth.

Vocational guidance interventions also highlight the importance of exploring different career options to gain needed information (e.g., Stumpf, Colarelli, & Hartman, 1983). Library research and informational interviews provide useful data-gathering tools in this regard. An image theory analysis would support the use of these techniques, albeit in an expanded way. Specifically, decision makers should be encouraged to seek information that goes beyond job duties and responsibilities. They should investigate the kinds of lifestyles (e.g., work hours, affluence, relative stress, typical work environments, etc.) afforded by occupations of interest. Seeing people in various occupations can be particularly helpful because it provides a holistic

TABLE 4.1

Career Development Exercise

Visualize yourself as you think you will be in 10 to 20 years. Use the questions below to help you flesh out your vision. Avoid thinking about what you or others close to you wish for; consider only what you can envision yourself doing and being.

1. What do you think you will look like? What will be your typical style of dress when working (e.g., business suits, jeans & tee-shirt, etc)?

2. About how much money (annually) do you see yourself making?

3. How much responsibility do you see yourself as taking—for others (e.g., subordinates), for organizations? Do you see many, few, or no people reporting to you? To what extent do you see yourself as reporting to others (e.g., a boss)?

4. What do you see as being your primary work activities? Do you see yourself as working primarily with people, with information, or with machines, or tools? Do you see yourself as a leader of others, as part of a team, or working by yourself?

5. How active do you see yourself as being? Are you likely to have a desk job or a job that requires getting out from behind a desk? Do you see yourself as traveling a lot, a little, or not at all?

6. What sort of work environment do you see for yourself (e.g., office, outdoors, home, etc.)? In what geographic region do you see yourself living?

7. What type of primary relationship (if any) do you see for yourself? Do you see yourself as having and raising children? If so, about how many children do you visualize having?

8. About how much time per week do you see yourself spending with family members, friends, on community service activities, in church or religious activities, in work or job-related activities?

picture that can be used in making decisions ("Can I see myself doing what this person is doing?"). As the example at the beginning of the chapter suggests, the reality of working in a particular occupation can be at odds with decision makers' visions of what it would be like to work in that occupation.

In practice, helping people to clarify their preferences and explore career possibilities may involve a reciprocal process. That is, their preferences may become clearer as information about various opportunities becomes available; likewise, the information sought depends on one's preferences. Unlike rational choice models, however, image theory implies that the end result of this process can take several forms, including multiple viable career goals. This outcome can be beneficial, given the decline of stable, single-employer career tracks (Bridges, 1994). By recognizing multiple attractive career goals, people may respond more adaptively as they confront changing workplace norms. Thus, downsizing, mergers, and temporary employment might be seen as providing opportunities to pursue alternative career goals, rather than as obstacles to the pursuit of the "only" career goal.

Implementing Career Decisions

An image theory analysis suggests that two types of difficulties may be encountered when people attempt to implement their career decisions. The first problem area entails identifying appropriate plans and tactics for pursuing career goals. Career development and counseling programs and many self-help books address this problem by describing how to locate information, search for job openings, and interview for jobs. Some organizations supplement employees' knowledge through formal career ladders, job posting, and mentoring programs. Although these can be beneficial, image theory would suggest that mere knowledge of plans and tactics is insufficient for ensuring their use. Decision makers will adopt only plans or tactics that are compatible with the way they see themselves. Thus, these programs can be more successful if they help people envision themselves using recommended plans and tactics. Training methods such as cognitive and behavioral modeling and role-play exercises can be particularly effective in this regard.

The second problem area people may encounter when implementing career decisions stems from difficulty in monitoring their progress. Deficiencies include ignorance of the need to monitor progress (or the need to monitor it more frequently), inability to forecast outcomes, or lack of knowledge about how to make corrections when progress is insufficient. Image theory suggests that career counseling and development efforts can be more effective if they address these issues. For example people can be taught both how and when to assess their career progress by identifying milestone events, tracking their progress regularly, seeking interim feedback, and forecasting probable outcomes. Jungermann and Thüring (1987) have outlined a four-step scenario construction model that can be used to help people improve their forecasting skills. Specifically, instruction can focus on each step: helping people determine what knowledge is relevant to their career progress (i.e., develop an appropriate frame), constructing causal (if–then) links between plans and possible outcomes (e.g., if additional training is pursued, then new projects can be undertaken), determining how different plausible conditions will affect the outcomes of each plan (e.g., What if the training is not available? What if new projects are undertaken without the prerequisite training?), and assessing the desirability of these plausible outcomes and thus overall plan adequacy.

Several interventions can help people gain the knowledge they need to make appropriate midcourse corrections to their career plans. One effective (if humbling) option is to have decision makers conduct feedback interviews with several people of their own choosing (e.g., respected coworkers, supervisors). These interviews can be structured to elicit interviewees' opinions about two strengths and two weaknesses that the interviewer possesses, given the interviewer's career goals. When this information is compiled across several interviewees, needed midcourse corrections often become apparent. A second option is to provide instruction in self-management principles (Frayne, 1989). These include anticipating obstacles to career goal attainment, planning how to overcome those obstacles, setting intermediate goals to overcome identified obstacles, monitoring (i.e., recording) interim progress, and rewarding goal attainment. Self-management is highly effective in helping people stay on course when attempting to overcome career-damaging habits (i.e., chronic absenteeism; Frayne, 1989).

Making Career Transitions

A final area in which people may experience difficulty involves making career transition decisions, including decisions associated with job loss, reaching career plateaus, or coping with midcareer dissatisfaction. In image theory terms, these transitions are marked by changes in the decision frame: New information indicates that the status quo is no longer viable. In some cases, changes in the decision frame are internally generated; one realizes that the current career track is at odds with her or his desires or vision of the self and future. These changes are often subtle and accumulate gradually over time. In other cases, the changes are forced by external circumstances such as loss of a promotion, job, or even one's employer. These changes are abrupt and often require time to adjust.

Regardless of the underlying cause, a change in the decision frame can be traumatic. The decision frame represents one's current understanding of the world as it pertains to a particular sphere of life. Frames are constructed initially with some difficulty; once in place, they are reinforced by subsequent information and decisions. Changes in the decision frame, especially if abrupt, remove familiar guideposts for understanding and interpreting events. This explains some of the paralysis people may feel when confronted with such changes (e.g., as the example of the uncle illustrates).

Coping with career transitions requires action on three fronts: clarifying the self-concept, vision of the future, and career goals; constructing a new decision frame; and developing plans and tactics for pursuing new goals. A fundamental issue for people facing career transitions involves changing their self-perceptions. People's occupations are often incorporated into their identities; therefore, changes in their occupations necessitate changes in the way they see themselves. It is often important to help people understand that there is more to who they are than what they do to earn a living. Revising the self-concept may also require values clarification: What tradeoffs between different underlying principles, values, and beliefs can be made? For example, Chris may need to decide whether it is more important to find new challenges in the same organization (but at the same level) or to find another job (possibly in management) at a new organization. As the self-concept and values become clearer, it also becomes easier to revise one's vision of the future and identify a new set of career goals.

As decision makers clarify their self-concepts and career goals, they must simultaneously construct a new decision frame. In some cases, the process must begin by convincing the person that the old frame can no longer work. In the example at the beginning of the chapter, the uncle must realize that his standards for evaluating options are inappropriate; he cannot expect to find a comparable job at similar pay and remain in the same location. In counseling people who are in this situation, it may be necessary to suggest new ways of interpreting the situation and to help them test the interpretations they develop.

Finally, the development of plans and tactics to implement new career goals represents a culmination of efforts to determine a new direction. The decisions involved at this stage include determining whether previous plans and tactics apply to the new direction one is taking. It may also be necessary to assist decision makers in visualizing themselves implementing new plans and tactics. Especially in the case of job loss, low self-confidence can inhibit the tendency to risk rejection or persist in the face of obstacles. Again, training in self-management principles can be effective in prompting people to make progress.

CONCLUSIONS

In summary, image theory provides a useful framework for understanding how people make career-related decisions. First, it is consistent with existing occupational choice and vocational development theories, thereby helping to integrate the insights from all three literatures. Second, image theory describes where and why people experience difficulty when making career-related decisions. This leads to the suggestion of several unconventional but promising intervention strategies, such as visualization techniques, training in scenario construction processes, and self-management principles.

Predictions for the future indicate that traditional career paths are rapidly being replaced by project-based, temporary, and part-time employment relationships. Adapting to these changes requires greater flexibility in people's career goals and plans as well as in counselors' intervention strategies. With its recognition of multiple, hazy goals and emergent plans, image theory provides a strong basis for interpreting and responding proactively to the changing workplace opportunities of the future.

REFERENCES

Bartol, K. M. (1976). Expectancy theory as a predictor of female occupational choice and attitude toward business. *Academy of Management Journal, 19*, 669–675.

Bridges, W. (1994, September 19). The end of the job. *Fortune, 130*, 62–64, 68, 72, 74.

Bolles, R. N. (1995). *What color is your parachute?* Berkeley, CA: Ten Speed Press.

Brooks, L., & Betz, N. E. (1990). Utility of expectancy theory in predicting occupational choices in college students. *Journal of Counseling Psychology, 37*, 57–64.

Brown, D. (1990). Models of career decision making. In L. Brown & L. Brooks (Eds.), *Career choice and development: Applying contemporary theories to practice* (2nd ed., pp. 145–196). San Francisco: Jossey-Bass.

Frayne, C. (1989, Summer). Improving employee performance through self-management training. *Business Quarterly, 54*, 46–50.

Greenhaus, J. H. (1987). *Career management.* Chicago: Dryden Press.

Hansen, J. C., & Campbell, D. P. (1985). Manual for the Strong Campbell Interest Inventory (4th ed.). Palo Alto, CA: Consulting Psychologists Press.

Holland, J. L. (1959). A theory of vocational choice. *Journal of Counseling Psychology, 6*, 35–44.

Jungermann, H., & Thüring, M. (1987). The use of causal knowledge in inferential reasoning. In J. L. Mumpower, O. Renn, L. D. Phillips, & V. R. R. Uppuluri (Eds.), *Expert judgment and expert systems* (pp. 131–146).Berlin: Springer-Verlag.

Lichtenberg, J. W., Shaffer, M., & Arachtingi, B. M. (1993). Expected utility and sequential elimination models of career decision making. *Journal of Vocational Behavior, 42*, 237–252.

Mitchell, T. R., & Beach, L. R. (1976). A review of occupational preference and choice research using expectancy theory and decision theory. *Journal of Occupational Psychology, 49*, 231–248.

Pitz, G. F., & Harren, V. A. (1980). An analysis of career decision making from the point of view of information processing and decision theory. *Journal of Vocational Behavior, 16*, 320–346.

Stumpf, S. A., Colarelli, S. M., & Hartman, K. (1983). Development of the Career Exploration Survey (CES). *Journal of Vocational Behavior, 22*, 191–226.

Super, D. E. (1953). A theory of vocational development. *American Psychologist, 8*, 185–190.

Super, D. E. (1980). A life-span, life-space approach to career development. *Journal of Vocational Behavior, 16*, 282–298.

Taylor, M. S., & Giannantonio, C. M. (1990). Vocational guidance. In C. L. Cooper & I. T. Robertson (Eds.), *International Review of Industrial and Organizational Psychology* (Vol. 5, pp. 281–323). Wiley.

5

SUPERVISION AND JOB SATISFACTION

Byron L. Bissell
Lee Roy Beach
University of Arizona

Lisa slowly opened her closet door and absently stared at her meager wardrobe. What should she wear today? What difference did it make anyway? If today was like most days, she would be close to tears by noon, and how she looked would not count for much. The problem was her supervisor, Ruth, who just did not seem to know her job. Ruth seemed to think of herself as a manager, not a supervisor—always soliciting her people's opinions, always soft-spoken and polite, always making sure everyone understood "the big picture." It was ridiculous. What was needed here was firmness, direction, and backbone. Lisa had worked many places and had never seen anyone like Ruth, had never worked under someone who had less of a clue about what supervision was all about. It was all Lisa could do to hold her tongue and not take over herself, and the constant strain was killing her. She wondered whether that factory in Kansas City was still hiring, they at least would have supervisors who knew how to supervise. Now that she thought about it, she not only disliked Ruth, she was beginning to hate both her job and the whole damned company. It clearly was time to move on.

Studies of leadership, management, organizational culture, quality of work life, and organizational satisfaction have focused almost exclusively on managers and employees. Little attention has been given to supervisors and supervision, even though the role of first-line supervision frequently is identified as fundamental to the success of modern organizations (Doud & Miller, 1980; Kerr, Hill, & Broedling, 1986).

This oversight results, at least in part, from the failure to differentiate between management and supervision. The traditional view sees management as consisting of planning, controlling, and organizing segments of the larger organization in order to develop systems that will achieve the goals of the organization. Newer views add creating a context for change, encouraging commitment, and balancing stability and innovation (Jonas, Fry, & Srivastva, 1990).

In contrast, supervision involves directing and influencing the behavior of individuals and small groups within the organization (Imundo, 1980). Its function is to induce members of the organization to adopt attitudes and behaviors consistent with the systems developed by management, thereby contributing to achievement of the organization's goals. This is accomplished through the reconciliation and coordination of the needs and goals of the supervisee with those of the organization (Mann, 1965). Indeed, supervision is the intermediary between management's grand schemes and the line employee's efforts to implement those schemes.

At first glance there appears to be greater intellectual appeal in studying management: the formulation of goals and the design of plans to achieve them. By contrast, supervision appears to be rather pedestrian: the mere conveyance of managerial directives to employees. However, closer examination reveals that "the processes through which supervisor expectations are translated into changes in supervisee behavior is considerably more complex and problematic than has been commonly believed" (Sutton & Woodman, 1989, p. 943).

For most supervisees, the supervisor is the point of contact with the larger structure of the organization. As such, the supervisor's behavior (supervisory strategy) serves as a form of communication from and reflection of that larger organization. Therefore, it is reasonable to expect that a supervisee's attitudes, beliefs, and/or opinions about the organization will be strongly influenced by his or her perceptions of the messages communicated by the supervisor's behavior (Graen, Dansereau, & Minami, 1972; Kelley & Michela, 1980), making satisfaction with supervision an intermediary for satisfaction with the organization. Indeed, research shows that the employee's relationship with his or her supervisor (satisfaction with supervision) influences the psychological commitment to the organization (DeCotiis & Summers, 1987; Katz & Kahn, 1978), and that employee turnover intentions are more strongly related to attitudes toward the organization (organizational satisfaction) than to attitudes toward specific jobs (Shore, Newton, & Thornton, 1990).

A FRAMEWORK FOR STUDYING SUPERVISION

The Supervisor's Perspective.   Successful supervision involves three distinct skills: ability to deal knowledgeably and skillfully with technical task-related issues, ability to coordinate activities to achieve the desired organizational ends, and ability to interact effectively with and influence supervisees (Mann, 1965; Scarpello & Vandenberg, 1987). This third skill, commonly labeled *human relations* or *interpersonal skill,* is typically identified by supervisors as being the most difficult, causing the most problems, and requiring the most time. Indeed human relations training is typically ranked as the top training priority for supervisors (Mahoney, Jerdee, & Carroll, 1965; Richards & Inskeep, 1974; Solem, Onachilla, & Heller, 1961).

The Supervisee's Perspective.   Graen, et al. (1972) observed that "leadership style does make a difference within organizations. This difference may be not so much in terms of what the leader does but may be in terms of how it [leadership style] is interpreted by his members." (p. 235). Generalizing this idea to supervision, by watching the behavior of the supervisor the supervisee evaluates the meaning of the supervisor's behavior in terms of his or her own idea (image) of how the supervisor ought to behave. The supervisee then uses this evaluation to derive his or her satisfaction with supervision and, through this, his or her satisfaction with the organization.

This leads to two rather straightforward hypotheses: The greater the incompatibility between the supervisee's image of the ideal supervisory strategy and his or her perception of the strategy being used by his or her supervisor, (a) the less the supervisee's satisfaction with the supervision he or she receives and (b) the less the supervisee's satisfaction with the organization.

A Research Perspective.   The situation to be examined is employees' job satisfaction as a function of the compatibility between their ideal images of supervision and their images of the supervision they actually are receiving. From the image theory viewpoint, this is a good situation in which to study the diagnostic function of the compatibility test because it is common and reasonably circumscribed. Previous research on image theory (see chapter 1) has focused upon the role of the compatibility test in screening options prior to choice of the best option from among the survivors. However, compatibility also provides a way of evaluating whether the existing situation (persons, objects, events) does or does not meet the decision maker's standards. If it does, all is well. If it does not, the decision maker experiences negative emotions, often expressed as dissatisfaction with the situation (Beach, 1990). If conditions permit, these emotions motivate decision activity: search for alternatives, screening, and choice of the best option to remedy the unsatisfactory situation. In short, compatibility also serves a diagnostic function; it tells the decision maker when the situation falls short of his or her standards. Research that examines the compatibility between supervisees' ideal supervisory strategies and their views of their supervisors' actual strategies, then relates the difference to supervisory and organizational satisfaction affords a test of the usefulness of the compatibility test in diagnosing the quality of existing situations. In doing so, such research expands our view of the role of compatibility in decision making.

From an applied viewpoint, knowledge about the determinants of satisfaction with supervision provides guidance for the design of interventions to increase supervisee commitment and decrease employee turnover. As a beginning, if the results were to support the prediction of a positive relationship between compatibility of the actual and ideal images and satisfaction with supervision, this would suggest that actions that increase compatibility would also increase satisfaction with supervision, hence increasing satisfaction with the organization.

METHOD

Our research strategy was similar to that employed by Shockley-Zalabak and Morley (1989) who found decreased satisfaction with the organization to be a function of the difference between employees' "values, beliefs, and assumptions about ideal organizational life" and "their perceptions of organizational reality" (p. 487). In the present case the counterpart of "ideal organizational life" is the employee's ideal image of supervisory strategy, which was measured by asking how his or her ideal supervisor would behave. The counterpart of "perceived organizational reality" is the supervisee's image of his or her supervisor's actual strategy, which was measured by asking for a description of the supervisor's behavior. "Satisfaction" was measured by having the supervisee evaluate both his or her satisfaction with the supervision received and his or her overall satisfaction with the organization. Using the compatibility equation (see chapter 1), I (a number that becomes increasingly negative as incompatibility increases) was calculated for the descriptions of the ideal and actual supervisory images. Also, across supervisees, I was correlated with the evaluations of satisfaction with supervision and satisfaction with the organization (partialing out the variance shared with supervisory satisfaction).

Corresponding to the hypotheses described above, the first prediction was that there would be a significant negative correlation between I and the supervisee's satisfaction with supervision. The second prediction was that whereas there would be a positive correlation between satisfaction with supervision and satisfaction with the organization, there would be little or no correlation between I and satisfaction with the organization (controlling for the correlation between satisfaction with the supervisor and satisfaction with the organization).

Participants.   Participants were employees of two cooperating organizations. Group 1 consisted of 88 employees of the controller's office in a large state agency. Group 2 consisted of 34 employees of the pretrial services office in the justice department of a large urban county. The data from each group were analyzed separately. In effect, the study was done twice.[1]

Materials.   Ideal and actual supervisory behaviors were measured using a questionnaire consisting of 30 examples of supervisory behavior obtained from in-class exercises in a series of MBA courses in management (Bissell, 1992). Participants from the two organizations each were given a copy of the questionnaire and asked to indicate how often each of the behaviors should be used by a supervisor (ideal image) by writing a 0 for *never*, 1 for *sometimes*, and 2 for *often*. Then they received another copy of the questionnaire and did the same thing for how often their own supervisor actually used each behavior.

Satisfaction with the supervisor was measured using the Satisfaction With My Supervisor Scale developed by Scarpello and Vandenberg (1987). The scale consists of 30 items about one's supervisor; each item is rated on a 1 to 5 point scale, and overall satisfaction is the mean of the ratings across the 30 items. Satisfaction with the organization was measured using King's (1960) About Your Company questionnaire. This scale consists of 11 items about what it is like to work for the organization; each item is rated on a 1 to 7 point scale and overall satisfaction is the mean of the ratings across the 11 items.

---

[1]Although it would have been best to obtain importance weights for each of the 30 behaviors from each of the participants from the two organizations, because the experiment was run as part of a comprehensive organizational evaluation program, asking for weights in addition to all of the other things participants were asked to do risked imposing an undue burden. Therefore, weights were obtained from 49 employed MBA students who indicated the importance of each of the 30 supervisory behaviors in defining their ideal supervisor on a 1 to 7 point scale running from *very unimportant* to *very important*. The means of these ratings were used as the importance weights for computing incompatibility for each of the participants in each of the two experimental groups. It turned out that the results for both experimental groups using these weights were nearly identical to those reported earlier using no weights, a not uncommon finding (e.g., Beach & Strom, 1989; see Puto and Heckler, chapter 12, this volume). Therefore, these results are not reported.

Procedure   Participants from the two organizations were administered the questionnaires in groups of 2 to 15 people. Each participant filled out a questionnaire for their ideal supervisor, for their real supervisor, for satisfaction with their supervisor, and for satisfaction with their organization. The order of presentation for the latter two questionnaires was random across participants.

RESULTS

I was calculated by comparing each supervisee's response for the ideal image of supervisor behavior with his or her response for the actual supervisor behavior for each of the 30 behaviors. Identical responses on an item were scored 0; different responses were scored minus 1 (i.e., they were scored as violations). Then the (negative) sum of the violations was computed across the 30 examples for each subject. This sum, *I*, was then correlated across participants in each group with the participants' respective scores on the supervisory satisfaction scale and on the organizational satisfaction scale.

Obtained correlations of minus .61, $df = 86$, $p < .001$, in group 1 and minus .62, $df = 32$, $p < .001$, in group 2 between *I* and satisfaction with supervision support the first prediction. That is, the more the supervisor's behavior is seen by the supervisee to violate his or her ideal image of how a supervisor ought to behave, the less satisfied he or she is with the supervisor's behavior.

The obtained correlation of .63, $df = 86$, $p < .001$, in group 1 between satisfaction with supervision and satisfaction with the organization suggests that the latter may derive from the former. However, this correlation was only .07, $df = 32$, *ns*, for group 2. In light of the analysis described in the next paragraph, this disparity in results suggests that supervisory satisfaction was swamped by other factors in determining organizational satisfaction for the participants in group 2.

Because satisfaction both with supervision and with the organization are correlated, for group 1 at least, a semipartial correlational analysis was performed to ascertain the degree to which each of these two variables is uniquely correlated with the incompatibility (*I*) of the ideal and actual supervisory images. The resulting semipartial correlation for satisfaction with supervision was minus .39, $df = 86$, $p < .001$, for group 1 and minus .60, $df = 32$, $p < .001$, for group 2 while the semi-partial correlation for organizational satisfaction was minus .12, $df = 86$, $p = ns$, for group 1 and minus .18, $df = 32$, $p = ns$, for group 2. In short, the unique relationship between I and supervisor satisfaction was statistically significant for both groups, but the unique relationship between I and satisfaction with the organization was statistically insignificant, suggesting that the latter derives from the former rather than deriving directly from image compatibility.

The functional relationship between I and satisfaction with supervision is shown in Fig. 5.1. Recall that satisfaction with supervision was summarized as the mean for each participant of his or her ratings of 30 supervisor behaviors on 5-point scales. For any participant, a mean of more than 3.0 indicates overall satisfaction with supervision. Grouping participants according to the magnitude of I and then calculating the proportion in each grouping who are satisfied with supervision as a function of decreasing compatibility between the ideal image and perceived supervisory behavior leads to the graph in Fig. 5.1. (Sample sizes for the points are, left to right, 5, 18, 25, 28, 19, 18, 9.)

Figure 5.1 shows that as compatibility decreases (i.e., as the sum of violations increases), satisfaction also decreases slowly up to 10 to 12 violations, and then falls quickly. The apparent break in the curve suggests that for these group data the rejection threshold is roughly 10 to 12 violations.

IMPLICATIONS

The present results underscore the theoretical implications of other studies (see Dunegan, this volume): The incompatibility between decision makers' standards and what they actually experience influences their interpretation of the situation and colors their reactions to it. In this case the discrepancy is between their ideal for supervision and the behavior of their supervisors. The result is decreased job satisfaction as a function of the discrepancy and decreased organizational satisfaction as a function of decreased job satisfaction.

The practical implications of the results is that the compatibility between employee expectations about supervision and actual supervisor behavior is important for employee morale. When turnover is particularly expensive, it is not far-fetched to imagine testing both supervisors and employees in order to produce the necessary match.

Short of this, managers might do well to look at other possibilities. The first author recalls consulting with a professional organization for which supervision had proved to be a major problem; supervisors saw themselves as monitors of their employees' behavior and, as a result, were regarded by their employees as too intrusive. Redefinition of the supervisors' jobs, with a change in title to program manager, led them to think more globally; their

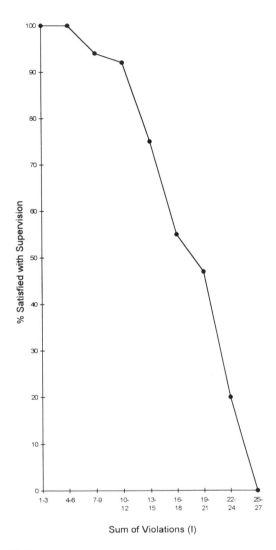

FIG. 5.1. Relationship between percentage of participants (combined groups, $n = 122$) who were satisfied with their supervisor's behavior as a function of I, where I is the incompatibility between participants' images of their supervisors' behavior and their ideal images of supervisory behavior.

old role behaviors no longer seemed appropriate to them. The new roles more closely fit their employees' image of what constituted proper supervision in a professional organization. Soon turnover decreased to near zero, absenteeism went down, morale increased dramatically, trust of management increased, and both the quantity and quality of customer service improved.

The relationship between management and employees has always been important, but historically it has been treated as though it were relatively simple. What is different today, and what makes the relationship so much more complicated, is that a better educated workforce is increasingly unwilling to simply follow orders. This unwillingness makes it difficult to induce the kind of behavior that management needs in order to move the organization forward. Many, or most, of the seemingly endless waves of managerial innovations are attempts to deal with this social phenomena. But most of these innovations fail to live up to their billing because they give little attention to establishing an effective management-supervisor-employee relationship that supports the kinds of behaviors that are desired. The present data suggest that a significant aspect of building this relationship is in having supervisory processes that meet employee standards. Until attention is given to this weak link in the organizational chain, we can expect a gap between management's requirements and employees' willingness to deliver.

REFERENCES

Beach, L. R. (1990). *Image theory: Decision making in personal and organizational contexts.* Chichester, UK: Wiley.

Beach, L. R., & Strom, E. (1989). A toadstool among the mushrooms: Screening decisions and image theory's compatibility test. *Acta Psychologica, 72,* 1–12.

Bissell, B. L. (1992). *Relationship between incongruity of supervisory strategy and satisfaction with the organization and/or supervision.* Unpublished doctoral dissertation, University of Arizona, Tucson.

DeCotiis, T. A., & Summers, T. P. (1987). A path analysis of a model of the antecedents and consequences of organizational commitment. *Human Relations, 40,* 445–470.

Doud, E., Jr., & Miller, E. (1980). The first-line supervisors: The key to improved performance. *Management Review, 69,* 18–24.

Graen, G, Dansereau, F., Jr., & Minami, T. (1972). Dysfunctional leadership styles. *Organizational Behavior and Human Performance, 7,* 216–236.

Imundo, L. V. (1980). *The effective supervisor's handbook.* New York: AMACOM.

Jonas, H. S. III, Fry, R. E., & Srivastva, S. (1990). The office of the CEO:Understanding the executive experience. *Academy of Management Executive, 4,* 36–48.

Katz, D., & Kahn, R. L. (1978). *The social psychology of organizations.* New York: Wiley.

Kelley, H. H., & Michela, J. L. (1980). Attribution theory and research. *Annual Review of Psychology, 31,* 547–501.

Kerr, S., Hill, K. D., & Broedling, L. (1986). The first-line supervisor: Phasing out or here to stay? *Academy of Management Review, 2,* 102–117.

King, D. C., (1960). The multiplant factor analysis of employees' attitudes toward their company. *Journal of Applied Psychology, 44,* 241–243.

Mahoney, T. A., Jerdee, T. H., & Carroll, S. I. (1965). The job(s) of management. *Industrial Relations, 4,* 97–110.

Mann, F. C. (1965). Toward an understanding of the leadership role in formal organizations. In R. Dubin, (Ed.), *Leadership and productivity* (pp. 289–301). San Francisco: Chandler.

Richards, G. L. & Inskeep, G. C. (1974, Spring). The middle manager, his continuing & and the business school. *Collegiate News and Views*, 5–7.

Scarpello, V., & Vandenberg, R. J. (1987). The Satisfaction With My Supervisor Scale: Its utility for research and practical applications. *Journal of Management, 13,* 447–466.

Shockley-Zalabak, P., & Morley, D. D. (1989). Adhering to organizational culture: What does it mean? Why does it matter? *Group & Organization Studies, 14,* 483–500.

Shore, L. M., Newton, L. A., & Thornton, G. C., III, (1990). Job and organizational attitudes in relation to employee behavioral intentions. *Journal of Organizational Behavior, 11,* 57–67.

Solem, A. R., Onachilla, V. J., & Heller, K. Z. (1961). The posting problems technique as a basis for training. *Personnel Administration, 24,* 22–31.

Sutton, C. D., & Woodman, R. W. (1989). Pygmalion goes to work: The effects of supervisor expectations in a retail setting. *Journal of Applied Psychology, 74,* 943–950.

6

WHY EMPLOYEES QUIT

Thomas W. Lee
University of Washington

Voluntary employee turnover has been of interest to managers since the beginning of the 20th century (e.g., Barnard, 1938). Driven in part by this managerial attention, organizational scholars have also shown a long-standing academic interest in understanding the dynamics of employee turnover (e.g., March & Simon, 1958). Since 1977, numerous psychological theories of employee turnover have been proposed (Hom & Griffeth, 1995; Hulin, 1991; Mobley, 1977; Mobley, Griffeth, Hand, & Meglino, 1979; Price & Mueller, 1886; Steers & Mowday, 1981). Correspondingly, a large number of empirical studies that test these turnover models have been reported as well. Given this sizable amount of information, it may be timely to pause and take stock of the more recent thinking on employee turnover. Thus, this chapter, based on the most recent interpretations of the academic research evidence, offers coherent explanations for why people voluntarily quit their organizations. Consider the following examples.

Case 1: A productive and job satisfied employee quits in a routinized (and almost casual) fashion. In the ski resort industry, for example, many employees enter with the idea of working for a fixed period of time. When that period of time ends, such an employee quits almost automatically.

Case 2: A productive and long-term employee abruptly and unexpectedly quits with no immediate job opportunities at hand. In the health care industry, for instance, major efforts at cost containment have led to significant changes in the relationships between nurses and their patients. Some nurses consider these changes to be so abhorrent that they simply quit when the hospital implements these new cost-containing nurse–patient practices.

Case 3: An employee suddenly begins evaluating the current and alternative jobs. Often, employees are basically satisfied with their jobs and committed to their organizations. On occasion, an unsolicited job opportunity presents itself in the form of an inquiry of interest or outright offer. These unexpected opportunities can often prompt a comparison between the current and potential job, which can then result in some relative disaffection, increased likelihood of future job searches, and eventual quitting.

Case 4: Over time, an employee grows and slowly changes differently from what the job requires. A semiskilled unionized craftsperson once described the widely shared vision for the career as follows: "You hook-on at 19 or 20. You make journeyman in a year or two. Then, you wait to retire. Sometimes, the sameness just makes you crazy." The experienced "sameness" can often result in an employee's quitting.

The psychological theories of voluntary employee turnover typically espoused in the organizational sciences do not explain these different cases very well. In fact, these traditional theories tend to be somewhat narrow in their approach to explaining employee turnover. In a review of the literature, Hom and Griffeth (1995) argued that traditional turnover theories have been too narrowly focused and that new approaches are needed. Thus, traditional theories may miss much of the variety in these quitting events. Recently, the unfolding model of voluntary employee turnover (UMVET), which is based in part on image theory (Beach, 1990), was proposed as a new and alternative way to understand quitting behavior (Lee & Mitchell, 1991, 1994a, 1994b).

CONCEPTUAL ANALYSIS OF VOLUNTARY EMPLOYEE TURNOVER

Traditional Turnover Theories

A detailed review of the major psychological theories of employee turnover that appear in the organizational sciences is beyond the scope of this chapter. However, the most influential turnover theory from this literature is undeniably Mobley's (1977) model of the "intermediate linkages between job satisfaction and employee turnover." Mobley's model is described here to illustrate how voluntary employee turnover has been commonly conceptualized. For an excellent and a comprehensive treatment of the literature on employee turnover, see Hom and Griffeth (1995).

Based on March and Simon's (1958) landmark ideas about the perceived ease and desirability of movement, the Mobley (1977) model depicts the process of employee turnover as a series of sequential stages. The process begins with an employee's (a) evaluation of the job, which is theorized to result in the experience of (b) job dissatisfaction. In turn, the experienced dissatisfaction prompts (c) thoughts of quitting, which then lead to a rational evaluation of the (d) expected utility of searching for another job and the (e) cost of quitting. Presuming that utility and costs are acceptable, (f) an intention to search for alternatives, followed by (g) the actual searching for alternatives and (h) the rational evaluation of the located alternatives are posited to occur. Next, (i) a comparison between the located alternatives and the present job is made. Finally, (j) an intention to stay and actual staying or (k) an intention to quit and actual quitting occur, depending, of course, on the outcomes of the rational analyses.

The empirical support for the Mobley (1977) model has been mixed. In general, the antecedents to actual employee turnover (or staying) have been related to one another in the theorized manner (Hom, Griffeth, & Sellaro, 1984; Lee, 1988). However, the final and most important link from the intention to leave (or stay) to actual leaving (or staying) has been modest in magnitude (Hom & Griffeth, 1995). Although the empirical evidence can be taken to be somewhat supportive, substantial opportunity to improve the model is also indicated. Moreover, the theory's focus on the intermediate links between job dissatisfaction and employee turnover may be overly restrictive. Other situations and factors may operate systematically on employee turnover and need to be included.

Consider, for example, the four cases described earlier. The Mobley (1977) model, as well as the other traditional theories, might aptly describe the turnover behavior of the semiskilled craftsperson in case 4, but may only partially explain the quitting of the job satisfied and organizationally committed employee in Case 3. However, the Mobley model, as well as the other traditional theories would not seem well suited to explain the turnover behavior of the employees in the ski resort industry described in Case 1 or the nurse's quitting described in Case 2. In order to increase the explanatory power of the disciplines' turnover models, the UMVET has been offered as an alternative to the traditional theories. It is important to note from the outset that most of the alternative theories, in general, and the UMVET, in particular, seek to complement and not to compete with the traditional turnover models.

The UMVET

Relationship to Image Theory (Beach, 1990).   In part, the UMVET seeks to lessen the heavy emphasis held by traditional turnover theories on the rational or intentionally rational comparison of alternatives (e.g., steps d, e, h, & i from Mobley's model). As such, Lee and Mitchell (1994a) applied principles from image theory (Beach, 1990) to better understand the process of employee turnover. Detailed later, the UMVET postulates that employee turnover occurs via four distinct processes called decision paths. In three of these four decision paths, employees are theorized to apply compatibility tests, instead of more rationally based comparisons, as part of the quitting process. Moreover, the immediate outcomes of these compatibility tests vary by decision path; only in decision path 3, for example, does a profitability test follow a compatibility test. Thus, portions of the UMVET derive directly from image theory, somewhat analogously to Mobley's (1977) model being derived from March and Simon's (1958) "decision to participate."

Shocks to the System.   The UMVET also seeks to expand the research from its heavy emphasis on attitude-driven turnover (e.g., job dissatisfaction begins the quitting process in Mobley, 1977) to a broader set of initiating variables. In three of the four decision paths, a "shock to the system" serves as the conceptual mechanism that initiates the turnover process. A *shock* is defined as a very distinguishable and jarring event that pushes an employee toward deliberate judgments about his or her job. These judgments involve the compatibility among the shock itself and the employee's values, goals, and plans toward goal attainment (e.g., the images from image theory). It is important to reiterate that a shock's key characteristics are distinctiveness, disruptiveness, and the prompting of deliberations. Thus, not all events are shocks, but all shocks must clearly disrupt an employee's ongoing status quo. Much like the disturbance notion used in the statistical method called time series analysis, a shock need not surprise the employee; it can be expected. Additionally, a shock does not imply a negative event; it can be positive, neutral, or negative. Lee and Mitchell's (1994a) UMVET is depicted in Figs. 6.1 and 6.2.

Decision Path 1 (Fig. 6.1).   In Decision Path 1, a shock to the system (diamond a) prompts a decision frame (box b) and memory probe (box c) for the recollection of a virtually identical shock situation and acceptable response (i.e., staying or leaving). If recalled, a match (diamond d) is said to occur, and the acceptable response is enacted in a scripted fashion (box e). If a highly similar memory cannot be recalled, another decision path is

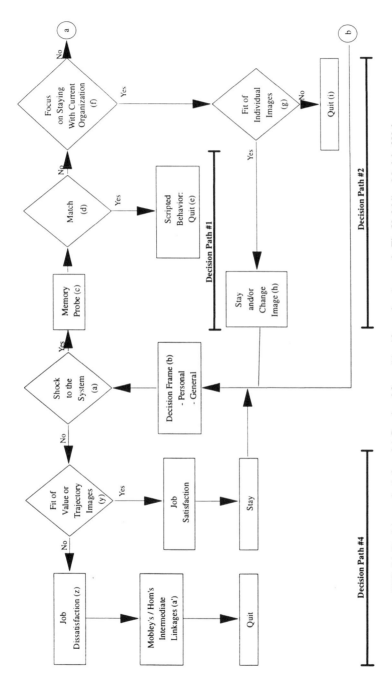

FIG. 6.1. Decision paths 1, 2, and 4. Reprinted from "An Alternative Approach: The Unfolding Model of Voluntary Employee Turnover," by T. W. Lee and T. R. Mitchell, 1994, *Academy of Management Review, 19*, p. 62. Copyright 1994 by the Academy of Management. Reproduced permission of the Academy of Management.

77

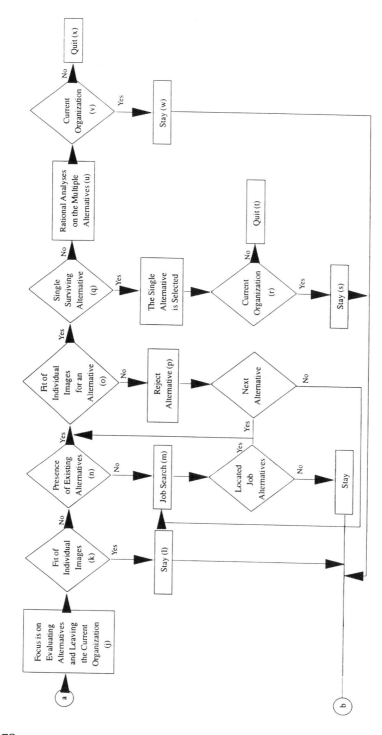

FIG. 6.2. Decision Path 3. Reprinted from "An Alternative Approach: The Unfolding Model of Voluntary Employee Turnover," by T. W. Lee and T. R. Mitchell, 1994, *Academy of Management Review, 19,* p. 63. Copyright 1994 by the Academy of Management. Reproduced permission of the Academy of Management.

initiated. Take for example, the employees from the ski resort industry in Case 1 developed prior. These individuals likely entered the job with a preexisting and scripted set of behaviors about how and when to leave. They may hold that they will leave when a certain amount of money is saved, when a certain time has elapsed, or when the snow goes bad. When the certain amount of money is actually accumulated, the particular date arrives or the given snow condition first occurs, these shocks to the system can prompt the onset of the scripted response of quitting. Note that a shock must be distinctive, disruptive, and prompting of deliberations; a shock need not surprise nor be negative.

Decision Path 2 (Fig. 6.1). In Decision Path 2, a shock to the system (diamond a) prompts a reassessment of the employee's basic attachment to the current organization; in other words, one focuses on how much one wants to stay with the current organization (diamond f). Moreover, the reassessment occurs in the absence of particular alternatives in mind. The specific process for the reassessment is image theory's compatibility test (Beach, 1990). The shock, situation, value-image, trajectory-image and strategic-image are assessed for fit (diamond g). If the shock, situation, and images fit, the employee stays (box h). If the shock, situation and images do not fit, the employee simply quits (box i). For instance, recall the nurse from Case 2. The shock to the system was the actual implementation of the cost-containing practices that altered the long-standing nurse–patient relationship. These shocks were abhorrent and incompatible with a nurse's basic values about patient care (i.e., violation of the value image). Additionally, these changes contradicted the nurse's beliefs about how to perform her required job tasks properly (i.e., violation of the trajectory image), and because these changes were perceived as permanent, the nurse–patient relationship was also permanently altered (i.e., violation of the strategic image).

Decision Path 3 (Fig. 6.2). In Decision Path 3, a shock to the system prompts an assessment of whether the employee could form a basic attachment to another company; in other words, the employee focuses on alternatives and leaving the current organization (box j). Note that these assessments occur with specific alternatives in mind. Here, three sets of decisions are theorized to occur. First, a compatibility test is conducted on the shock, situation, and images (diamond k). Unlike its counterpart application in Decision Path 2, the outcome in Decision Path 3 is to stay for a fit decision (box l), but there is some level of disaffection for a *not-fit* decision and a search for alternatives (diamond n and box m). Second, the compatibility test is then applied to the located alternatives (diamond o). A judgment of *not-fit* leads to the deletion of an alternative from further consideration; a judgment of fit leads to further evaluations on the surviving alternatives. Thus, this second compatibility test produces a subset of alternatives that will subsequently be analyzed by the individual. Third, these surviving alternatives are subjected to a more intentionally rational form of analysis (diamond q, box u; e.g., a profitability test). The particular alternative judged to be best is selected (diamond v, box w, and box x). Recall, for example, the job-satisfied and organizationally committed employee who received an unsolicited job feeler in Case 3, which provides a simple example of Decision Path 3. Note that the shock to the system is also the single alternative to the current job. A job search becomes unnecessary, but an evaluation occurs between the single alternative and the current organization. Thus, this hypothetical employee did not compare a dissatisfying job with the unsolicited job feeler; instead, this individual compared a good situation with the feeler. Rather than getting away from a bad job, this person might be going from a good job to a better job. Note that these comparisons only occur because of the precipitating shock to the system.

Decision Path 4 (Fig. 6.1).   In the fourth decision path, there is no shock to the system to prompt scripted behavior (Decision Path 1), no reassessment of one's attachment to the current organization (Decision Path 2) or no assessment of whether an attachment could form with an alternative company (decision path 3). Instead, the job is perceived as ongoing with few demarcations. Over time, some people grow or change in ways different from the natural evolution of the job. Rather than a prompting shock, a compatibility test involving the value and trajectory images occurs gradually (diamond y). A judgment of *fit* leads to job satisfaction, but a *not-fit* judgment leads to job dissatisfaction (box z), and in a sequence specified by Mobley (1977) or Hom and Griffeth (1995), lower organizational commitment, more job search activities, clearer perception of the ease of movement, stronger intention to leave, and higher likelihood of actual employee turnover follow. Recall, for instance, the semiskilled craftsperson in Case 4. At age 20, he believed that job security, good pay, and a comfortable life were all he wanted. By age 40, however, he had achieved his image of the "good life," but it was now insufficient; he wanted more. In his case, the value image had become incompatible with what the job could provide, and job dissatisfaction followed. Making only a minimal inferential leap, the onset of the sequences specified by the Mobley (1977) and Hom and Griffeth (1995) models occurred, and this particular craftsperson eventually quit the job.

UNIQUE CONTRIBUTIONS
OF THE UNFOLDING MODEL

A New Theoretical Basis

Lee and Mitchell (1994a) identified five particular contributions of the Unfolding Model. Perhaps most important, the Unfolding Model represents a major change in underlying theory. As noted earlier, traditional turnover theories have relied heavily on March and Simon's (1958) ideas about the perceived ease and desirability of movement (i.e., the decision to participate). Although a great deal has been learned from the perceived ease and desirability of movement, significant conceptual advances seem to be slow in coming. Indeed, some researchers have suggested that the traditional models tend to be quite similar (e.g., Hulin, 1991; Hulin, Roznowski, & Hachiya, 1985) because they represent only modest variations of March and Simon (1958). In contrast, the Unfolding Model derives, at least in part, from image theory (Beach, 1990). Instead of an almost sole reliance on rational evaluations, or evaluations intended to be so, concepts of compatibility and fit supplement the more "profitability-like" judgments found in the traditional models. Thus, one result is the redirection of the thinking about employee turnover. Moreover, a natural by-product of new theory is the corresponding novel directions for the empirical research and the application of alternative analytic methods (Hom & Griffeth, 1991; Morita, Lee, & Mowday, 1989, 1993; Peters & Sheridan, 1988). Over time, a great deal of understanding about this organizational behavior should accrue.

Scripted Behaviors

Automatic behaviors, labeled by psychologists as *habits, scripts* and *schemas*, typically have not been considered by turnover theorists or researchers. Yet, such routinized behaviors are no small part of organizational, as well as everyday, life. Perhaps, the reason for this omission in the turnover literature is an over-reliance on assumptions about rational mental processes, or those intended to be rational. As a result, such "nonoptimizing" deliberations and scripted behaviors cannot be easily explained by the traditional theories. In the UMVET, Decision Path 1 represents an explicit recognition and a statement of its centrality within the turnover process. Furthermore, Decision Path 1 may most validly apply to a much neglected portion of the workforce, namely, the secondary or contingent worker (Belous, 1989; Hulin, 1991). Given the decade-long growth of the service sector and the enduring strength of job creation in the small business sector of the American economy, for instance, Decision Path 1 and the contingent worker may become an increasingly important process and group of employees, respectively, to study and understand.

Shocks to the System

In our thinking about employee turnover, shocks offer a conceptual mechanism to make us consider the role unsolicited job offers (Case 3 above), random events (e.g., a 45-year-old colleague dies from a sudden heart attack), and personal luck (denial of tenure). Additionally, shocks can jar an employee out his or her inertial state. Sometimes, people simply move along comfortably in life, and opportunities (job and otherwise) go unnoticed because of the constant demands from work, home, and family responsibilities. Shocks can refocus attention beyond one's daily routine.

In a probing commentary, Cappelli and Sherer (1991) argued that scholars of organizational behavior were losing sight of the external context to which our concepts apply. In particular, turnover theorists and researchers were minimizing the role that the organization and other factors external to the employee have in the quitting process. In the UMVET, shocks to the system are conceptualized as being tightly linked to the context in which organizational behavior occurs. As a result, the concept of shocks encourages turnover researchers and theorists to stay closely focused on the role of the environment on quitting. Such refocusing on the organization and external environment should serve to remove an alleged gap between academic and managerial interests.

Multiple Pathways

Although multiple pathways have been recognized, traditional turnover theories and the corresponding empirical research have focused on a single and sequential process (e.g., Mobley's intermediate links between job dissatisfaction and quitting). Certainly, highly focused attention can result in substantial understanding, which has undeniably occurred in the research on employee turnover (cf, Hom & Griffeth, 1995). At some point, however, it is timely to redirect attention. The UMVET specifies shocks, memory probes, match versus not-match judgments and image fitting to distinguish four pathways. Thus, the UMVET now offers potential refocusing of our collective attention.

Differing Psychological Foci

In keeping with the idea of a single pathway, most of the traditional models have, understandably, focused attention on staying or leaving the current organization. The first step in Mobley's (1977) model, as we recall, is an employee's dissatisfaction with the current job. In subsequent links, a strong connection to the current job is also found. For instance, subsequent evaluations involve utilities and costs relative to the current job. Thus, the "anchor" (or object of attention) is the current job. In contrast, the UMVET's four decision paths direct attention to varying anchors. Decision path 1 involves a shock, memory probe, and match judgment. As such, the object of attention is the shock itself and the constructed decision frame. Decision Path 2 involves a shock, no alternatives in mind, and image fitting. The object of the employee's attention is on staying with the current company; in other words, the focus is on whether sufficient organizational commitment and job satisfaction exists to justify staying. Decision Path 3 involves a shock, alternatives in mind, and (potentially multiple) image fitting; the focus is on whether sufficient organizational commitment and job satisfaction could form with the alternative in mind to justify leaving. Decision Path 4 involves no shock and the slow (and possibly random) onset of a feeling of job dissatisfaction. The object of the employee's attention is the current company itself; there is no necessary focus on staying or leaving; there is no necessary job search or evaluation of alternatives. In sum, the UMVET explicitly recognizes and delineates different psychological foci and processes that can lead to employee turnover.

FURTHER IMPLICATIONS OF THE UMVET

Voluntary Staying

In traditional models, voluntary employee turnover is, quite naturally, the outcome variable of interest. That is, researchers want to understand and predict it. For example, the primary concepts in Mobley's model are antecedents to leaving (e.g., dissatisfaction, thoughts of quitting, cost of quitting, cost of search for alternatives, expected utilities for these alternatives relative to the present job). However, an emphasis on the understanding and prediction of a particular event (i.e., voluntary quitting) likely diverts attention away from another theoretically specified and potentially more important outcome, namely, voluntary staying. In traditional turnover models, voluntarily staying is seen as the conceptual opposite of leaving.

Voluntary staying has no uniqueness and is implied only to occur when leaving is not justified. Moreover, voluntary staying has no particular psychological or social mechanism beyond "not leaving" in most turnover theories.

In addition to explaining employee turnover, the UMVET is also a theory about voluntary staying. More specifically, it suggests possible and unique psychological or social mechanisms that prompt staying. Consider Case 5.

> *Case 5: Sequential decision paths.* Suppose that the hypothetical employee from Case 3 had ultimately turned down the unsolicited job feeler. Suppose further that two additional unsolicited job feelers arrived soon afterwards and were declined with minimal mental deliberations or changes in job attitudes.

In a narrow sense, Decision Path 1 might have occurred. That is, the first of the two recent job inquires was a shock to the system. The subsequent memory probe identified the experience and behavior described in Case 3 as a match. Staying was the scripted response. Also in the narrow sense, Decision Path 1 may have occurred again with the second of the recent job inquiries. That is, the second job inquiry was another shock to the system; the subsequent memory probe identified both the experience in case 3 and the just completed judgments resulting from the first job inquiry as additional matches; staying was again the scripted response. In a somewhat broader sense, these episodes should perhaps be viewed not as relatively distinct events. Instead, these episodes might be better viewed as strongly linked, with the prior experiences and judgments serving as the "raw materials" for subsequent Decision 1 matching and for the subsequent formation of schemas. In a broader sense still, the accumulation of decision path 1 experiences might, over time, constitute the process of voluntary staying. For instance, the repeated decision to stay because of Path 1 circumstances may lead both to a general desire to stay and to a cognitive schema oriented around staying (e.g., "I can't realistically imagine living anywhere else in the country than here."). Most broadly, the UMVET might serve as a conceptual tool for understanding and predicting additional organizational outcomes. In addition to voluntary leaving or staying, other outcomes might include duration of company tenure, voluntary entry into semi retirement, or voluntary shifts to part-time employment.

Shifting Paths

As noted earlier, voluntary employee turnover has been typically conceptualized to occur via one, but not more than two, pathways. In contrast, UMVET delineates four processes. In contrast to the single pathway, the advent of multiple pathways leads to questions about changing decision paths while they are unfolding. That is, what if one begins Decision Path 3 but changes midway to Decision Path 2? Consider the following case:

Case 6: Changing decision paths

A hypothetical individual is denied promotion to full professor and begins to search for another job. The denied promotion would constitute a shock to the system. Presumably, a subsequent memory probe did not produce a match decision; a compatibility test was conducted, a not-fit judgment was made, and a job search began (e.g., permission to list other professors as references, inquires to professional colleagues). In short, decision path 3 was begun. Suppose further that early during the process of job search, the hypothetical associate professor changed his or her images such that the prior not-fit judgment became a fit decision. Correspondingly, the decision to stay would follow. Whereas Decision Path 3 was begun, Decision Path 2 actually was completed.

Several conceptual issues arise. For example, might there be systematic reasons why there is a change of one or more images rather than completion of an already initiated search plan? When the images are changed such that a *not-fit* judgment becomes a fit decision, might there be a greater receptivity on the individual's part toward future unsolicited job inquires? Suppose Decision Path 4 were unfolding, and a shock propelled an employee into Decision Path 2. Would that individual be more likely to quit than had Decision Path 4 not been occurring? Because numerous interactive effects are plausible, the opportunity to expand the model's application and increase our understanding of employee turnover seems great.

MANAGERIAL IMPLICATIONS
OF THE UMVET

Managing the Turnover Process

Most turnover models in the organizational sciences assume that employees' voluntary leaving is dysfunctional for the firm. Early on, however, most managers recognized that at least some employee turnover was, in fact, functional for the organization (e.g., Simon, 1945). For example, employee turnover can allow for creative ideas that often come with new personnel; it can allow for promotion and transfer opportunities for current employees; and it can strengthen the work force when less productive employees move to better-suiting jobs. Thus, managers have been more recently advised not merely to minimize company turnover, but instead, they should seek to manage the process (Mowday, Porter, & Steers, 1981).

In the last decade or so, human resource specialists have advised managers to distinguish between functional and dysfunctional (to the organization) turnover (Dalton, Tudor, & Krackhardt, 1982) and between avoidable and unavoidable turnover (Abelson, 1987). More recently, managers have been advised to consider, in combination, functional versus dysfunctional and avoidable versus unavoidable turnover (Hom & Griffeth, 1995). In particular, functional but avoidable turnover implies that those who leave are less valuable to the organization and that managers have some ability to affect the quit decisions; under these conditions, managers should actively encourage the departures. Dysfunctional and avoidable turnover implies that the leaving employees are more valuable to the organization and that, again, managers can affect the quit decisions; here, managers should actively discourage the departures. Functional but unavoidable turnover may sometimes imply that managers have minimal ability to affect the quit decisions of less valuable employees; under these conditions, managers should take no action to encourage or discourage the departures, but should take action to minimize disruptions to the organization. If, however, dysfunctional and unavoidable turnover implies that the leaving employees are more valuable, but that managers can not affect the quit decisions, then managers should take no action to discourage departures, but should act to minimize the disruptions to both the leaving employees and the organization. Via its shocks to the system, image fitting, and decision paths, the UMVET can offer some advice on managing the turnover process; more specifically, it can suggest when to encourage, discourage, or take no action about an employee's departure.

Managerial Actions

Monitor Shocks. Because shocks initiate three of the four decision paths, managers might be well advised to become sensitive to their occurrence in employees' lives. Recall that shocks are defined as clearly distinguishable and jarring events. Managers (as well as coworkers, family, and friends) should recognize them easily when they happen. An observed shock can signal to a manager that an upcoming decision for employees to leave or stay is likely. At the very least, then, the manager is positioned to make additional judgments about whether it is worthwhile to encourage or discourage an actual quit or a decision to stay. In other words, managerial actions based on assessments of whether the quit behavior would be functional or dysfunctional, avoidable or unavoidable become timely. Consider the nurse in Case 2. Several months before implementation of the cost containing changes to the nurse–patient relationship, the nurse began making hostile comments about the organization's management and health care industry. Even a casual observer, let alone a manager or an immediate coworker, could recognize the magnitude of the anger by the tone of her conversation. It is suggested that her manager might have observed the angry tone, investigated the meaning of these comments (e.g., "What's going on here?") and decided upon a course of action (e.g., encourage leaving, discourage quitting, take no action because turnover was unavoidable, and/or preempt the rumors that would naturally have occurred).

Monitor Images. In the UMVET, compatibility tests occur in three of the four decision paths. The value, trajectory and strategic images can serve as an interpretive framework when (or if) mangers elect to monitor shocks, anticipate employee's judgments about compatibility or predict their subsequent reactions.

In particular, the manager might infer the value image from an employee's frequent statements about his or her broad, general goals. For example, a certain value image may be indicated when sincere statements are made by an employee about wanting to be an entrepreneur and some day owning a software company. His or her value image may then correspond to, and predict, long-term movement toward a career emphasizing learning, decision making, and work situations with strong performance–reward contingencies.

The manager might infer a trajectory image from an employee's frequent statements and actions about distal but more specific goals. For instance, a certain trajectory image may be inferred from actions taken by this entrepreneurial oriented employee who is interested in owning a software company. Such actions might include pursuing jobs that provide opportunities to write software, to experience the conditions that facilitate or inhibit software production, or to interact with successful owners of software companies.

The strategic image might be inferred from statements and actions about more proximal and very specific goals. The entrepreneurial oriented employee, for example, might regularly take college courses on computer programming, entrepreneur ship, and small business management; routinely attend major trade shows involving software companies; or enter social circumstances in which contact with software entrepreneurs is likely. Shocks then might be interpreted as facilitating or inhibiting the enactment of broad and general goals (i.e., value image), distal but more specific goals (i.e., trajectory image), or proximal and specific goals (i.e., strategic image). Those shocks that facilitate goal attainment should lead to *fit* decisions, whereas shocks that inhibit goal enactment should lead to *not-fit* decisions. When taken together, monitoring shocks and images might allow for meaningful explanation and anticipation of functional or dysfunctional and avoidable or unavoidable turnover.

Monitoring Mechanisms

Management by Wandering Around (MBWA).   MBWA was first recommended by Peters and Waterman (1982) in their insightful book *In Search of Excellence.* As the name suggests, to employ this mechanism managers should spend at least some portion of their day and week simply wandering around the workplace. By watching, talking, and generally interacting, the manager maintains contact with the people that matter most, namely, the employees. Understanding, empathy, and trust likely follow. In addition to being a good idea in general, MBWA provides an excellent means for a manager to monitor an employee's shocks and images. Recall the semiskilled craftsperson from example Case 4. Had his supervisor practiced MBWA, which he did not, the craftsperson's job dissatisfaction would have been recognized. Because his job performance was deemed good (as indicated by his official performance appraisals), the craftsperson's eventual turnover was organizationally dysfunctional. Moreover, his quitting could have been avoided had someone in the company simply discussed how long-term career goals might be identified (e.g., help clarify a value image) and attained (e.g., help devise trajectory and strategic images).

Measurement.   Pfeffer (1994) recommended the frequent measurement of organizational practices. In addition to knowing what actually is occurring within the company, measurement focuses employees' attention (i.e., "what gets measured, gets done"). From the perspective of the UM-VET, frequent measurement of employee attitudes, reactions, and values would also allow a manager to monitor shocks and images efficiently in a broader and more formal manner than would MBWA. Via frequent employee surveys in conjunction with MBWA, employees' attention would be forcefully directed toward shocks, images, and their compatibility. Over time, discussion of shocks, images, and fit would could become almost second nature.

Managers' Performance Appraisal.   Often, managerial performance includes the development of employee commitment and loyalty to the organization. It is only a small inferential leap to envision that a portion of the manager's performance appraisal could include the development of employees' commitment and loyalty as a formally evaluated component. Monitoring shocks, images, and fit could easily be incorporated into a "development" dimension on a manager's formal performance appraisal.

CONCLUSION

In prior presentations, we focused on the theoretical and research implications of the UMVET (e.g., Lee & Mitchell, 1991, 1994a, 1994b). In those papers, we concluded that only a surface understanding had been achieved and that much more remained for the academic scholar; that judgment still holds. Here, we considered some applied implications, and two conclusions appear evident. First, only a surface understanding of the applied value for the UMVET has been achieved. Managers and applied researchers may gain considerable insight on voluntary employee turnover from further study of the UMVET. Second, the old adage, "the best tool is good theory," may also provide wise guidance. In order to achieve even greater understanding of voluntary employee turnover, managers and applied researchers might also try to improve the UMVET.

REFERENCES

Abelson, M. A. (1987). Examination of avoidable and unavoidable turnover. *Journal of Applied Psychology, 72*, 382–386.

Barnard, C. I. (1938). *The functions of the executive.* Cambridge, MA: Harvard University Press.

Beach, L. R. (1990). *Image theory.* New York: Wiley.

Belous, R. S. (1989). *The contingent economy.* Washington, DC: National Planning Association.

Cappelli, P., & Sherer, P. D. (1991). The missing role of context in OB: The need for a meso-level approach. *Research in Organizational Behavior, 13*, 55–110.

Dalton, D. R., Tudor, W. D., & Krackhardt, D. M. (1982). Turnover overstated: A functional taxonomy. *Academy of Management Review, 7*, 117–123.

Hom, P. W., & Griffeth, R. W. (1991). Structural equations modeling test of a turnover theory: Cross-sectional and longitudinal analysis. *Journal of Applied Psychology, 76*, 350–366.

Hom, P. W., & Griffeth, R. W. (1995). *Employee turnover.* Cincinnati, OH: Southwestern.

Hom, P. W., Griffeth, R. W. & Sellaro, C. L. (1984). The validity of Mobley's (1977) model of employee turnover. *Organizational Behavior and Human Performance, 34*, 141–174.

Hulin, C. L. (1991). Adaptation, persistence, and commitment. In M. Dunnette & L. Hough (Eds.), *Handbook of industrial and organizational psychology in organizations* (Vol. 2., 2nd ed., pp. 445–506). Palo Alto, CA: Consulting Psychologists Press.

Hulin, C. L., Roznowski, M., & Hachiya, D. (1985). Alternative opportunities and withdrawal decisions: Empirical and theoretical discrepancies and an integration. *Psychological Bulletin, 97*, 223–250.

Lee, T. W. (1988). How job dissatisfaction leads to employee turnover. *Journal of Business and Psychology, 2,* 263–271.

Lee, T. W., & Mitchell, T. R. (1994a). An alternative approach: The unfolding model of voluntary employee turnover. *Academy of Management Review, 19,* 51–89.

Lee, T. W., & Mitchell, T. R. (1994b). Organizational attachment: Attitudes and actions. In J. Greenberg (Ed.), *Organizational behavior: the state of the science* (pp. 83–108) Hillsdale, NJ: Lawrence Erlbaum Associates.

Lee, T. W., & Mitchell, T. R. (1991). The unfolding effects of organizational commitment and anticipated job satisfaction on voluntary employee turnover. *Motivation and Emotion, 15,* 99–121.

March, J. G., & Simon, H. (1958). *Organizations.* New York: Wiley.

Mobley, W. H. (1977). Intermediate linkages in the relationship between job satisfaction and employee turnover. *Journal of Applied Psychology, 62,* 237–240.

Mobley, W. H., Griffeth, R. W., Hand, H., & Meglino, B. M. (1979). Review and conceptual analysis of the employee turnover process. *Psychological Bulletin, 86,* 493–522.

Morita, J. G., Lee, T. W., & Mowday, R. T. (1989). Introducing survival analysis to organizational researchers: A selected application to turnover research. *Journal of Applied Psychology, 74,* 280–292.

Morita, J. G., Lee, T. W., & Mowday, R. T. (1993). The regression-analog to survival analysis: A selected application to turnover research. *Academy of Management Journal, 36,* 1430–1464.

Mowday, R. T., Porter, L. W., & Steers, R. M. (1981*). Employee-Organizational Linkages.* New York: Academic Press.

Peters, L. H., & Sheridan, J. E. (1988). Turnover research methodology: A critique of traditional designs and a suggested survival model alternative. *Research in Personnel and Human Resources Management, 6,* 231–262.

Peters, T. J., & Waterman, R. H. (1982). *In search of excellence.* New York: Harper & Row.

Pfeffer, J. (1994). *Competitive advantage through people.* Boston: Harvard Business School Press.

Price, J. L., & Mueller, C. W. (1986). *Absenteeism and Turnover of Hospital Employees.* Greenwich, CT: JAI Press.

Simon, H. A. (1945). *Administrative Behavior.* New York: Free Press.

Steers, R. M., & Mowday, R. T. (1981). Employee turnover and post-decision accommodation processes. *Research in Organizational Behavior, 3,* 235–282.

7

AUDIT DECISIONS[1]

Lee Roy Beach
University of Arizona

James R. Frederickson
Indiana University

In 1984, Waller and Felix proposed a new model for describing how financial auditing decisions are made. Their thesis was that the auditor reaches an opinion about the absence of material error in a set of financial statements through a series of revisions and modifications of his or her knowledge structure. These revisions and modifications are made in light of audit evidence about account balances and about the procedures used by the client to collect and store accounting information. The auditor's knowledge structure both guides the search for and the interpretation of the evidence that modifies it, and the structure's modified form represents the current state of that evidence vis-à-vis the requirements that the client's data and procedures must meet.

The Waller and Felix (1984) analysis was quite bold, especially because behavioral accounting has enthusiastically adopted the concepts provided by classical decision theory and the heuristics and biases research (Ashton, 1982). Their analysis was a profound departure from the established view, but because it rejected the classical view, it lacked a decision model to which it could be tied. Since then, image theory has been developed. What follows is an extension of Waller and Felix's thinking using image theory.

[1]From "Image Theory: An alternative Description of Audit Decisions," by L. R. Beach and J. R. Frederickson, 1989, in *Accounting, Organizations and Society, 14*, pp. 101–112. Reproduced by permission of Pergamon Press.

Waller and Felix divided the audit process into four steps:

1. Deciding to perform the audit
2. Gaining an understanding of the client and a preliminary evaluation of internal accounting controls
3. Planning and execution of audit activities
4. Forming an opinion.

Step I involves deciding about the "auditability" of the potential client. Step 2 involves obtaining information about how the client's accounting information system actually transforms economic activity into accounting numbers. What is learned here sets the criteria that must be met by evidence obtained during the execution of the audit. Step 3 involves planning and execution of the audit. Step 4 involves assessing the implications of what is learned in the implementation of the audit (in step 3) in regard to the presence or absence of material error in the client's financial statements. The apparent presence of error warrants continued audit work or a recommendation that the client adjust the financial statements. If neither of these courses of action produces appropriate results, then a qualified opinion must be issued.

THE IMAGE THEORY ANALYSIS

The image theory analysis is done from the viewpoint of an accounting firm member who is primarily responsible for the audit. This auditor's decisions are about whether to accept or retain a client and whether the client's financial statements are without material error. In this we adopt Schandl's (1978) view that "the purpose of the audit is to see if events conform to some desired state of affairs [in which] the norms used are the image or images of the desired state of affairs" (p. 69).

The Images

The auditor shares with others in the auditing firm an idea of what constitutes the firm's *value image*: its principles, including business principles (e.g. profits, clientele), acceptable accounting principles, and acceptable auditing standards and techniques (appropriate compliance and substantive tests). The latter two, which are part of the frame that defines the focal activity as an audit, will be called the firm's *audit principles*.

The *audit trajectory image* consists of multiple, but similar, goals: a correct audit for each of the auditor's clients. The goal in the present frame is a correct audit for this particular client. A *correct audit* is defined as one in which the audit process supports an unqualified opinion (i.e., lack of material error in the client's financial statements). For convenience we shall call this a *successful audit;* an *unsuccessful audit* is one in which an unqualified opinion is not supported by the audit.

The *audit strategic image* consists of the audit plans for examining the auditor's different clients' financial statements in order to render an opinion. It includes the plan for the present client that is unique to that client's particular circumstances. The plan consists of major tactics, individual audit steps aimed at producing satisfactory progress toward the larger goal of a successful audit. The plan's minor tactics are more or less assumed: ascertaining where information is filed, footing columns of numbers, making phone calls, and the rest of the day-to-day activities that make a plan work but that are not necessarily thought out at the time the plan is formulated.

Each plan on the audit strategic image generates forecasts that are used to assess the audit's progress. That is, as the plan is implemented through execution of its component tactics, its forecasted results are tested for their compatibility with the criteria for a successful audit. Forecasted success leaves the plan in place. Forecasted failure results in adjustments to the tactics, such as revising the audit steps or increasing the extent of substantive testing. If adjusting the tactics does not reduce anticipated failure, then the plan itself must be revised. If plan revision provides no remedy, the goal must be rejected. Goal rejection means that the auditing firm cannot affirm without qualification that the client's financial statements are free from material error.

Types of Decisions

Let us examine the auditor's decisions within this framework. First, the auditor must decide whether to accept a potential new client for his or her firm (or to retain a present client). That is, the first decision is an adoption decision—whether or not to adopt the candidate client, which is the same as adopting the goal of a successful audit for that client. This adoption decision depends on the compatibility of the client's attributes with the firm's audit principles. Do the client's attributes violate any of the firm's relevant principles? Information about these attributes is drawn from records, from inquiries made of previous auditors, from governmental agencies, and so forth. (Waller & Felix, 1984). If the information indicates that the client's auditability is acceptable, and that the audit is an appropriate undertaking for the firm in other respects (e.g. it does not impede the firm's business goals), the client will be adopted or retained. Once adopted, the client and its successful audit become a constituent of the firm's audit trajectory image, with its location on the trajectory being determined by the deadline for completion of the audit.

The second decision is the error decision—whether the audit evidence supports an unqualified opinion about the lack of material error in the client's financial statements. As outlined by Waller and Felix, the first step in making the error decision is a preliminary evaluation of the client's internal accounting controls. Here again the firm's audit principles are brought to bear on the decision, except that this time they are used to set the criteria to be met before the goal can be regarded as having been achieved. Poor internal controls prompt more stringent criteria in terms of the timing and extent of substantive tests. Moreover, it is during this step that the major tactics of the plan begin to take shape. The general form of the plan is fairly clear from the beginning: It is dictated by generally accepted auditing standards and by prototypic audit plans developed by the audit firm. However, the prototypic audit plan is modified in light of the preliminary evaluation of internal controls and the resulting criteria for each client. It is during this step in the auditing process that the task requirements begin to become clear and the process begins to be crafted to fit the unique characteristics of the particular client and the environment in which the client operates. The second step toward the error decision is the implementation of the audit plan. Each tactical activity is aimed at seeing whether the information that it examines advances the audit toward achievement of the various criteria for goal accomplishment. When a criterion is met, tactical activity related to it stops. If prolonged activity does not produce progress toward meeting a criterion, the tactic is reviewed and changed if some alternative seems more promising. If the new tactic produces no progress, and no alternative to it appears promising, the plan itself must be reviewed. If the plan does not appear to be faulty or if no alternative can be adopted to replace it (perhaps there simply is no way to obtain necessary information or the client refuses to cooperate in some important way), the goal must be rejected.

Goal rejection means that the error decision is negative; the firm must propose adjustments to the client's financial statements or, lacking client support for adjustments, it must attach qualifications to its report on those statements. Usually, a negative error decision is negative because the plan could not produce events that met the criteria. In most cases the plan's lack of progress accurately reflects the gap between the client's financial statements and the supporting evidence. Thus the plan's default leads to rejection of the goal of a successful audit and, therefore, to the conclusion that the client's financial statements are not materially correct. Criteria that are unmet indicate where qualification is required.

SETTING CRITERIA

Criteria for a particular audit are addressed by the substantive and compliance tests that are the major tactics comprising the audit plan. If the tests yield results that meet all of the criteria, the goal of a successful audit is regarded as having been achieved, and the auditor can issue an unqualified opinion. The question is: What is meant by *criteria* and how are they set?

Criteria addressed by substantive tests are the amounts reported in the client's financial statement. Criteria addressed by compliance tests are dictated by the firm's audit principles—its image of appropriate accounting procedures and internal controls. As described by Waller and Felix, meeting substantive criteria is of primary importance; meeting compliance criteria merely allows the auditor to rely upon the client's internal controls, thereby allowing a reduction in the extent and/or timing of substantive testing.

Theoretically, decisions about whether criteria have been met often are described as Bayesian, sometimes short-circuited by judgmental heuristics. Practically, such decisions often appear to rest on tests of the null hypothesis that the amounts adduced from the audit evidence are not significantly different from the financial statements. Probably neither of these accurately reflects how the decisions actually are made. The process of setting criteria and making decisions about whether criteria have been met cannot properly be described using statistical concepts because both are influenced by variables that have no counterparts in statistics. Although a parallel exists between these activities and what statisticians do, the resemblance is superficial and can be misleading.

Indeed, it is highly unlikely that audit evidence is used in a strictly Bayesian manner, or even in a heuristic manner, nor are statistical tests really very germane to the error decision. The auditor's judgments of what constitutes "close enough" or materially correct are determined by many nonstatistical variables. In contrast, these judgments govern the decision about when a criterion has been met and when there has been progress toward achieving the goal, so they are important to the understanding of audit decisions.

SOME RESEARCH QUESTIONS

The foregoing analysis raises interesting research questions, the answers to which could be of service in the further development of both behavioral accounting research and image theory. The questions fall into two categories, those involving images and those involving the implementation of the audit and the decisions that result from the audit.

Questions About Images

The first question is about the auditing firm's value image, about the constituent principles and how they differ from one kind of firm to another. It has been found that for both persons (Brown, Mitchell, & Beach, 1987) and organizations (Beach, Smith, Lundell, & Mitchell, 1988) it is possible to discover constituent principles. Moreover, it has been found in both cases that it is possible to use knowledge of these principles to predict subsequent decisions. Auditing firms present an especially interesting setting for such research because, although each firm is unique, they nonetheless are quite similar in many ways. That is, some of their principles are unique to the business environment in which each of them operates, but other principles are similar across firms because of the strong norms and guidelines for the auditing profession. To be credible, research findings must reflect this diversity and similarity.

A second question is about the degree to which ethical principles pervade the various spheres of the firms' and the individual auditors' activities. That is, are ethical principles applied more directly in the evaluations of clients than in the determination of the firm's own activities? Do firms' ethical principles (and one assumes, their practices) reflect the instruction, or lack of it, received in the programs in which the partners received their training? How are ethical principles, as well as the other constituent principles, transmitted to newcomers to the firm—how does acculturation take place?

A third question is about the image of the successful audit and its role in audit decisions. Even though achieving a correct opinion is the abstract goal, if an unqualified opinion is the concrete goal toward which the audit is oriented, what sort of biases does this introduce? It is widely accepted that anchor points have an effect on subsequent decision making, although the effect to be expected is not always clear. In the present case, the audit is seen as needing to marshal evidence in order to achieve the goal of a successful audit. In this view the thrust is from doubt and ignorance toward affirmation, which according to the anchoring and adjustment hypothesis (Tversky & Kahneman, 1974) might induce a bias against goal attainment.

In contrast, one could construct a case for the effects of the thrust, the striving toward the goal, that produces the opposite bias. It really is not at all clear which bias, if any, is to be expected, and that is why research is needed.

A fourth question is about how forecasts are created. This is a general question for image theory, but auditing is a particularly appropriate arena in which to investigate it. The forecast is the anticipated results of the audit at any moment during the audit. The concept assumes a mechanism for bridging the gap between that moment and the future so that progress can be assessed. The question is how bridging takes place. Is it accomplished, for example, by merely extrapolating the present in some simplistic linear fashion? It probably is not. Is it accomplished, as suggested by Beach (1990) and Beach, Jungermann, and De Bruyn (chapter 11, this volume) by constructing a story about how events might unfold to form a path from here to there? Perhaps in some cases, but in auditing, this description may be more elaborate than what is needed or what actually happens. Clearly, research is called for.

Questions About Implementation

The first question about implementation actually is about the prior issue of how clients are adopted or retained. Because clients are usually considered one by one (it is seldom a question of retaining this client or that one), their adoption or retention is a decision about optional change. Optional change decisions are those in which the auditor has the option of doing nothing at all, thus staying with the status quo (Beach, 1990). In this case staying with the status quo either means not taking on the new client or retaining the old client. Research shows that in optional change decisions the status quo tends to be favored over change (e.g. Samuelson & Zeckhauser, 1988). This suggests that, business concerns aside, auditors may tend to be biased against accepting slightly incompatible new clients, while at the same time being equally biased toward retaining slightly incompatible old clients. The possible paradox is that, all else being equal, a firm might retain a client that it would not adopt were it a new candidate, and it might reject a new candidate that it might retain were it an old client. A corollary of this may be that, because progress decisions are optional decisions, there may be a bias toward staying with an unsuccessful audit (the status quo) longer than an outside observer would recommend, perhaps pouring even more re-sources into it in an effort to make it work (e.g., Staw, 1981; Dunegan, chapter 14, this volume).

The second question about implementation involves how evaluations of the client's internal controls influence both the judgment about how close is close enough for meeting criteria and the structure of the audit plan. Clearly, the course of the entire audit is conditional based upon the quality of the client's internal controls. During preliminary evaluation, the apparent quality sets preliminary tolerances for meeting criteria, thus determining the major tactics of the audit plan. As the audit proceeds and compliance tests are performed, if the preliminary evaluations of the controls are revised, there must be a complementary revision in the tolerances and tactics that comprise the plan. It is tempting to couch these revisions in Bayesian terms, but as explained earlier, this will not do. There are too many nonstatistical considerations operating in these revisions, from hard data to gossip. Perhaps a better starting place would be the attitude change literature. Although criterion tolerances may not be attitudes in the strict sense, they are not very different. They have the evaluative aspect of attitudes, and they have strong implications for behavior in that they influence both the formulation (and reformulation) of plans as well as the precision of those plans in terms of meeting criteria. Hence, attitude change may be an appropriate perspective for thinking about tolerance revision.

The final research question about implementation involves how implementation results in decisions. Ignoring the complications implied by the questions raised previously, the adoption–retention decision about clients is more straightforward than the materiality decision. It is customary to think of it as a routine business decision dominated by financial considerations. However, this may reflect an inaccurate stereotype about how business is done. Certainly the firm's profit is a large factor in the decision, and a firm that needs business may let this factor dominate. But principles other than solvency may also play a large role in adoption–retention decisions, and it is important to examine their contributions. Of course, the decision about material error is our primary interest. The image theory description of how this decision is made is quite different from the usual cost–benefit, expected utility description. In the present analysis the decision actually is about progress toward the goal rather than about the goal itself. Insofar as costs, benefits, probabilities, or utilities are involved at all, they influence the tolerances for meeting the criteria rather than being properties of or outcomes of the goal. No doubt some readers will regard this description as distressingly unparsimonious. However, a parsimonious description of unparsimonious events may be a Pyrrhic victory of style over substance.

Of course, because of its importance, all of the research questions outlined here have implications for the error decision. However, additional questions involve the criteria that comprise the goal, the manner in which tactics are designed to address these criteria, and whether some criteria are primary to the goal whereas others are secondary or whether all are of equal status. Finally, there is the question of how compliance tests contribute to the goal. Is the contribution direct or is it through influencing the criteria that must be met by the substantive tests?

SUMMARY

We have presented an image theory interpretation of audit decisions based on an analysis of auditing by Waller and Felix (1984; Felix and Kinney, 1982). The purpose has been to provide the reader with an elaborated example of the application of the image theory view to a specific business decision environment. The analysis is quite different from that provided by the conventional application of classical decision theory, which is the view that presently dominates behavioral accounting research. It is our opinion that because of the explicitness of the process and because of the importance of the task, auditing provides a potentially valuable arena for the investigation of decision making in the workplace.

REFERENCES

Ashton, A. H. (1982). The descriptive validity of normative decision theory in auditing contexts. *Journal of Accounting Research, 20*, 415–428.

Beach, L. R. (1990). *Image theory: Decision making in personal and organizational contexts.* Chichester, UK: Wiley.

Beach, L. R., & Frederickson, J. R. (1989). Image theory: An alternative description of audit decisions. *Accounting, Organizations and Society, 14*, 101–112.

Beach, L. R., Smith, B., Lundell, J., & Mitchell, T. R. (1988). Image theory: Descriptive sufficiency of a simple rule for the compatibility test. *Journal of Behavioral Decision Making, 1*, 17–28.

Brown, F., Mitchell, T. R., & Beach, L. R. (1987). *Images and decision making: The dynamics of personal choice* (Tech. Rep. No. 87–1). Seattle, WA: University of Washington, Department of Psychology.

Felix, W. L., & Kinney, W. R. (1982). Research in the auditor's opinion formulation process: State of the art. *The Accounting Review, 57*, 245–249.

Samuelson, W., & Zeckhauser, R. (1988). Status quo bias in individual decision making. *Journal of Risk and Uncertainty, 1*, 7–59.

Schandl, C. W. (1978). *Theory of auditing.* Houston: Scholars Book Company.

Staw, B. M. (1981). The escalation of commitment to a course of action. *Academy of Management Review, 6*, 557–588.

Tversky, A., & Kahneman, D. (1974). Judgment under uncertainty: Heuristics and biases. *Science, 221*, 1124–1131.

Waller, W. S., & Felix, W. L. (1984). Cognition and the auditor's opinion formulation process: A schematic model of interactions between memory and current audit evidence. In S. Moriarity & E. Joyce (Eds.), *Decision making and accounting: current research.* (pp. 27–48). Norman, OK: University of Oklahoma Press.

8

SCREENING OF CLIENTS BY AUDIT FIRMS

Stephen K. Asare
University of Florida

At the heart of a free enterprise system is the free flow of reliable information by which creditors, investors, and regulators make informed decisions about the allocation of resources or the need for governmental action. The banker deciding whether to approve a loan, the investor making a decision to buy or sell securities, the local congressman evaluating the fairness of utility rates–all are relying on information provided by others. In many of these situations, the goals of the providers of information differ from those pursued by users of the information (Watts & Zimmerman, 1986). For instance, in reporting on its own administration of a business, management can hardly be expected to be entirely impartial.

This line of reasoning highlights the social need for independent auditors—individuals of professional competence and integrity who will attest to the veracity of the information on which key decisions are predicated. In this vein, the auditing function is critical to the success of a free enterprise system. Audits increase the credibility of information and allow decision makers to use information with more confidence. By reducing information risk, audits reduce the overall risk of making various types of economic decisions and facilitate resource allocation (Ashton & Ashton, 1990).

Although professional auditors attest to the reliability of a wide range of information, including financial forecasts and advertising claims, the financial statement audit is by far the most common attest engagement (Pany & Whittington, 1994). In a financial statement audit, the auditor undertakes to gather evidence and provide a high level of assurance that the financial statements follow generally accepted accounting principles (GAAP). The initial phase of a financial statement audit involves a decision to accept (or decline) the opportunity to become the auditor of a new client or to continue as an auditor of an existing client (Waller & Felix, 1984). Although auditors provide a socially useful service whose restriction can affect resource allocation, they are not obligated to perform a financial statement audit for any entity that requests it, any more than an insurance company is expected to write a policy for an undesirable customer.

The client-screening decision, which is the focus of this chapter, presents an interesting dilemma to auditors. The recession in the 1980s and the sluggish economic recovery in the 1990s brought in their wake considerable competition among accounting firms for clients, including that of clients seeking an audit for the first time and clients seeking a change in auditors. This competition has propelled accounting firms to find innovative ways to attract new clients and retain old ones. For instance, Hock (1993) reported that accounting firms are resorting to "telemarketing, long resisted by accountants, to unabashedly steal clients." Moreover, once inside the door opened by the phone banks, there is considerable lowballing—promising to take work for next to nothing in the first year in hopes of keeping the client permanently. In one instance, reported by Hock (1993), a local accounting firm bid $31,000 for a job held by one of the largest accounting firms (hereafter, the Big Six). The Big Six firm had held the job for $50,000. To the chagrin of both the local firm and the Big Six firm, the winning bid came in at $16,000. In the face of such intense competition, the ability to retain old clients and attract new ones is a vital ingredient for accounting firms' growth and profitability. Little wonder that this ability continues to be an important component in the firms' compensation and promotion decisions (Asare & Knechel, 1995).

Although obtaining clients is essential to growth and profitability, it is also true that association with undesirable clients could lead to serious adverse consequences. These consequences include litigation, sanctions imposed by public or private regulatory bodies (e.g., the Securities and Exchange Commission [SEC], the American Institute of certified Public Accountants [AICPA], and other professional societies), and impaired professional reputation that can occur as a result of litigation, sanctions, or adverse publicity (Brumfield, Elliot, & Jacobson, 1983). As an indication of this problem, the Big Six spent $477 million to settle and defend lawsuits in 1991 (Arthur Andersen & Co., et al. 1992). In 1992, one of these firms faced a $338 million jury verdict (Pickering & Okell, 1992), and another one negotiated a $400 million settlement with the Federal Deposit Insurance

Corporation (Telberg, 1992). Thus, there appears to be no end to the continuous upward spiral in liability arising from association with undesirable clients.

To minimize business risk (i.e., the likelihood that association with a client would lead to adverse consequences), professional standards establish broad principles, and accounting firms set specific goals to govern the client-screening decision. The ultimate decision is delegated to a senior member of the accounting firm, who in essence, tests whether the acceptance (adoption) of the client is compatible with these principles and goals.

The professional standards, promulgated by the AICPA, articulated three broad principles that serve as rigid guides for the screening decision. The first principle states that "the audit is to be performed by a person or persons having adequate technical training and proficiency as an auditor" (AICPA, 1994, SAS 1, section 210). Thus, before accepting an engagement, an auditor, acting on behalf of the firm, must determine whether the firm has the personnel and expertise to complete the engagement. The second principle states that "in all matters relating to the assignment, an independence in mental attitude is to be maintained by the auditor or auditors" (AICPA 1994, SAS 1, section 220). Independence has always been a fundamental concept in the auditing profession, because without it, the auditing opinion is of little value to those relying on it. Finally, the third principle states that "due professional care is to be exercised in the performance of the audit and the preparation of the report." Thus, an engagement should be declined if due professional care cannot be exercised.

In addition to these broad principles, the professional standards provide that "policies and procedures should be established for deciding whether to accept or continue a client in order to minimize the likelihood of association with a client whose management lacks integrity" (AICPA, 1994, QC, section 90.16). The auditor's goal of providing a competent audit in conformance with generally accepted auditing standards (GAAS) can be severely retarded if the client's management lacks integrity. The standards also provide examples of appropriate policies and procedures; however, with few exceptions, the extent to which each accounting firm may employ those policies and procedures is a matter of professional judgment.

The specific policies and procedures established and the nature and extent to which they may be documented vary from firm to firm (Huss & Jacobs, 1991). At some firms, a lengthy form must be completed, typically consisting of numerous yes–no questions and requiring additional explanation for the no answers. Other firms utilize open-ended questionnaires that allow the auditors to summarize their efforts and findings. Firms differ in the level of approval (e.g., office managing partner or regional partner) required for obtaining or continuing any given client relationship. Most firms also articulate a general firm philosophy to accompany the specific client screening policies and procedures (Asare, Hackenbrack, & Knechel, 1994). An auditing firm may, for example, state that clients accepted by the firm should not be engaged in a certain line of business.

Although the specific policies and procedures vary by firm, research suggests that most client-screening decisions encompass four distinct phases: practice development, acceptance analysis, acceptance decision, and continuation analysis (Asare et al., 1994). These phases are depicted in Fig. 8.1. The process starts with practice development, whose purpose is to disseminate information about the services provided by the firm and ultimately to cultivate potential clients. Practice development is usually continuous with a low profile, although it may be aggressive, as when specific target companies are identified and actively cultivated. Size of company, auditing fee, prestige, exposure, opportunity for consulting, and timing of

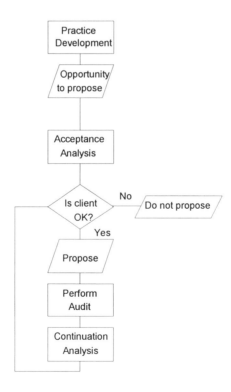

FIG. 8.1. Flowchart of the client acceptance and continuation decision process.

the work are among the engagement attributes that accounting firms consider when targeting prospective clients. Successful practice development provides opportunities for auditors to offer their services to prospective clients, often in the form of a proposal.

When presented with an opportunity to propose, the auditor performs a series of procedures hereafter referred to as acceptance analysis. The acceptance analysis may result in a decision not to propose, which terminates the process. Alternatively, if the analysis does not reveal any significant violation of the firm's principles or goals, the auditor will submit a proposal. The proposal is a verbal or written offer to provide services; if accepted by the prospective client, it signifies the "go ahead" to perform the audit.

The final phase is the continuation analysis— the decision to retain an existing client. Once the auditor has completed the audit engagement, a decision must be made about whether to continue the relationship with the client. There are a number of reasons why an auditor might choose to discontinue an existing client relationship. Invariably, the decision to disassociate from a client involves consideration of information that becomes available during the course of the audit. If the auditor and the client decide to continue their professional relationship, they will enter into an indefinite cycle of auditing the company and reviewing the relationship. The rest of this chapter elaborates and provides an image theory interpretation of the activities in the four phases.

PRACTICE DEVELOPMENT

The main role of practice development is to market the firm's services to the set of prospective clients whose attributes are not in obvious violation of the firm's principles (i.e., its value image) and goals (i.e., its strategic image). The marketing tools employed by accounting firms include institutional and target advertising; involvement in civic, business, charitable and social organizations; personal contacts; survey of clients; referral by existing clients; and submission of unsolicited bids to target companies.

Advertising, which until 1976 was banned by the accounting profession, is now a formidable component of firms' practice development (Wallace, 1994). Most of the international accounting firms now have an advertising campaign on national television that seeks to highlight their commitment to service. For instance, Deloitte and Touche has a slogan that emphasizes that its approach goes "Beyond the Bottom Line." Arthur Andersen advertised during the broadcast of the 1990 superbowl, and KPMG Peat Marwick International emphasized its global message.

Although firms routinely employ advertising, a recent survey reveals that most firms are funneling most of their marketing funds into special events. Both the international and local firms are reported to be spending more and more on profile-raising events such as symphony concerts and golf tournaments. Sponsored events include the Mobil Cotton Bowl Classic (Arthur Anderson), PGA of America's 1995 and 1997 Ryder Cups (Coopers and Lybrand, at a cost of $2.5 million a year), Habitat for Humanity (Deloitte and Touche), United States Olympic Committee 1992–2000 (Ernst and Young), NCAA College World Series (KPMG Peat Marwick), and the Michael Jordan/McDonald's Charity Golf Classic (Price Waterhouse).

It must be emphasized that not all potential clients are targets of a firm's practice development. That is, firms' principles and goals are used to define which clients to cultivate. Firms consider only those clients that can be serviced in accordance with professional standards and regulatory and governmental restrictions. Some companies may be omitted from consideration because they are in a high risk industry (e.g., casinos, savings and loans), are potentially unlawful (e.g., an importer of cut flowers from Colombia), or are of questionable repute (e.g., a 900 telephone service or adult bookstore). Finally, some clients are excluded because of the auditing firm's current client portfolio. For instance, the auditors of Coca-Cola company will exclude Pepsi-Cola company from its practice development efforts. Indeed, upon the merger that gave birth to Ernst and Young, the firm suddenly became auditors of both cola giants. However, Ernst and Young was told by Coca-Cola company that it could not stand for reelection as the auditor for both companies. Subsequently, Ernst and Young reluctantly informed Pepsi officials that they must withdraw as auditors for Pepsi. The Pepsi engagement had an estimated auditing fee of $9 million in 1990. Thus, practice development can also be considered as a prescreening mechanism.

ACCEPTANCE ANALYSIS

This phase of the screening decision is devoted to gathering and evaluating evidence to establish the fit between a prospective client and the firm's principles and goals. As discussed earlier, the strong norms and guidelines in the accounting profession (e.g., GAAS, etc.) lead accounting firms to have similar principles and goals that govern the client-screening decision. For instance, there is a good deal of agreement about principles, large portions of which are codified in the professional code of conduct (ET 52 to ET 57, AICPA 1994). These common principles engender the common goal of performing a competent audit in accordance with GAAS for each client.

In essence, the auditor applies specific procedures to evaluate whether the engagement can be completed in accordance with GAAS or, in image theory parlance, whether providing an audit for this prospective client is consistent with the firm's strategic image. To give some perspective to the balance of this section, the following issues are developed:

1. Firm independence and expertise
2. Management integrity
3. Anticipated profitability of the engagement
4. Client financial status
5. Auditability.

Firm Independence and Expertise

Professional standards require that the auditing work be performed by an auditor who is independent of the client. Also, the auditor or the auditing firm must have the requisite expertise to handle a specific engagement. As such, one of the earliest considerations is for auditors to evaluate the firm's independence and ability to service the prospective client.

With respect to independence, a designated auditor must consider whether any members of the firm has any financial interests or relationships that impair the appearance of the firm's independence from the client. Interpretation 101-1 of the professional code of conduct provides various examples of transactions, interests and relationships that result in lack of independence (AICPA, 1994). Among others, it indicates that independence will be impaired if a member or a member's firm had any loans to or from the enterprise; was connected to the enterprise as a promoter, underwriter, or voting trustee; or had or was committed to acquiring any direct or material indirect financial interests in the enterprise.

Two issues warrant additional clarification. The first is whether all employees of a certified public accounting (CPA) firm are required to be independent of the prospective client. Interpretation 101-1 clarifies that the independence requirement applies to all partners (or stockholders) of the accounting firm, all managerial employees assigned to an office that significantly participates in an engagement, and all professional staff personally participating in the engagement. Thus, the independence of a large CPA firm is not necessarily impaired merely because one employee of the firm is not independent of the client. If the employee does not have managerial responsibilities, the problem can be resolved by assigning the employee to other engagements. If the employee does have managerial responsibilities, it will be necessary to transfer the employee to an office of the firm that is not significantly involved with the auditing engagement.

The second issue relates to the way independence is affected by the financial interest or business position held by a relative of an auditor. Not surprisingly, the answer depends on the closeness of the family relationship and on whether the auditor works in a firm office that participates in the audit. The general rule is that the financial interests and business relationships of an auditor's spouse and dependents (including relatives supported by the auditor) are attributed directly to the auditor. As such, if the auditor's spouse owns even one share of a prospective client's stock, the situation is evaluated as if the auditor owns the stock (i.e., the auditor's independence is impaired). Whether the firm's independence is also impaired depends on the earlier discussion: Independence is not impaired unless the individual in question is a partner, a managerial employee assigned to an office that significantly participates in the engagement, or a professional staff member who personally participates in the audit. Independence may also be impaired by the business position held by the spouse or the dependent, by the financial interest or business relationships of other close relatives, and in some instances, by that of other relatives. An exhaustive treatise of the subject is probably beyond the scope of this chapter. Suffice it to say that a useful heuristic adopted by accounting firms is to determine whether acceptance of the client would lead a reasonable person to question the firm's independence.

Accounting firms vary in the procedures employed to verify independence. In some firms, independence is verified with a "negative confirmation." That is, a list of clients is periodically distributed to all auditing staff, but only those who have a conflict of interest with a client need to respond. Other firms use a "positive confirmation." The client list is made available to appropriate staff, who sign a form indicating that they are independent. Some firms retain investment bankers to supervise the stock portfolios of their auditors. When the firm decides to accept a new client, it instructs the banker to sell any stock the firm's auditors have in the new client's company. Regardless of the system used, independence problems caused by direct or indirect ownership interests must be resolved by disposing of the interests in question.

Consideration is also given to whether the partners and staff have appropriate training and experience to competently complete the engagement by the deadline desired by the client.

Management Integrity

As discussed previously, the primary purpose of a financial statement audit is to express an opinion on management's financial statements. Accordingly, it is important that an auditor accepts an engagement only when the client's management can be trusted. When management lacks integrity, there is a greater likelihood that the financial statement will be misleading. Furthermore, inquiry of management, which is a common and necessary auditing procedure, becomes of dubious value. The case of ZZZZ Best, a California carpet cleaning business, illustrates the futility of doing an audit of a client whose management lacks integrity. When an auditor demanded to see a ZZZZ Best job site, an employee of ZZZZ Best led the unsuspecting auditor to an unfinished San Diego building. Later, when the auditor demanded to see the finished job, the client leased the building with a $500,000 security deposit and spent another $1 million to put the building in shape. The auditor visited and was again misled.

Assessing management integrity involves inquiring about the general reputation of high ranking employees, influential directors, and shareholders. Circumstances that auditors will consider as raising questions about management integrity include a poor attitude toward compliance with outside regulatory obligations and evasive or uncooperative responses to inquiries. The professional standards and firm manuals identify many routine sources of references for prospective clients. These sources include attorneys, bankers, stockbrokers, ex-employees of the company, alumni of the accounting firm, business acquaintances of the company's management, other clients, colleagues in the firm (especially tax and consulting personnel), and mutual friends.

When routine sources are lacking, auditors employ more rigorous and formal investigations. They may check with the SEC for complaints, review arrest records, or hire an investigation service. If these investigations reveal anything of importance, management is usually given the opportunity to respond or explain.

In evaluating a potential client that has been audited previously by another accounting firm, a primary source of information is the prospective client's predecessor auditor. Professional standards recognize this and require the successor auditor to communicate with the predecessor auditor. The initiative for the communication rests on the successor auditor who inquires about the integrity of management, disagreement with management as to accounting principles or auditing procedures, and the predecessor's understanding as to the reasons for the change in auditors. To avoid problems of confidentiality, the successor auditor must request that the potential client authorize the predecessor auditor to respond to these inquiries. Of course, the client may refuse to grant this permission, which must be taken into account in evaluating the client.

The predecessor auditor is required to respond fully and promptly to the successor auditor. In some instances, legal problems or other unusual circumstances may preclude the predecessor from providing a full response. Again, such a limited response becomes a cue to the inquiring auditor. The form of communication may be oral or written. If the client is an SEC client, the auditor will read the Form 8-K which reports the termination of the predecessor auditor, including the predecessor auditor's response .

Evidence that will be at cross purposes with the goal of a successful audit for the client will include disagreement with the previous auditor over accounting principles or practices, resignation of the previous auditor or no clear reason for the cessation of the client relationship, refusal of other accounting firms to serve the prospective client, or insistence of the prospective client on a specific accounting treatment of an economic event—opinion shopping.

Anticipated Profitability of Engagement

Another consideration in screening a prospective client is the willingness and ability of the prospective client to pay an acceptable fee. Research suggests that most engagements result in little or no profit in the first year (i.e., lowballing). In submitting a proposal, firms focus not on first-year profits but rather on the prospect for future profits from repeat engagements and on opportunities for spinoff work such as consulting or tax accounting.

Client Financial Status

Auditors are not interested in accepting a client on the verge of bankruptcy because such cases tend to end up in costly litigation and high up-front costs that cannot be recouped. Further, the incentive for management to overstate operating results is increased when the client company is in a weak financial position or is in dire need of additional capital. Accordingly, the client's financial status is thoroughly assessed prior to proposing. The client's annual reports, interim financial statements, registration statements, filings of Form 10-K, reports to regulatory agencies, and income tax returns are carefully reviewed. The review of these statements also enables the auditor to gain a better understanding of the client's business and operations. The auditor will consider whether the client's business is compatible with the firm's statement of philosophy and goals.

Reviewing a client's financial status does not mean that companies in financial difficulty are totally avoided. Auditors also evaluate management plans for dealing with the identified difficulties. In such situations, the key questions become: Is the business legitimate and does the product or service make sense? Is management competent and honest? Does the company have a reasonable business plan? Is undercapitalization the main cause of the company's difficulties? Although not interested in short-term clients, accounting firms stand to gain much from start-up companies with a reasonable plan because these may eventually require more accounting services.

Auditability

A key concern that auditors often address early in the decision process is whether the prospective client is auditable. As used here, auditability refers to whether the client's accounting practices and control structure are conducive to accurate and complete recordkeeping. Concerns about the accounting system may cause the auditor to conclude that it is unlikely that sufficient competent evidence will be available to support an opinion on financial statements. The auditor will also consider management's response to observations about or suggestions for improvement in the internal controls made by the predecessor auditor, the internal auditor, or both.

The auditor will also obtain an understanding of the client's business and operations and evaluate whether the services required by the client are compatible with the firm's policies. Needless to say, the factors that will be relevant or considered will vary in each client situation. As such, it is not possible and probably not desirable to discuss all the potential factors that will be considered. Table 8.1 enumerates other circumstances that will be regarded as violations in the client-screening setting. It is important to emphasize that the presence of any one of these factors does not make a prospective client an automatic candidate for rejection.

Acceptance Decisions

"Most of the [acceptance] decisions are fairly easy" and "95 percent [of the time we] are going to accept the client—it is a matter of documenting what we are doing." These were comments made by auditing partners interviewed by Asare, et al. (1994). Auditors want to "get to yes." Turning away a client is a difficult choice for auditors to make because successful recruiting of clients is one criterion often used to judge the promotability of a manager to partner or to determine a partner's share of profits. But even

TABLE 8.1
Circumstances That Are Considered to be Violations of the Strategic Image

Engages in activities indicative of lack of integrity	Depends on a limited number of customers or suppliers.	Has a low entry barrier.
Is prone to engage in speculative ventures.	Is experiencing a financial or liquidity crisis.	Is subject to high competition, product obsolescence, or declining demand.
Displays a poor attitude toward compliance with regulations.	Operates in countries where business practices are questionable.	Has high operating leverage.
Engages in complex transactions whose effects on the financial statements are subjective.	Is vulnerable to rapidly changing technology.	Is undergoing rapid change.
Lacks a proven track record.	Has products that are new and unproven.	Is highly cyclical or countercyclical.
Is evasive or uncooperative.	The entity is prone to a high number of lawsuits or controversies.	Is facing regulations that will adversely impact profitability.
Is dominated by a single individual.	The entity plans an initial public offering.	
Places an undue emphasis on meeting earnings projections.	The financial statements will be used in connections with an acquisition or disposal of a business or segment.	
Compensation based to a significant degree on reported earning.	Has an understaffed accounting department.	
	Is experiencing difficulty in meeting restrictive debt covenants.	
	Has publicly traded debts that are below investment grade.	

the most aggressive auditor realizes that there are significant risks associated with accepting some prospective clients.

Consequently, little negative evidence is needed to reject the client. This suggests that auditors can be characterized as "hungry yet cautious." Being "hungry," the auditor adopts the operating hypothesis that all prospective clients are acceptable. However, because the auditor is cautious, very little negative evidence is required for this hypothesis to be abandoned. In this vein, auditors can be characterized as using a noncompensatory decision strategy, with rejection decisions influenced solely by violation.

Asare and Knechel (1995) tested this proposition by asking 29 auditors to screen 4 prospective clients. For each prospective client, participants were provided with background information and were allowed to obtain additional cues via computer to help in their evaluation. Different cue profiles were provided for each of the four clients. The cue set was all positive for client P and all negative for client N. For the remaining two clients, the participants received a sequence of either 8 positive cues followed by 8 negative cues (client M8) or an alternating sequence of 4 positive and 4 negative cues (client M4). As in actual practice, the participants controlled how many cues to evaluate before making a final decision (up to 16 cues, the maximum allowed for each client). The computer kept track of the number of cues and the decisions made by each participant.

All 29 participants rejected client N after processing an average of 7 negative cues. In contrast, auditors required an average of 14 positive cues to accept client P. Moreover, 18 auditors in the all-positive sequence used up all the cues compared to only three in the all-negative sequence. This suggests that rejection decisions are based on far fewer cues than are acceptance decisions. Further, if there was a stopping threshold for an acceptance decision, about 60% of the decisions required 16 or more cues for it to take effect. With respect to client M4 and M8, the mean number of negative cues processed prior to the 42 rejection decisions was 7, the same as the average number of cues required to reject client N. Finally, for the two mixed sequences, decisions to reject the client were more frequent than decisions to accept the client.

These results suggest the use of a noncompensatory decision strategy, with rejection decisions influenced solely by violations. They also suggest that auditors' rejection decisions are consistent with a simple tallying heuristic. That is, auditors will seek information about a prospective client until the tally of violations reaches a critical threshold or an external event (such as a deadline) compels them to make a decision. The rule of thumb is always to accept the client unless the tally indicates that the threshold has been reached.

Continuation Analysis

Rapid changes in the business environment make it necessary for auditors to evaluate existing relationships with clients. An auditor will withdraw from an existing relationship with a client when it has become apparent that the values of the auditor and client are at odds. The same matters considered when the client was accepted are reconsidered in light of the cumulative experience with the client in order to highlight issues such as management integrity, changes in management behavior, deteriorating financial condition, or rapidly changing operational conditions. The main difference in the acceptance and continuation decisions lies in the sources of information for the decisions. After completing an engagement, the accounting firm has more information upon which to base its decision. This suggests that external sources of information, such as business or legal references, are less important when the firm has extensive firsthand information. The three key issues that auditors consider when deciding to continue a professional relationship are now discussed.

Significant Changes in Client Characteristics.   Conditions that would have led an accounting firm to reject a prospective client may develop and lead to a decision to discontinue the engagement. For example, a client company may expand on an international scale to the extent that the current auditors do not have the competence to continue with the audit. Other significant changes may occur in the client's management, legal status, financial condition, nature of the client's business, and the client's ownership.

Audit Results and Client Relations.   The performance of the audit will reveal information relevant to the continuation decision and may lead to conflict between the auditor and the firm personnel or management. Situations involving voluminous related-party transactions, client-imposed scope limitations, and accounting disagreements that cannot be satisfactorily or amicably resolved may lead auditors to conclude that they should withdraw their services. Other situations may be more subtle, such as when management ignores the auditor's comments or when the control structure is deteriorating.

Profitability.   After an audit has been performed, the firm is able to analyze whether the engagement was profitable. Fees, costs, and expenses are all known with relative certainty at that point. The mechanism for determining profitability is the realization rate, computed by dividing the total fees collected for the job by the person-hours employed. This rate is then compared to the "official" billing rates of the auditing team. Realization rates in the first, and even second year of an engagement may be relatively low. However, if the realization rate is not close to 100% by the fourth year, it will suggest the need to reevaluate and probably terminate the relationship.

CONCLUSIONS

In explicating the working hypothesis of image theory, Beach and Strom (1989, p. 2) borrowed this example from Peeters (1986):

> Assume that there is a creature who lives solely on fungi; mushrooms are abundant and edible and toadstools may or may not be abundant but they are poisonous. The creature holds as its working hypothesis that every fungus is a mushroom. However, if the fungus has one or more attributes of a toadstool, that working hypothesis is quickly rejected. The reverse logic does not apply: a fungus that has many of the attributes of a toadstool must not be eaten even if it has one or more attributes of a mushroom. Hence the negative attributes of a particular fungus determine the decision about its edibility.

The analogy is certainly appropriate in the client-screening context. Auditing firms (the creature) depend on clients (the fungi) for their growth and profitability. Most clients present little risk (the mushrooms) to auditing firms and are acceptable. However, there are a few high-risk clients (the toadstools) who present substantial business risk to the auditing firm. For instance, a jury verdict of $338 million was awarded against Price Waterhouse in the audit of Miniscribe. Under these circumstances, the auditor's screening decision rule can be characterized as "hungry yet cautious." Positive evidence does not counterbalance the effect of negative evidence. Given that perfect discrimination of prospective clients is not possible, this screening strategy is safest because it favors false negative decisions (rejection of low-risk clients that have attributes of high risk clients) over false positive decisions (acceptance of high-risk clients that have attributes of low-risk clients).

There is no mystery about auditors' posture in the screening decision. In recent years, accounting firms have had to pay millions of dollars to settle claims alleging that their audits did not uncover financial problems. Accounting firms are routinely sued when they are involved in an initial public offering that goes sour. A position paper on legal reform, issued by the Big Six firms, indicated that there are about $30 billion in damage claims currently facing the profession as a whole. In the same paper, the firms indicated they are reducing the threat of litigation by avoiding what are considered high-risk auditing clients and even entire industries. High-risk categories include financial institutions, insurance companies, and real estate investment firms.

Although the screening strategy may be reasonable from the viewpoint of auditors, it presents a conundrum for prospective clients and indeed for the economic system as a whole. With respect to prospective clients, they may be forced to buy auditing services from accounting firms less used to assessing their industry. As such, they may not be getting the quality of auditing services needed by them and their investors. Clients "fired" by their auditors as a result of the client continuance decision may also be faced with a double jeopardy. That is, not only do they lose their auditors, but they also have to contend with suspicious investors who often interpret loss of auditors as a signal of "crooked accounting." The position paper by the Big Six firms included high technology, midsize companies, and private companies making initial public offerings as "high-risk" companies. Restricting auditing services to these companies, who are key sources of innovations and jobs, has detrimental effects for the economy as a whole.

Conspicuously missing from the discussion thus far are any notions of probabilistic processing or maximization. This is not an oversight. These notions have been found to be inadequate descriptors of auditors' decisions.

REFERENCES

American Institute of Certified Public Accountants (1994/June). *AICPA professional standards* (Vols. 1 & 2). Chicago: Commerce Clearing House.

Arthur Andersen & Co., Coopers & Lybrand, Deloitte & Touche, Ernst & Young, KPMG Peat Marwick, Price Waterhouse (1992/August). *The liability crisis in the United States: Impact on the accounting profession, A statement of position.* New York: AICPA.

Asare S., Hackenbrack, K., & Knechel, R. (1994). *Client acceptance and continuation decisions.* Paper presented at the XII Deloitte & Touche/University of Kansas Symposium on Auditing Problems, University of Kansas, Lawrence, KS. 163–178.

Asare, S., & Knechel, R. (1995). Termination of information evaluation in auditing. *Journal of Behavioral Decision Making, 8*, 21–31.

Ashton, R., & Ashton, A. (1990). Evidence responsiveness in professional judgment: Effects of positive versus negative evidence and presentation mode. *Organizational Behavior and Human Decision Processes, 46*, 1–19.

Beach, L. R., & Strom, E. (1989). A toadstool among the mushrooms: Screening decisions and image theory's compatibility test. *Acta Psychologica, 72*, 1–12.

Brumfield, C., Elliott, R., & Jacobson, P. (1983). Business risk and the audit process. *Journal of Accountancy, 155*, 60–68.

Hock, S. (1993/April 19). Telemarketing heats Chicago rivalries. *Accounting Today, 7*, 1, 44.

Huss, H., & Jacobs, F. (1991/Fall). Risk containment: Exploring auditor decisions in the engagement process. *Auditing: A Journal of Practice and Theory, 10*, 16–32.

Pany, K., & Whittington, R. (1994). *Auditing.* Boston: Irwin.

Peeters, G. (1986). Good and evil as softwares of the brain: On psychological "immediates" underlying the metaphysical "ultimates." *Interdisciplinary Studies in the Philosophy of Understanding, 9*, 210–231.

Pickering, J., & Okell, B. (1992/June). PW verdict rocks profession: Arizona jury levies $338 million penalty in audit case. *Accounting Today, 6*, 1, 35.

Telberg, R. (1992/December). Ernst deal marks new era. *Accounting Today, 6*, 1, 29.

Wallace, W. (1994). *Auditing.* Boston: PWS-Kent.

Waller, W., & Felix, W. (1984). Cognition and the auditor's opinion formulation process: A schematic model of interactions between memory and current audit evidence. In S. Moriarity & E. Joyce (Eds.), *Decision making and accounting: Current research* (pp. 27–48). Norman, OK: University of Oklahoma Press.

Watts, R., & Zimmerman, J. (1986). *Positive accounting theory.* Englewood Cliffs, NJ: Prentice-Hall.

9

ORGANIZATIONAL CULTURE AND DECISION MAKING

Kristopher A. Weatherly
The Walt Disney World Co.

Lee Roy Beach
University of Arizona

It really had seemed like a good idea, but it clearly was not working. He had seen it work in his last job, but trying to do it here merely resulted in chaos. How many times had he read that "empowerment" was good, that it would result in happiness and profit and all the rest? Moreover, he had seen it work before. True, the people at his last job had been working together for a long time and had a clear idea of what the company was about and how to do things. Here everyone seemed to march to a different drummer, to make up the rules as they went along. Only one thing was clear, empowering this bunch was going to cost him his job and cost the organization a fortune to get things straightened out again. Still, it had seemed like a good idea at the time.

In this chapter we examine the relationship between an organization's culture and the decisions made within that organization. The chapter has two goals: first, to provide a theoretical link between culture and organizational decision making and second, to test some of the implications of this link.

An organization's culture consists of the organizationally relevant beliefs and values that are mutually understood and subscribed to by its members (see Schein, 1985, Schneider, 1990, and Trice & Beyer, 1993, for detailed discussions). As such, the culture prescribes what is true, necessary, and

117

desirable and, therefore, the goals one ought to pursue and how one ought to go about pursuing them (Beyer, 1981; Campbell & Nash, 1992). By the same token, it proscribes what is false, unnecessary, and undesirable, and, therefore, the goals and actions that one ought not to pursue oneself and that one ought to resist when proposed by others (Beyer, 1981; Sathe, 1983).

Building upon earlier work by Mitchell, Rediker, and Beach (1986) and Beach and Mitchell (1990), Beach (1993a) analyzed the implications of culture and its imperatives for decision making and decision implementation within the context of image theory. This analysis focused on the ways in which an organization's culture influences decisions made by its members and the ways in which it influences its members' acceptance or rejection of decisions made by its leaders. The theoretical mechanism of primary interest involves assessment of the compatibility of a decision option with the organization's culture—where an option is defined as a possible course of action in the case of a member who is making a decision, or a proposed course of action in the case of a decision that has been made by leaders. Image theory predicts that when compatibility is low, the option will be rejected. This means that when an acculturated member is making decisions for the organization, he or she will tend not to make decisions that are incompatible with its culture; when leaders make culturally incompatible decisions, the organization's members will tend not to endorse the decision.

At the level of the individual decision maker, there is a growing body of research on the implications of incompatibility for one's own decisions (Beach, 1993b) and for the acceptance of others' decisions (van Zee, Paluchowski, & Beach, 1992), all of which is congruent with the image theory predictions described above. In contrast, only two image theory studies of organizational decision making have been done (Beach, Smith, Lundell, & Mitchell, 1988; Rediker, Mitchell, Beach, & Beard, 1993); together with a closely related study (Shockley-Zalabak & Morley, 1989), these are now described.

AN IMAGE THEORY ANALYSIS
OF ORGANIZATIONAL CULTURE

Fig. 9.1 contains the organizational counterpart of the image theory structure presented in chapter 1. To begin with, the three boxes at the top of Fig. 9.1 are the organizational counterparts of the individual decision maker's three images. The organization's *culture* is the beliefs and values that are shared, to one degree or other, by the members of the organization. Like the

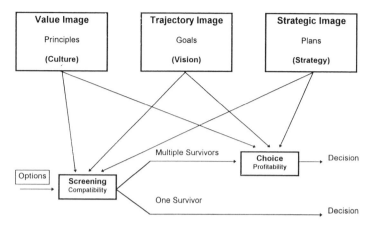

FIG. 9.1. Relationship between images and decision making as described by image theory.

value image at the individual level, at the organizational level this image provides answers to the question, "Who are we and what do we stand for?" The trajectory image is the organization's *vision,* the concrete and abstract goals that the organization is seeking to attain. This image provides answers to the question, "Where are we going and what are we trying to become?" The strategic image is the organization's *strategic plan,* the blueprint for actions aimed at attaining the goals that comprise the organization's vision. This image provides answers to the question, "How are we striving to achieve the goals that constitute our vision?"

As is the case for individual decision makers, images guide organizational decision making. Potential goals for inclusion in the vision and tactics for inclusion in the strategic plan must not violate the organization's culture, its existing vision, or its existing plan(s). That is, new ideas about where to go and how to accomplish things must be compatible with the members' image of themselves as an organization, their image of what the organization is to become, and their image of the path the organization has laid out for pursuing the future (see Mudd, 1989, for an example of culture change over time). Moreover, when the organization's members broadly share these images, the decisions they make in light of them will tend to be compatible, even without deliberate coordination.

Decision making in organizations is accomplished by application of both the compatibility test and the profitability test (Fig. 9.1), in precisely the same way as for individual decision makers. This is because the organization's culture, vision, and strategic plans are possessed by its members; there is no "organizational mind" that retains these images and makes decisions (Beach, 1990).

The primacy of individual members as possessors of the organizationally relevant images is crucial to the theory. Indeed, much turns upon the degree to which the various individual members possess similar images. Specifically, the key element is the extent to which the culture is shared among an organization's members and the implications of this for decision making within the organization, particularly for acceptance or rejection of proposed courses of action.

As stated above, there are only two studies of image theory per se at the organizational level, and one related study that we discuss later. In the first of the two image theory studies, Beach, et al. (1988) examined three businesses that varied in the degree to which their cultures were broadly shared by their executives. After the general dimensions of the cultures were captured, hypothetical plans for introducing a new product were presented to the executives who were asked to rate each plan's acceptability. It was found that the less broadly the organization's culture was shared by its members, the greater the disagreement among the organization's executives about the acceptability of the various plans. A culture in which values are broadly shared is called *unified,* and one in which they are not is called *fragmented* (Beach, 1993a). The implication is that coordinated action among executives may be made more difficult when they do not share images about what is of fundamental importance to the organization.

In the second image theory study, Rediker, et al. (1993) had business students play the role of CEO of a firm that was considering six alternative candidate companies for acquisition. Information was provided about the degree to which the firm's culture was unified or fragmented. Considerable information was presented about the candidates for acquisition, in which it became clear that some candidates were more compatible with the culture of the firm than others. The subjects rated the attractiveness of each candidate and selected the candidate or candidates about which they would like to have more information prior to choosing one for acquisition.

Results showed that, across subjects and conditions, as compatibility between the candidates and the firm decreased, evaluated attractiveness also decreased, $r = .95$, $p < .01$. However, the variance in the attractiveness evaluations was 1.81 times greater when the firm's culture was fragmented than when it was not. Most subjects rejected the three least compatible of the six candidates and retained the three most compatible candidates for further investigation.

In the related study that was not inspired by image theory, Shockley-Zalabak and Morley (1989) interviewed employees of a computer manufacturing company about the ". . . values, assumptions, understandings, and implicit rules that govern day-to-day behavioral expectations" in the company (p. 489). It was found that the greater the discrepancy between these statements about the company's culture and the employees' statements about their own values, the less satisfied the employees were with their jobs, career progress, pay, opportunity to contribute, and similar evaluations, and they gave lower estimations of the company's chances of survival.

The foregoing discussion raises four testable hypotheses about organizational decision making.

The first hypothesis is that different groups can be demonstrated to have different degrees of cultural fragmentation, and that this will either reflect or be reflected in their general well-being and success in pursuit of their goals. The commonsense notion is that cultural fragmentation either occurs in stressed organizations or perhaps may give rise to the stress. In either case, the idea is that some organizations will have more fragmented cultures than others and that this can be measured.

The second hypothesis is that the more compatible an option is with an organization's culture, the more likely it is that the members of that organization will choose that option.

The third hypothesis is that an organization's members will be more willing to accept decisions made by its leaders if the goal or plan decided on is congruent with its culture.

The fourth hypothesis is that when an organization's culture differs from what its members think it ought to be, members will be less committed to the organization, less satisfied with their roles (jobs) in the organization, and more inclined to leave the organization.

RESEARCH

In order to do research on organizational culture, one must be able to measure it. Beach (1993a) introduced the Organizational Culture Survey (OCS), which consists of 15 features of organizational culture that subjects use to describe the culture of the organization to which they belong.[1] Table 9.1 contains the 15 features divided into three groups of related items. This instrument has been shown to produce diverse results for diverse organizations, thereby demonstrating that its results are not merely the result of

---

[1] The Organizational Culture Survey (OCS) was called the Organizational Culture Inventory (OCI) in Beach (1993a). The name has been changed to distinguish it from Cooke and Rousseau's (1988) OCI.

TABLE 9.1

The Elements of the Organizational Culture Survey (OCS)

Values centering on how employees should be treated and the opportunities afforded them:

1. Respect
2. Growth
3. Rewards
4. Communication
5. Fairness

Values centering on professionalism and support of efforts to do a good job:

6. Effectiveness
7. Efficiency
8. Support
9. Innovation
10. Enjoyment

Values centering on how the organization interfaces with its environment and strives to accomplish its mission:

11. Achievement
12. Competitiveness
13. Resourcefulness
14. Judgment
15. Integrity

---

stereotyped responses; it is reliable across different groups of subjects from the same organization; it has a mean individual subject test–retest reliability of .72 (Weatherly, 1995).

The OCS yields a profile across the 15 features that describe the subject's judgment of the relative salience of each feature in the organization's culture. These profiles can be averaged across subjects in order to make comparisons among groups or between organizations. For an individual subject, salience for any single feature could range from 0 (if it were wholly absent from the culture) to 100 (if it were the only salient feature of the culture); all features would receive 6.67 were they all deemed to be of equal salience.

Study 1

The purpose of study 1 was to test the hypothesis that different organizations have different degrees of cultural fragmentation and that this can be measured using the OCS.

Subjects. Employees of two commercial organizations participated in the study. The first organization, GFC, is a successful corporate financial services business. At the time of the study it was fairly small (approximately 150 employees) and was housed on one floor of an office tower. Both then and now, it takes pride in having good internal communications, and its CEO makes a point of articulating GFC's mission and its values.[2]

The second organization, XQC, is a small utility company. It is, however, much larger than GFC (approximately 1400 employees). It is housed on many floors of its own building. At the time of the research, XQC was in the process of trying to avoid bankruptcy after a long, difficult reorganization at the executive level, and the entire organization was stressed.

Procedure. In each organization the employees were asked to describe their views of the culture of their organization using the OCS. GFC employees did so as part of a business education course offered first to the executives, next to the top-level managers who reported directly to the executives, then to the managers who reported to the top-level managers, and so forth. The result was that 6 levels (all nonclerical employees) of the organization took part in the research, one level at a time over the course of a year.

In contrast to GFC, the data from XQC management and employees were gathered at the worksite rather than in the classroom. By the use of its organizational chart, it was possible to stratify XQC into 6 levels, comparable to the levels in GFC.

Results. Fig. 9.2 contains the mean profiles for the different levels of the two organizations. As can be seen in the top panel of the figure, with the exception of one point for one group, the profiles for the six groups of GFC employees are remarkably similar. This means that the employees at all levels of the organization described GFC's culture similarly, which we interpret to mean that GFC has a unified culture.

Although it is not readily apparent from this figure, close examination of the profiles for XQC, in the bottom panel of Fig. 9.2, reveals that there are two fairly distinct views about its culture. The executives and top-level managers see responsibility and personal growth as the most salient aspects of the XQC culture whereas the lower-level employees see the company's achievement and competitiveness as most salient. That is, there appear to be at least two cultures in XQC as perceived by the employees at the top

---

[2]GFC has since been renamed The Finova Corporation.

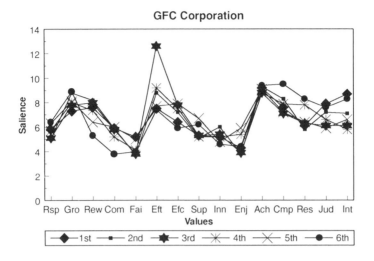

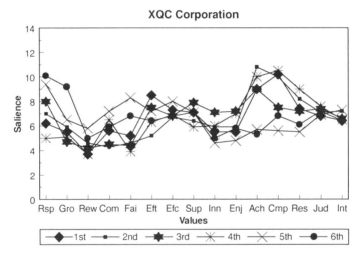

FIG. 9.2. OCS profiles for an organization that has a unified culture (GFC, top panel) and for one that has a fragmented culture (XQC, bottom panel).

and by the employees at the bottom of the organization. (The existence of these two cultures in XQC also was revealed in the results of an employee survey done by an independent consulting company.) These results are in marked contrast to the similarity of views in GFC, as evidenced by the profiles in the top panel of Fig. 9.2.

The overall degree of fragmentation in GFC's culture can be measured by calculating the variance of the six GFC groups' salience scores around each of the 15 points on the profiles in the top panel of Fig. 9.2, the mean of which across the 15 points is .86 (range = .06 to 3.91, median = .71). The comparable mean variance for XQC is 1.74 (range = .08 to 5.14, median = 1.29). The probability that the difference between these two means is due to chance alone is .059 using the Mann–Whitney U test. GFC's variance exceeds XQC's on 5 of the 15 points by a mean of 1.08; XQC's variance exceeds GFC's on 10 of the 15 points by a mean of 1.87.

Based on the mean variances (.86 for GFC and 1.74 for XQC), XQC's culture is twice as fragmented as GFC's culture, thus illustrating that organizations that might be expected on prior grounds to have different degrees of fragmentation in their cultures, do in fact differ considerably in the profiles that they yield. Moreover, the two organizations do not have the same culture, although GFC's profiles are more similar to the profiles for XQC's lower-level employees than to the profiles for its higher-level employees.

Study 2

The purpose of study 2 was to examine the hypothesis that the more compatible an option is with an organization's culture, the more likely it is that the members of the organization will choose that option.

Procedure. Subjects were 58 middle-level managers from XQC who had completed the OCS one to two weeks before the experiment was conducted. They were told to consider the hypothetical situation in which XQC's management decided that the company's values should be more clearly articulated, particularly to help new employees understand the culture. Although management wanted to present XQC in the best light, it did not want new employees to undergo culture shock when they took up their jobs (i.e., the values presented to them should accurately reflect the XQC culture).

Management had hired two consultants, each of whom proposed a list of values that they thought characterized the most salient features of XQC's culture. The Board decided that the XQC employees were the best judges of which list was most accurate, and therefore decided to do a survey.

Subjects were asked to read both lists and to distribute 10 points (votes) between the two to indicate the degree to which each list accurately reflected XQC's culture and, therefore, the degree to which they thought the list ought to be the one chosen.

Results. The first step was to calculate the degree to which each list of values was compatible with each subject's perceptions of XQC's culture. To do this, each subject's profile of XQC's culture was derived from an earlier administration of the OCS. Next, the salience scores from the subject's profile were summed for each of the (elements) values on each of the two lists, thus indicating each list's compatibility with the subject's perception of his or her organization's culture. Then the number of points the subject had assigned to each list was paired with the sum of his or her salience scores (compatibility) for each list. Finally, the mean number of points was computed across the subjects for ranges of compatibility (note that each subject is represented twice, once for each of the two lists).

The results are presented in Fig. 9.3. As can be seen, the more compatible an option is with individual subjects' perceptions of their organization's culture, the greater the number of points assigned to the option.[3]

Study 3

Study 3 examined the hypothesis that the greater the compatibility between a decision made by management and employees' perceptions of their organization's culture, the greater the degree of employee acceptance of the decision.

Procedure. The subjects were the 27 members of the sixth group from GFC and 27 volunteers from the Distribution Services group from XQC. Each of the subjects had anonymously completed the OCS a week or more earlier as part of study 1.

Subjects were asked to consider a hypothetical situation in which their Board of Directors wanted to increase the size of the organization by acquiring a small company in the same industry and merging the two operations. The Board had decided on a particular candidate and wanted to know if the employees agreed with decision. The employees of each candidate company had filled out the OCS, a summary of which was enclosed for each subject's inspection. Each subject responded to management's decision by indicating "Yes" or "No. "

Subjects in group 1 ($n = 27$, 14 from GFC and 13 from XQC) were given a description of the culture of the proposed company in which its "highly emphasized" elements were the 5 highest-scoring elements for their own cultures and its "less emphasized" elements were the 5 lowest-scoring elements for their own cultures. Subjects in group 2 ($n = 27$, 13 from GFC and 14 from XQC) were given a description in which the five lowest-scoring elements of their own cultures were the proposed company's "highly emphasized elements," and the 5 highest-scoring elements of their own cultures were the candidate's "less emphasized" elements.

---

[3]Further analyses showed that the spread of the points was not related to the difference in the sums of profile numbers for the two lists; indeed, the only relationship obtained between sums and number of points is the one shown in Fig. 9.3.

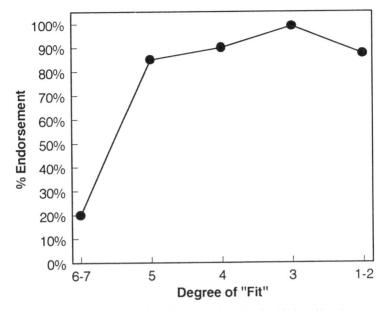

FIG. 9.3. Mean points assigned to a list as function of its fit with the subjects' company's culture.

Results. In group 1, 96% (26) of the subjects endorsed management's decision to acquire the company when its culture was similar to that of their own company. In contrast, 59% (16) of the subjects in group 2 endorsed acquisition when the company's culture was different from that of their own company, $Z = 37.00$, $p < .001$. In short, the organizations' members were more likely to endorse management's decision if the features of the decided-upon option were compatible with the features of their organization's culture.

Study 4

Study 4 examined the hypothesis that the greater the difference between how an organization's members see its existing culture and how they think that culture ought to be, the less committed they will be to the organization, the less satisfied they will be with their jobs, and the more inclined they will be to leave the organization.

Procedure. Subjects were 49 employees from throughout XQC. In addition to filling out the OCS for XQC's culture as it is now, these subjects were asked to fill it out again for the culture as it ought to be. Profiles were constructed for both sets of answers for each subject, and the absolute differences between each of the 15 points on the two profiles were summed to yield a discrepancy score.

After filling out the OCS twice, subjects answered a series of questions aimed at measuring their commitment to the organization, their satisfaction with their job, and their inclination to leave their job. Commitment was measured by using O'Reilly and Chatman's (1986) 12-item organizational commitment scale.

Job satisfaction was measured by using Kunin's (1955) Faces Scale together with a 2-item measure from the University of Michigan Quality of Employment Survey (Quinn & Staines, 1979) used by Gutek and Winter (1990). The 2 items measure global job satisfaction: "All in all, how satisfied would you say you are with your job?" (answered on a 5-point scale from *not at all* to *very*) and "Knowing what you know now, if you had to decide all over again whether to take the job you have now, what would you decide?" (answered on a 3-point scale from *definitely would not take the same job*, through *would have some second thoughts*, to *would decide without any hesitation to take the same job*). Job satisfaction was the sum of the answers to all of the items.

Intention to leave was measured using a single item; "How strongly do you feel about leaving or staying in your present job?" (answered on a 5-point scale from *strongly inclined to stay* to *strongly inclined to leave*).

Results. The subjects were divided at the median of their discrepancy scores. Then *t* tests were conducted between the scores on the commitment measure, the job satisfaction measure, and the intention to leave measure for subjects who had high-discrepancy scores and those who had low-discrepancy scores.

For commitment, the high-discrepancy mean was 44.20 and the low-discrepancy mean was 55.12, $t = 3.40$, $p < .001$ one tail, $df = 47$. That is, when there was a low discrepancy between how the culture is now and how it ought to be, subjects reported themselves to be significantly more committed to the organization than when the discrepancy was high.

For job satisfaction, the high-discrepancy mean was 10.00 and the low discrepancy mean was 11.38 ($t = 2.04$, $p = .02$ one tail, $df = 47$). That is, when the now-ought discrepancy was low, subjects reported themselves to be significantly more satisfied with their job than when it was high.

For intention to leave, the high discrepancy mean was 1.58 and the low-discrepancy mean was 2.16, $t = 1.97$, $p = .03$ one tail, $df = 47$. That is, when the now-ought discrepancy was low, subjects reported themselves to be significantly more inclined to stay in their present job than when the discrepancy was high.

SUMMARY AND PRACTICAL IMPLICATIONS

Using image theory, we presented a theoretical framework for examining the influence of organizational culture on decision making. Then we presented four studies that tested some implications of the theory.

Study 1 found that the OCS is sensitive to cultural fragmentation, in that it produced different results for two organizations that, on prior grounds, were expected to differ in fragmentation.

Study 2 found support for the hypothesis that the decisions of an organization's members are influenced by the degree to which the features of the options are compatible with the features the organization's own culture.

Study 3 found that an organization's members are more likely to endorse a management decision if the features of the decision are compatible with the features of the organization's culture.

Study 4 found that the greater the difference between subjects' assessments of an organization's culture as they perceived it to be now and as they thought it actually ought to be, the less committed they reported themselves to be to the organization, the less satisfied they reported themselves to be with their jobs, and the more inclined they reported themselves to be to leave their jobs. These results are similar to those obtained by O'Reilly, Chatman, and Caldwell (1991) for the relationship between person–organization fit and satisfaction and inclination to leave, as well as those cited previously by Shockley-Zalabak and Morley (1989) for the relationship between the size of the discrepancy between ideal organizational life and perceived organizational life on the one hand and employees' satisfaction with the organization and estimations of its quality and overall effectiveness on the other. The results also echo the results obtained by Bissell and Beach (chapter 5, this volume) for the discrepancy between ideal supervision and perceived supervision on the one hand and job and organizational satisfaction on the other.

While acknowledging that there is much to be done and that these experiments are preliminary, we conclude from these results that the image theory characterization of organizational culture and its influence on decision making holds promise for further research on organizational decision making. Moreover, by tying culture to decision making, the practical, managerial implications of studying culture become clearer. For example, in light of the trend in business to flatten organizational hierarchies and empower lower-level employees, the role of culture as a metalevel coordinator of decision making becomes of considerable interest. The research we described suggests one line of inquiry; empowerment should be more successful in organizations that have less fragmented cultures than in organizations that have more fragmented cultures. Moreover, practical methods of promoting cultural unity become important.

On the other hand, a unified culture could be as much an obstacle to an organization's survival as a fragmented culture. A unified culture could be a detriment if it promoted decisions by individuals that, however coordinated and unsurprising, failed to address the organization's internal or external problems. A unified culture also could be detrimental if it promoted rejection of leaders' proposals for needed reforms, however large the consensus about rejection may be.

Fragmented cultures also may have management implications. A highly fragmented culture may promote anarchy if supervisory control is insufficient to assure coordination among members' activities; it would be like trying to herd cats. In this circumstance, management would have to make decisions and work diligently to assure implementation, which would argue for a bureaucratic structure that could impose the necessary control. In contrast, a fragmented culture may discourage coalescence of opposition to management decisions, although it might not promote their acceptance either.

Of course, wholly unified cultures are rare. Therefore, the degree of unity and fragmentation is likely to be of interest more often than whether an organization has a unified culture or a fragmented culture. Because of this, it is important to be able to measure the degree of cultural unity or fragmentation.

The results reported earlier suggest that leaders must know their organizations' cultures in order to obtain internal endorsement of the decisions they make for the organization. When their decisions are incompatible with the culture, members will be less inclined to accept them; at some point incompatibility may be so great that it engenders active opposition to implementation of the decisions.

Organizational change, at best a difficult task, may be greatly complicated by the fact that significant change almost always requires cultural change. Techniques for easing organizational change may best be centered on ways of inducing cultural change, perhaps through appropriate design of a vision that will save the most important parts of the culture and change the peripheral parts.

In short, future research should focus on establishing the conditions under which a unified culture is in the best interests of an organization. Then it should study ways of inducing the changes necessary for creation of an appropriate unified culture for the organization, perhaps with emphasis on constructing a vision that offers an attractive future that is a logical extension of what is most important about the existing culture. This should be followed by efforts to design methods for helping members to understand the vision, accept it (and the cultural changes it will entail), and implement it in a manner that helps the organization to prosper while retaining the integrity of the core beliefs and values in its culture.

REFERENCES

Beach, L. R. (1990). *Image theory: Decision making in personal and organizational contexts.* Chichester, England: Wiley.

Beach, L. R. (1993a). *Making the right decision: Organizational culture, vision, and planning.* Englewood Cliffs, NJ: Prentice-Hall.

Beach, L. R. (1993b). Broadening the definition of decision making: The role of pre-choice screening of options. *Psychological Science, 4,* 215–220.

Beach, L. R., & Mitchell, T. R. (1990). Image theory: A behavioral theory of decisions in organizations. In B. M. Staw & L. L. Cummings (Eds.), *Research in organizational behavior (Vol. 12)* pp. 1–41). Greenwich, CT: JAI Press.

Beach, L. R., Smith, B., Lundell, J., & Mitchell, T. R. (1988). Image theory: Descriptive sufficiency of a simple rule for the compatibility test. *Journal of Behavioral Decision Making, 1,* 17–28.

Beyer, J. M. (1981). Ideologies, values, and decision making in organizations. In P. C. Nystrom & W. H. Starbuck (Eds.), *Handbook of organizational design* (pp. 166–197). New York: Oxford.

Campbell, A., & Nash, L. L. (1992). *A sense of mission: Defining direction for the large corporation.* Reading, MA: Addison-Wesley.

Cooke, R. A., & Rousseau, D. M. (1988). Behavioral norms and expectations: A quantitative approach to the assessment of organizational culture. *Group and Organizational Studies, 13,* 245–273.

Gutek, B. A. & Winter, S. J. (1990). Computer use, control over computers, and job satisfaction. In S. Oscamp & S. Spacapan (Eds.), *People's reactions to technology in factories, offices, and aerospace* (pp. 121–144). Newbury Park, CA: Sage Press.

Kunin, T. (1955). The construction of a new type of attitude measure. *Personnel Psychology, 8,* 65–78.

Mitchell, T. R., Rediker, K. J., & Beach, L. R. (1986). Image theory and its implications for organizational decision making. In H. P. Sims & D. A. Gioia (Eds.), *The thinking organization* (pp. 293–316). San Francisco: Jossey-Bass.

Mudd, S. (1989). Organizational image assessment in the health and human services sector. *Journal of Applied Social Psychology, 19,* 30–49.

O'Reilly, C. A., III, & Chatman, J. (1986). Organizational commitment and psychological attachment: The effects of compliance, identification, and internalization of prosocial behavior. *Journal of Applied Psychology, 71,* 492–499.

O'Reilly, C. A., III, Chatman, J., & Caldwell, D. F. (1991). People and organizational culture: A profile comparison approach to assessing person-organization fit. *Academy of Management Journal, 34,* 487–516.

Quinn, R. P., & Staines, G. L. (1979). *The 1977 quality of employment survey.* Ann Arbor, MI: Institute for Social Research.

Rediker, J, Mitchell, T. R., Beach, L. R., & Beard, D. W. (1993). The effects of strong belief structures on information-processing evaluations and choice. *Journal of Behavioral Decision Making, 6,* 113–132.

Sathe, V. (1983, Autumn). Implications of corporate culture: A manager's guide to action. *Organizational Dynamics,* 5–23.

Schein, E. H. (1985). *Organizational culture and leadership.* San Francisco: Jossey-Bass.

Schneider, B. (Ed.). (1990). *Organizational culture and climate.* San Francisco: Jossey-Bass.

Shockley-Zalabak, P., & Morley, D. D. (1989). Adhering to organizational culture: What does it mean? Why does it matter? *Group and Organizational Studies, 14*, 483–500.

Trice, H. M., & Beyer, J. M. (1993). *The cultures of work organizations.* Englewood Cliffs, NJ: Prentice-Hall.

van Zee, E. H., Paluchowski, T. F., & Beach, L. R. (1992). The effects of screening and task partitioning upon evaluations of decision options. *Journal of Behavioral Decision Making, 5*, 1–23.

Weatherly, K. A. (1995). *The rapid assessment of organizational culture using the Organizational Culture Survey: Theory, research, and application.* Unpublished doctoral dissertation, University of Arizona, Tucson.

MITIGATING CULTURAL CONSTRAINTS ON GROUP DECISIONS

Kenneth R. Walsh
University of Arizona

Chapter 9 described how image theory characterizes the effects of culture on organizational decision making. The thesis is that a unified culture promotes decisions that are consistent across the organization. A danger of this consistency is that the organization may be unable to adequately address threats and opportunities resulting from changes in its environment. That is, if the appropriate measures are incompatible with the organization's culture, those measures may be rejected out of hand, leaving the organization vulnerable and unable to respond.

The present chapter examines another danger inherent in unified cultures, the danger that good or bad ideas may never arise at all. If ideas (options) are rejected because they are incompatible with the culture, at least they have had their moment in the spotlight and have received some consideration, however minimal. The possibility always exists that their merits for addressing the issue at hand may be recognized and steps be taken to promote changes in the culture to permit their accommodation and adoption.

However, if ideas never even make it to the table, they are unlikely to have any impact at all. It long has been an axiom in group decision making that a large number of options for consideration is better than a small number (Osborn, 1963). Therefore, in what follows, we examine the effect of culture on what in current parlance is called the "surfacing" of ideas, particularly in group decision tasks. Then we examine the possible benefits of new computer collaboration technologies, group support systems (GSS), for helping ideas survive cultural repression. To do the latter, we focus on the University of Arizona's GroupSystems™ group support system.

SCREENING AND THE COMPATIBILITY TEST

Image theory describes the adoption of ideas about how to address an issue as a two-step process. In the first step, screening, each idea is compared with the individual's images to see if it is reasonably compatible (the compatibility test). If not, it is rejected. If it survives screening, the idea passes to the second step, choice (the profitability test). Beach (1993) suggested that screening serves to eliminate implausible options, thereby reducing the opportunity for a bad choice farther down the line. In contrast, screening also may reject options that might be very good, even though they are incompatible with the images. Indeed, this may well be a sign that images need revision in light of changes in reality. These lost options can be regarded as a cost to the decision maker, and in an organizational setting the cumulative cost across a group of decision makers, each of whom is repressing possibly good ideas, may well be substantial.

GROUP DECISION MAKING

When individuals, as members of organizations, consider new ideas, they each do their own screening using their own images about the organization. These images may not be the same for everyone; therefore, ideas rejected by one person might be acceptable to others. Because an organization's members make decisions for it, the negative effects of their conflicting images and conflicting decisions can be very serious. To reduce these effects and give order to the many decisions made in its name, organizations frequently spend a great deal of time, effort, and money developing vision statements that capture the essential reasons for their existence. The goal of the vision statement process, in image theory terms, is to align its members' images of the organization's beliefs and values, goals, and plans.

Group decision making differs from individual decision making in that individuals consider the images of other group members, as well as their own. When individuals make decisions, they use their own images to test ideas. When a group makes a decision, each member tests the group's ideas with his or her own images and also with his or her perceptions of other group members' images. If an individual regards an idea as good but incompatible with the other decision makers' images, he or she may not present the idea. An individual may decide that an idea fails the compatibility test based on a perception of others' images. These interactions are made more complex because the individuals' perceptions of the other group members' images are not wholly accurate.

Fig. 10.1 shows the images of three hypothetical members of two different organizations; one organization has a unified culture, and the other has a fragmented culture. Ideas that are compatible with the central region of the overlapping images would be regarded as compatible by all three decision makers. In the unified culture, this region is larger and makes up a higher percentage of the image of each decision maker. Therefore, a greater percentage of ideas that an individual decision maker considers compatible will also be compatible with ideas of others in the organization.

By contrast, the images in the fragmented culture have a small overlapping region that makes up a smaller percentage of the individuals image. In this situation, many courses of action regarded as good by one individual may be regarded as incompatible by others.

Many organizations appear to believe that having a unified culture is good. This belief, particularly for organizations that actively strive for a unified culture, may encourage individuals to focus on the intersection of their images and further enhance the consistency of the group. However, individuals in fragmented cultures may find it acceptable to explore ideas that are compatible with their own images with less regard for the intersection of the group's images. Together, the tendency to strive for closely aligned images and the tendency to focus on the intersection of those images can greatly enhance the consistency of different decision makers, but this consistency can come at a cost.

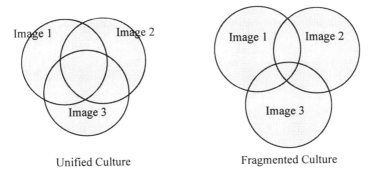

Unified Culture   Fragmented Culture

FIG. 10.1. Overlapping images in unified and fragmented cultures.

The danger for organizations with unified cultures is that their members may lose potentially profitable ideas by prematurely rejecting them. In the case of a unified culture facing a changing environment, the likelihood of eliminating alternatives that would benefit the organization can be increased. That is, the locus of mutually acceptable ideas broadens by unifying a culture, as shown by the intersection of the images in Fig. 10.1. However, the locus of ideas generated may narrow, as shown by the union of the images. One goal of idea generation tools, either older manual techniques or newer GSS techniques, is to allow unified cultures to make full use of their diversity when novel ideas are needed.

THE COSTS OF IDEA SCREENING

"From time to time, we must turn off our judicial mind and light up our creative mind. And we must wait long enough before turning up our judicial light again. Otherwise, premature judgment may douse our creative flames, and even wash away ideas already generated" (Osborn, 1963, p. 41). For organizations to gain competitive advantage from their superior ideas, they must not only generate those ideas, but also allow them to develop before subjecting them to the collective "judicial minds" of the organization. This implies that, under some circumstances, the screening and the compatibility test may remove ideas too quickly from consideration.

To better understand this problem, we must expand the screening process to look at different stages of application of the compatibility test. Each stage is a finer screen that reduces the number of ideas to be considered at the following stages as shown in Fig. 10.2. Idea generation is clearly important, but ideas will never be considered if they are screened out by one of the three stages of the compatibility test. The first two stages are performed by the individual whereas the last stage is performed by the decision making group.

The first stage, the unconscious compatibility test, is the most coarse of the tests. This test occurs at what many presume to be a nearly unconscious level at which ideas are rejected so quickly that they may never be consciously recalled. This stage rejects grossly incompatible ideas before they even reveal themselves. Individuals who are deeply acculturated or who have shared in the past successes that have built that culture are most vulnerable to this nearly automatic rejection of ideas that are even vaguely incompatible with the culture. Many organizations try to attain this level of acculturation by providing new employees with orientation exercises that

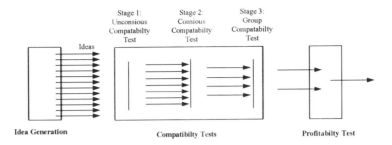

FIG. 10.2. Three levels of the compatibility test.

describe the history of the organization and what made it successful. The point of these exercises is to improve the efficiency of the unconscious compatibility test by framing the solution space that can be considered.

The second stage, the conscious compatibility test, is applied to the ideas that have survived the unconscious test before the individual shares the ideas with the group. In this case, the individual is consciously considering his or her own ideas and whether they are good enough to share with the group. At this level, individuals' own images and their interpretation of the group's images both function as screening criteria. During this stage, individuals may think of ideas that they feel are innovative and good for the organization, but they may fear sharing them because they think the ideas are incompatible with what they perceive to be the other group members' images.

The final stage is performed on all ideas that individuals were willing to put forth. The group as a whole evaluates the ideas. This test is the most rigid because the ideas must be compatible with the group's image, which is the intersection of the individuals' images; the intersection is smaller than any individual's image. This stage should not be confused with group alternative evaluation techniques used in the profitability test. Rather, this test screens ideas before bringing them to the profitability test and occurs subtly as the group does not acknowledge the incompatible ideas. This can be observed in meetings when one individual puts forth an idea, another instantly criticizes it, and the group largely ignores the exchange. This type of exchange not only blocks the idea but also can block future ideas as it increases group members apprehension about putting forth further ideas.

The foregoing decomposition of the compatibility test helps us to understand different processes all of which contribute to idea rejection and each of which needs to be addressed if the most innovative ideas are to survive for more deliberative consideration. Also, each process implies different tactics that may be valuable in reducing the blocking.

A cost of the unified culture is the ideas that are never fully considered. The magnitude of this cost depends on the degree to which an organization's culture is unified and the degree to which an organization needs innovative ideas. The more unified the culture, the more ideas will be blocked and lost from consideration. If the organization is facing a changing environment and stiff competition, those lost ideas may be critical.

Another way to consider the costs and benefits of the compatibility test is to consider all ideas as falling into one of three categories: compatible, incompatible but profitable, and incompatible and unprofitable. The compatibility test approves of only compatible ideas. It can be considered beneficial and efficient in that little time is wasted eliminating incompatible and unprofitable ideas. It also can be considered harmful and ineffective when incompatible ideas that are profitable are lost.

A unified culture seeks, in effect, to reduce the number of ideas that are compatible with decision makers' images in order for operation to be efficient and consistent. If the organization is faced with a static and predictable environment, the compatibility test will be effective because the profitable ideas will tend to be compatible with the culture. As the environment becomes more competitive and more unstable, the number of ideas that are both compatible and profitable may decrease, whereas the number of ideas that are both incompatible and profitable may increase. In the latter situation, overreliance on culturally correct decisions may cause the organization to miss profitable opportunities.

One way to reduce the blocking effects of the compatibility test in unified cultures is to use GSS. GSS are computer-supported collaborative meeting environments which have been shown to improve idea generation and that seem to reduce premature idea rejection in the three stages of the compatibility test.

GSS

Imagine a business meeting that is productive, involving 20 or more people. Imagine further that in this meeting every person contributes ideas, every person hears others' ideas, and no one person monopolizes the speaking time. In a 1-hour meeting, everyone may speak for half an hour each, a paradox that is possible with the use of GSS, a newly emerging collaborative computer technology.

A GSS combines anonymity, simultaneous input, and structured process techniques to greatly reduce many of the factors that hinder the productivity of meetings. Moreover, the GSS seems to make meetings even more productive than would be expected by just reducing the process losses of a typical meeting.

A GSS is networked computers and software designed to coordinate group work (Dennis, George, Jessup, Nunamaker, & Vogel, 1988; Nunamaker, Dennis, Valacich, Vogel, & George, 1991). The computer system supports idea entry by all participants at the same time and allows them to see other people's ideas as the ideas are generated. It generally has a number of different tools for generating and developing ideas as well as for reaching consensus on a choice of alternatives. Some of the tools offer unstructured data entry, which is good for unrestrained idea generation, whereas other tools offer structured electronic conversations for more focused ideas. Additionally, voting and organizing tools help synthesize the work.

GSS facilities are generally conference rooms equipped with networked microcomputers at each participant's seat, although the systems can be used without the participants being in the same room. For example the University of Arizona's room is equipped with an Intel 486 microcomputer at each of the 29 participants' workstations and 3 facilitator workstations. The workstations are connected via a Novell network to a file server. The University's GroupSystems™ software is the GSS software used.

GSS software allows groups of approximately 4 to 30 people to meet efficiently, reducing many of the obstacles to traditional face to face meetings. In the electronic meeting room, all participants can "talk" at the same time without missing what others have said. Participants type their ideas, comments, and questions on their workstations and the system distributes their input to all other stations for viewing, eliminating a common bottleneck in traditional verbal meetings.

Input to the electronic meeting system is usually anonymous. Ideas are entered into the systems, discussed, and prioritized without attaching authors' names to the ideas.

Electronic brainstorming (EBS) is one tool in the GroupSystems™ software and is used by groups to create new ideas in a similar but more effective manner than that of older manual techniques. Research on manual brainstorming techniques has shown little evidence that the great productivity gains envisioned by Osborn are realized. However, GSS research, replicated over many studies, has shown GSS to generate significantly more ideas than nominal groups, which are sets of individuals working separately (Dennis & Valacich, 1993; Gallupe et al., 1992; Valacich, Dennis, & Connoloy, 1994). The research strongly supports EBS as an effective tool in helping groups generate ideas, but the reasons why the tool is effective are not fully understood.

GSS AND CULTURAL CONSTRAINTS

Although cultural constraints on idea generation have not been studied in the GSS literature, indirect evidence exists showing that people can behave in a more "socially unacceptable" manner when using an anonymous electronic communication media. One example is "flaming," or harshly and emotionally criticizing (Siegel, Dubrovski, Keisler, & McQuire, 1986). Although flaming is not generally a positive aspect of an electronic meeting, it does demonstrate that people are willing to state ideas that they would probably repress in a face-to-face, unsupported environment. Gallupe and Cooper (1993) referred to the importance of reducing evaluation apprehension in brainstorming. They do not study this directly, but note from their experience with electronic brainstorming that people are excited by "the enhanced ability to express innovative and off-the-wall ideas without having to wait or worry about being criticized" (p. 30).

Connolly, Routhieaux, and Schneider (1993) observed that reduction of production blocking is not enough to account for the success of the GSS tools. They noted that "in the electronic brainstorming context, each member works largely alone generating ideas, seeking inspiration (if he or she chooses) by reading over lists of ideas generated by others" (p. 493). They hypothesized that unusual ideas may stimulate other group members to new ideas. Their findings did not show that unusual ideas had an effect on group brainstorming, but they did demonstrate that large groups generate more ideas than nominal groups of equal size.

An alternative explanation for the success of EBS is that the use of EBS affects the way people use images to screen ideas. The anonymity allows individuals to express ideas consistent with their own images but not consistent with the intersection of the images of the group (see Fig. 10.1). Without anonymity, participants may feel as though they should stick with "safe" ideas with which they think most will agree, but with anonymity they only have to consider if what they think is valid.

In addition to anonymity, group members can view the ideas of others as they are entered. Seeing others' ideas, particularly those ideas not compatible with the intersection of the groups' images, may broaden the individuals' perception of what is acceptable. The combination of the two features, anonymity and idea viewing, may lead people to enter ideas somewhat outside their own image, but within the perceived image of another individual who may have submitted other ideas that look interesting. These features may lead groups to use the union of their images rather than just the intersection. This explanation is consistent with findings that large groups are more improved by the use of EBS than are small groups.

The features anonymity and idea viewing along with parallel input that keeps people from waiting for others help to reduce the screening effects of each of the three stages of the compatibility test (see Fig. 10.2.). This effect seems most clear at stage 2 in which group members are consciously screening ideas based on their own images as well as their perceptions of the groups' images. Because their idea entry is anonymous, they begin to put in ideas compatible with their own image, but perhaps incompatible with the groups' images. They do not have the same peer pressure to conform as in the verbal meeting. Then they view other group members' ideas that have been entered with a similar relaxation of constraints, and they expand their perception of what is compatible with the group. This relaxation of constraints and freedom of expression, then, seems to reduce the effects of stage 1 of the compatibility test. Finally, the effects of stage 3, the group compatibility test, are reduced because, unlike the experience in verbal meetings, ideas can be considered on their own merit and not criticized because of the feelings for the person who presented them or because of an emotional overreaction. Furthermore, a single person has less ability to criticize the idea and shelve further discussion because the idea is recorded and shared on all participants' screens.

It seems that the EBS process allows people to broaden their views of what is acceptable and frees them to be creative. One may not have expected the computer to be so useful in helping people communicate, but the energy developed in the GSS facility demonstrates how old notions of a computers place should be revised.

GSS groups have been proven very effective at producing ideas and, in fact, produce more ideas than would be expected from the use of parallel input alone. Some interaction between anonymity and viewing others ideas seems to create a synergy not found in any other method of brainstorming.

CONCLUSION

When considering the benefits of a unified culture and the efficiencies of screening, the costs should not be ignored. It is easy to see why organizations foster cultures that will keep large and dispersed work forces making decisions efficiently and effectively. However, these consistent decisions may not be adequate in the face of a changed environment.

Unified cultures are useful for organizations wishing to improve the consistency of decision makers. However, that same culture can reduce an organization's ability to adapt to a changing environment and generate novel ideas. GSS has been shown to be an effective tool for generating ideas, and it appears to reduce the blocking effects of the unified culture.

When individuals from unified cultures use GSS, they can begin to act as if they are from fragmented cultures, using the full extent of their diversity. When encouraging cultural unification, one no longer has to consider it a simple tradeoff between the benefits of unified culture and the benefits of a fragmented culture. Through creative use of GSS, individual meetings can be designed that take advantage of the culture type most useful at the time.

GSS seem to have more complex sociocognitive effects than just the ability to reduce production-blocking effects. GSS can also change the way images are applied. The interaction between the ability to enter ideas anonymously and the ability to read others' ideas seems to expand individuals' images of what is acceptable and allow groups to develop more ideas than groups without computer support.

REFERENCES

Beach, L. R. (1990). *Image theory: Decision making in personal and organizational contexts.* Chichester, UK: Wiley.

Beach, L. R. (1993). Broadening the definition of decision making: The role of prechoice screening of options. *Psychological Science, 4*, 215–220.

Connolly, T., Routhieaux, R. L., & Schneider, S. K. (1993). On the effectiveness of group brainstorming: Test of one underlying cognitive mechanism. *Small Group Research, 24*, 490–503.

Dennis, A. R., George, J. F., Jessup, L. M., Nunamaker, J. F., Jr., & Vogel, D. R. (1988). Information technology to support electronic meetings. *MIS Quarterly, 12*, 591–624.

Dennis, A. R., & Valacich, J. S. (1993). Computer brainstorms: More heads are better than one. *Journal of Applied Psychology, 78*, 531–537.

Gallupe, R. B., & Cooper, W. H. (1993/Fall). Brainstorming electronically. *Sloan Management Review,* 27–36.

Gallupe, R. B., Dennis, A. R., Cooper, W. H., Valacich, V. S., Bastianutti, L., M. &. Nunamaker, J. F., Jr. (1992). Electronic brainstorming and group size. *Academy of Management Journal, 35*, 350–369.

Nunamaker, J. F., Dennis, A. R., Valacich, J. S., Vogel, D. R., & George, J. F. (1991/July). Electronic meeting systems to support group work. *Communications of the ACM, 34*, 40–61.

Osborn, A. F. (1963). *Applied imagination: Principles and procedures of creative problem-solving* (3rd ed.). New York: Scribner.

Siegel, J., Dubrovski, V., Keisler. S., & McQuire, T. W. (1986). Group processes in computer mediated communication. *Organizational Behavior and Human Decision Processes. 37*, 157–187.

Valacich, J. S., Dennis, A. R., & Connolly, T. (1994). Idea generation in computer-based groups: A new ending to an old story. *Organizational Behavior and Human Decision Processes, 57*, 448–467.

11

IMAGINATION AND PLANNING

Lee Roy Beach
University of Arizona

Helmut Jungermann
Technical University of Berlin

Eric E. J. De Bruyn
University of Nijmegen

Sam sat at his desk lost in reverie. His landscape business was doing far better than he had dared to hope and it was time to do something to develop it even further. He and his wife had agreed to build the business until its sale could provide enough for their retirement. In his mind's eye he could see the two of them sitting on a beach somewhere in Greece, the setting sun bathing them in a golden light. He abruptly turned his thoughts to how he could achieve this blissful goal. Clearly the business had to be expanded, but there was not enough landscape business in town to go in that direction. He tried to make himself think in other directions. He imagined what might happen if he expanded his line of bedding plants—hard to imagine making enough profit. Perhaps he could supply plants for restaurants and hotels—he just could not see Roe Inc. letting him horn in on their business. Then it struck him! He could specialize in office plants specific to particular businesses: poppies for a drug manufacturer, venus flytraps for an adult bookstore, lilies for a funeral home, ivy for a physician's office, a wandering jew for a travel agent, jade plants for a jeweler, and palms for a fortune teller.[1] He could see it now, getting the exotic plants, selling the business managers on the idea, setting

---

[1]We thank Dr. David Tansik for suggestions about appropriate plants for the businesses.

up schedules for taking care of the plants, and selecting the advertising materials he would need for getting out the word. Then it struck him. Most of this picture involved working indoors, something he hated. Suddenly the plan lost its attraction. He considered it a moment or two longer and then rejected it, turning his attention to coming up with a different idea.

This chapter examines an important component of Sam's thought processes, the use of imagination in decision making, particularly in planning decisions.

For the most part, the decision literature, including image theory (Beach, 1990), has focused on deliberative decision making. However, underlying all of these forms of decision making is the ability of the decision maker to imagine both the outcomes of different courses of action and the intrinsic attractions of those actions themselves. Therefore, to understand decision making, be it automatic, intuitive, or deliberative, it is necessary to understand decision makers' ability to imagine alternative futures.

We begin by recalling that Mitchell and Beach (1990) identified *automatic decision* making as recognition of a familiar situation and application of a preformulated policy to it. That is, when the decision maker recognizes that he or she previously has encountered a situation similar to the one at hand, recollection of what he or she did in that previous situation provides a guide for action. Because recognition and recall are practically instantaneous, the decision appears to be automatic. However, the present situation is unlikely to be exactly the same as the previous one; the less the similarity, the less likely it is that the previous action will be appropriate this time. As the similarity decreases, the decision maker should be increasingly reluctant to behave automatically. (It is here that the many years of research on stimulus and response generalization have relevance to decision making.) At some point situational similarity is so low that the decision maker must pay attention to the unique characteristics of the present situation and the problems that might arise by using the existing policy. If these problems are nonnegligible, he or she must consider other means of dealing with the situation.

Intuitive decision making is different from automatic decision making, even though it too tends to be rapid (Mitchell & Beach, 1990). Subjectively, an option (a goal or plan) is "sensed" to be acceptable or unacceptable. In terms of image theory, the process underlying this "sense" is the compatibility test (see chapter 1). That is, the option's most salient features are compared to decision standards that derive from the decision maker's three images. If the features are compatible with the standards, the intuition is that the option is acceptable; if they are incompatible, the intuition is that the option is unacceptable.

Intuition also applies when progress toward an existing goal is monitored. Here the decision maker's intuitive feeling about where the plan is leading must include the goal of the plan (i.e., must be compatible with the goal), or the intuition is that something is wrong, that the plan must be rejected, and that another must be sought that can plausibly lead to goal achievement.

In either case, adoption decision or progress decision, it is not simply the features of the option nor the inclusion of the goal that dictates the decision. Rather, both processes are predicated on the decision maker's ability to imagine what would happen if he or she adopted a new plan or continued to implement an existing plan. If a new plan were adopted, what would other people think; what would be one's own emotional reaction (guilt, pride, etc); what would be involved in reaching the goal or implementing the plan; what would be the possible outcomes; and what opportunities or threats would the plan engender? If implementation of an existing plan were to continue, what would be required to make it work; what parts of it are under one's control and what parts are not; what would other people do that could help or hinder successful implementation; what barriers must be overcome, and how can events be managed in order to clear those barriers before they are encountered; and finally, is goal attainment a plausible possibility?

Deliberative decision making involves even more imagination, be it deliberative prechoice screening of options or deliberative choice of the best option from among the survivors of screening. At the extreme, decision making may be brought to a standstill by prolonged worry and pondering—usually in the form of imagined aversive scenarios about what might happen if this or that plan were selected. Short of the extreme, deliberation involves considerable investment of cognitive effort in imagining the results of screening and choice.

It is important to note that the imaginings associated with decision making are structured. Perhaps when stress is too great the structure may shatter, but for the most part, decision makers tell themselves reasonably coherent stories about the future, and decisions are informed by these stories. However, introspection reveals that the imagining process does not necessarily proceed in a linear manner. One's mind flickers from one scene to another, tries out different possibilities, selects some to further the story, integrates new insights or suppositions, and generally patches together a story about the future—or two or three alternative stories. It is presentationally inconvenient, if not impossible, to retain the erratic flavor of this process while trying to lay out a coherent argument about its role in decision making. Therefore, in what follows, we talk as though the imagination process is considerably more linear than it really is. Moreover, because the major function of imagination in decision making is to provide a glimpse of the future, we relieve readers who find themselves discomforted by references to imagination by henceforth using the word "forecast. "

The discussion begins with an examination of the role of forecasts in policy use, focusing on what happens when a policy fails or when the present situation is sufficiently different from previous situations to cast doubt on the policy's appropriateness. Then we turn to the role of forecasts in more deliberative decision making. Finally, we examine the practical implications of what has gone before.

FORECASTS IN POLICY USE
AND POLICY REPLACEMENT

Many treatments of decision making assume that all decisions involve clearly defined problems, that alternative solutions are readily available, and that the task is merely to choose the best solution. From the decision maker's point of view this is wrong. It often is easier to act than to think (i.e., to make an automatic decision rather than to figure out what the problem actually is, what the possible remedies are, and then to forecast the consequences of each of these remedies in order to screen out the worst and identify the best). Indeed, mere superficial identification of the situation often suggests an immediate course of action because the decision maker simply can do what he or she previously has done in similar situations (i.e., apply a preformulated policy).

The difficulty, of course, is that superficial identification of the situation may lead to using a policy that would not be used had the situation been more carefully examined, other options considered, and the policy's fore-casted consequences compared with forecasts for the other possible options

Klein (1996) presented considerable evidence of automatic, policy-driven decision making derived from field studies of fire fighters, tank platoon leaders, and design engineers, to name but a few. He found that from 39% to 80% of the decisions in his studies were what he called *recognition-primed* decisions. That is, the decision maker recognized the situation as one for which he or she had an existing policy and proceeded to implement the policy. Furthermore, the more familiar the situation, the more decision makers depended on automatic, policy-driven decisions. In situations that resembled familiar situations but that were discriminably unique, experienced decision makers focused on situational diagnosis rather than action options, and less experienced decision makers did exactly the opposite. Apparently experience both provides policies for recurring situations and provides the wisdom to perform situational diagnosis for nonrecurring situations. As in other studies of problem solving, novices appear to have acquired neither requisite policies nor the ability to look beyond the surface characteristics of the problem in order to design an appropriate plan for dealing with it.

The attraction of depending on policies is very strong, often taking precedence even when the decision maker knows that careful deliberation is required. De Bruyn (1992) has provided an example from clinical decision making (an example that also might describe the behavior of trouble-shooters when an organization or a piece of equipment malfunctions).

De Bruyn (1992) presents a logical model of clinical diagnosis that begins with *complaint analysis*, a consideration of the client's presenting symptoms. The second step, *problem analysis*, consists of identifying the particular behavioral or personality disorder reflected in the client's complaints. The third step, *diagnosis*, involves detection of the conditions that cause, elicit, or sustain the dysfunctional behavior or disorder. The fourth step, *treatment indication*, consists of considering the possible consequences of selecting one or another available therapies and choosing the most promising. The final step consists of *implementation* of the chosen therapy.

Even though this sequence of steps seems quite reasonable and would appear to be what is taught in clinical training, research shows that clinicians very often fail to proceed through the whole sequence (Pijnenburg & De Bruyn, 1993). It is true that they go from complaint analysis to problem analysis to diagnosis. But instead of proceeding to the next step, a decision about treatment based on their understanding of the causes of the problem and the forecasted effects of the available therapies, clinicians almost always go back to the problem itself and select some standard treatment for dealing with it. The treatment is a preformulated policy for dealing with the identified problem and the causal diagnosis is used merely to reinforce the accuracy of problem identification rather than as information that could contribute to precise evaluation of alternative treatments and selection of the one with the best potential.

FORECASTING WHEN POLICY FAILS OR NO POLICY EXISTS

Economy of cognitive energy argues for use of a policy until its failure seems imminent, whereupon the decision maker should abandon it and engage in deliberation (which includes forecasting) that leads to the choice of a new, more appropriate and promising plan. Of course, if the problem is not much like a problem faced before, there may be no policy available for use, in which case the decision maker is forced to generate and evaluate one or more new plans.

We turn now to the question of where new plans originate when policy is absent or is seen to be failing. This involves questions about how new plans are adopted and, once adopted, how they are changed or abandoned if they are seen to be failing. The key is that planning and monitoring of implementation progress requires the decision maker to forecast the future by constructing cognitive scenarios. (see also Pennington & Hastie's story model, 1986, 1988.)

Scenarios are mental representations of sequences of actions and events that connect the present and the future (see Jungermann, 1985). They take advantage of the decision maker's knowledge about the events that led up to the present decision as well as his or her beliefs about how things work and how people behave in order to generate forecasts of the future given the assumptions imbedded in the scenario.

Although scenario construction is a common practice in business forecasting, little is known about how it is done by individuals. Jungermann and Thüring (1987; Thüring & Jungermann, 1986) presented a four-step view of personal scenario construction based on the concept of mental models from cognitive science. In the first step, *activation of problem knowledge*, the frame within which the decision maker is working evokes relevant knowledge from memory. *Relevant* means knowledge that permits posing of if–then propositions, usually knowledge of causes or conditionalities (Beach, 1992).

In the second step, *construction of mental model*, a mental model is constructed consisting of elements (events or actions) and relations (if–then propositions). Construction uses both the known causal relationships retrieved from memory and inferred causal relationships. The latter rely on cues to causality (i.e., covariation of events, their temporal order, their spatial and temporal contiguity, and their similarity; Einhorn & Hogarth, 1982, 1986). In most cases the cause is an action that could be taken by the decision maker and the effect is a forecasted change in the situation that the decision maker would interpret as progress toward the goal.

In the third step, *simulation using the mental model*, the mental model is "run" by assigning plausible states to the if part of its if–then propositions. A different scenario is generated by each unique set of if states and the unique set of then states that are the logical consequences of the propositions. Not all possible sets are admissible because the causal relations as well as the frame of the situation impose severe constraints. As a result, the decision maker produces (mentally) a set of hypothetical but more-or-less plausible forecasted futures, each of which is, in effect, an answer to the question: "What if I did x?"

The mental model can be run either forward or backward (see Jungermann & Thüring, 1987). Any element of the model can be assigned a state, and the model can then be run forward to predict future states of other elements. Also, the model can be run backward to explain how the present state of this element could have come to be. In short, the decision maker can forecast (imagine) what will happen if he or she makes x occur, and also can imagine what might have happened in the past that makes it necessary to do something.

In the fourth step, *selection of a plan*, the set of scenarios produced by running the model results in a set of potential plans of action from which one plan must be selected. This fourth step links scenario construction to the strategic image in image theory. The plans that are the constituents of the strategic image are the scenarios that have been chosen for pursuing the goals on the trajectory image. This raises the question of why some scenarios (plans) are adopted and others are rejected.

DECIDING ABOUT PLANS

The construction of scenarios is constrained by both context and goals. Therefore, not all possible scenarios are constructed. In terms of image theory, as each scenario, and thus its forecast, is generated, it is screened for compatibility with the relevant standards from the decision maker's three images (value, trajectory, and strategic). The most important of these constituents is the goal of interest from the trajectory image, but moral issues about means to the end also are part of the standards. If the number of violations of the decision standards exceeds the decision maker's rejection threshold, the scenario is rejected; otherwise it is assigned to the choice set. (In most cases the goal that the plan addresses is such an important standard that its absence, a violation, from the forecast is sufficient to cause rejection of the plan).

If no scenario survives screening, the decision maker must rescreen the rejected scenarios using a higher rejection threshold, attempt to generate more acceptable scenarios, or change the goal. If only one scenario survives screening, it is adopted as the plan for pursuing the goal. If more than one scenario survives screening, the best of the survivors in the choice set must be selected by using the profitability test (Potter & Beach, 1994a, 1994b).

The end result is that the scenario producing a forecast that includes the goal and that does not violate too many other decision standards is adopted as the plan for pursuing the goal.

As outlined above, because the compatibility test is applied to scenarios and their forecasts as they are generated, relatively few scenarios survive to become full-fledged plans. However, when decision makers conscientiously try to be thorough and careful, it sometimes happens that the number of scenarios, and therefore the number of potential plans, is increased. One of these is chosen to become the plan and usually is implemented.

CHANGING PLANS

For adults at least, beliefs and values that comprise the value image are surprisingly stable across time. Many of them are learned in childhood and persist throughout life. Changes are extremely difficult to effect, even in the face of contradictory evidence and social pressure. Goals are more persistent, but only until they are achieved or until they prove to be unachievable—whereupon they give way to new goals. In contrast to values and goals, plans change very easily. Sometimes they fail to produce progress toward their goals. At other times they meet resistance from environmental forces, or the cost of implementing them exceeds the value of achieving their goal. Whatever the reason, plans are constantly being revised to meet unexpected contingencies or are replaced by more promising courses of action.

Because the future is uncertain and forecasts often are wrong, the vulnerability of plans is inevitable. Robotlike persistence in the execution of a plan when conditions change or when things turn out to be different than was forecasted would doom a plan to failure. Instead, most plans are monitored for progress toward goal achievement and are abandoned when progress is insufficient.

Efficient monitoring requires frequent updating of the original forecasts associated with the plan to make sure that continued implementation will in fact lead to the goal. Other things being equal, as long as the decision maker can forecast that the goal will be achieved, he or she is wise to retain the plan; when the goal no longer appears in the forecast, the plan should be relinquished.

When a plan must be replaced, the replacement need not be radically different from the plan itself; often only minor adjustments to the plan will be sufficient to make the plan acceptable. These minor adjustments permit the decision maker to fine-tune the plan so that it more perfectly fits the environment in which it is being implemented and becomes more capable of achieving its goal.

Attempts to replace a failing plan sometimes are to no avail. The decision maker is unable to imagine a scenario that forecasts successful goal attainment (i.e., that plausibly bridges the gap between the present situation and the goal). When "you can't get there from here," the attempt to achieve the goal must be abandoned, and the decision maker must reexamine the goal itself. Is it in fact worth all the effort? Is it still as desirable as it was when it was adopted? Can he or she settle for some other goal, or some modification of this goal? Does the unattainability of the goal indicate that the desired future represented by the trajectory image should be reconsidered—perhaps resulting in a major reorientation of the decision maker's view of his or her future?

Finally, it should be noted that plans sometimes change because goals simply change over time. Goals often become less pressing, less desirable, or less salient as time progresses, and implementation of plans to achieve them becomes less important. Perhaps without realizing it, the decision maker turns attention to other activities and the plans, while never actually abandoned, simply get set aside. The decision maker always means to get back to them, but somehow never does ("someday I will return to playing the cello, learning French, mastering my statistics package"). It would be difficult to say how often plans die this sort of obscure death, but it probably is common. The point is, plans may cease to be implemented without ever being abandoned or changed; they simply waste away.

PRACTICAL IMPLICATIONS

We have examined the role of imagination (forecasts) in decision making. The discussion has focused on forecasting the consequences of continuing to do what one already is doing (progress decisions) or of adopting a new plan (adoption decisions). In the context of image theory, both forecasts use the same mechanism, cognitive scenarios, and both decisions are made using the same mechanism, the compatibility test (although the profitability test may be used to break adoption ties). We also have noted the tendency of decision makers to rely on preformulated policies, bypassing much in the way of forecasts, and we have observed the advantages and drawbacks of doing so.

Policies

Let us begin with implications of heavy reliance on policies. The obvious advantage to using policies is that the decision maker need not devote time and energy to making new decisions each time a situation recurs. Because much of the day-to-dayness of life is repetitious (encounters with clerks, filling your gas tank, getting ready for work each morning, etc.), the use of policies allows one to operate more efficiently than one otherwise might. Indeed, human rote learning and rats running mazes provide the ideal analogy for policy use—experience provides rules for behaving, and we economically follow those rules.

The disadvantages of policy use are equally obvious. Bureaucratic obstinacy in the face of special circumstances is a familiar experience. So too is the experience of behaving inappropriately because our perception of a situation turns out to be wrong, such as mistaking a stranger for a friend and therefore behaving with undue familiarity.

An important part of any training program is to teach people to discriminate between those situations in which a policy is appropriate and those in which it is not. For example, employees who are being trained to deal with customer complaints must be taught to discriminate between legitimate and fraudulent complaints, and to use a different policy for dealing with each of them.

Finally, it is interesting to note that neurotic behavior can be interpreted as the persistent use of policies in situations in which an outside observer would deem them to be inappropriate. The classic notion is that the neurotic person treats discriminably different situations as though they were the same and applies a policy that may be (or may have been) appropriate to one of them but not to all of them. Thus, a policy of appeasement may have been appropriate for a child with bullying parents, but it is considered neurotic when applied to all authority figures later in life.

In the workplace, policies often seem to take on a life of their own. Because they frequently are followed by lower-level employees who do not understand their original goal, the absence of progress toward the goal goes unnoted. As a result, policies can become a threat to progress. Consider a policy designed to enhance customer service that instead degrades it, often ending up with elaborate and burdensome paperwork that counterbalances any benefit it may offer. We know of one office in which the supervisor enforces a very old policy requiring clerks to clear their desks of all objects before leaving for the day. Originally, the idea was to encourage workers to finish work on each day's projects. Instead, the policy merely results in unfinished projects being stuffed into drawers, and the time required to pack and unpack the desk each day is taken from productive work on the projects.

Forecasts

Scenarios for forecasting can be generated in two ways, and the results are not necessarily the same. One way is by starting with the goal and imagining a sequence of actions and events sufficient to bridge backward from the goal to the present situation. If such a sequence can be constructed, it becomes a feasible scenario worthy of being submitted to the compatibility test to see if it meets the decision maker's standards.

More commonly, however, the focus is less on the goal than on the present state of affairs and how they can be changed in order to achieve a goal. The resulting scenario bridges forward from the present to the goal. If such a sequence of actions and events can be constructed, it too becomes a feasible scenario worthy of being submitted to the compatibility test to see if it fits with the images.

This view of scenario generation has some interesting implications when a scenario is under consideration for adoption as a plan. For example, Jungermann (1985) suggested that those parts of the scenario that lie furthest in the sequence from the starting point tend to be the least clearly formulated. Thus we would expect that difficulties in implementing the scenario would be concentrated earlier or later, depending upon whether the scenario had been constructed backward or forward. Moreover, forecasts must be updated more frequently for plans that grew from forward-generated scenarios because, in contrast to the clarity of the goal in backward-generated scenarios, forward-generated scenarios are ambiguous in the vicinity of the goal, and it is not clear that continued implementation of the plan actually will achieve what is desired.

In the workplace the location of ambiguity in scenarios is readily apparent. Planning committees that begin with the goal and work backward often fail to get things started because they have no idea what the requisite first steps might be. Similarly, committees that work in the other direction may not specify what constitutes success. That is, because goals often are abstract states ("a leader in our industry"), it may be unclear how to know when you have achieved them. Because of this ambiguity, it may be extremely difficult to know if the plan is making progress, or, perhaps as bad, to know when to stop once you get there. For example, how many publications does it take for an academic unit to declare success in achieving scholarly competence, and how many are too many, causing a consequent drain of resources away from other goals, such as good teaching? If ambiguity in the vicinity of the goal makes it difficult to detect lack of progress, it also makes it difficult to detect success and the need to stop pursuit of the goal that has been achieved.

REFERENCES

Beach, L. R. (1990). *Image theory: Decision making in personal and organizational contexts.* Chichester, UK: Wiley.

Beach, L. R. (1992). Epistemic strategies: Causal thinking in expert and nonexpert judgment. In. G. Wright & F. Bolger (Eds.), *Expertise and decision support* (pp. 107–127). New York: Plenum.

De Bruyn, E. E. J. (1992). A normative-prescriptive view on clinical psychodiagnostic decision making. *European Journal of Psychological Assessment, 8,* 163–171.

Einhorn, H. J., & Hogarth, R. M. (1982). Predictions, diagnosis, and causal thinking in forecasting. *Journal of Forecasting, 1,* 23–36.

Einhorn, H. J., & Hogarth, R. M. (1986). Judging probable cause. *Psychological Bulletin, 99,* 3–19.

Jungermann, H. (1985). Inferential processes in the construction of scenarios. *Journal of Forecasting, 4,* 321–327.

Jungermann, H., & Thüring, J. (1987). The use of causal knowledge for inferential reasoning. In J. L. Mumpower, L. D. Phillips, O. Renn, & V. R. R. Uppuluri (Eds.), *Expert judgment and expert systems* (pp. 131–146). New York: Springer.

Klein, G. A. (1996). *Sources of power: The study of naturalistic decision making.* Manuscript submitted for publication.

Mitchell, T. R., & Beach, L. R. (1990). "...Do I love thee? Let me count..." Toward an understanding of intuitive and automatic decision making. *Organizational Behavior and Human Decision Processes, 47,* 1–20.

Pennington, N., & Hastie, R. (1986). Evidence evaluation in complex decision making. *Journal of Personality and Social Psychology, 51,* 242–258.

Pennington, N., & Hastie, R. (1988). Explanation-based decision making: Effects of memory structure on judgment. *Journal of Experimental Psychology: Learning, Memory and Cognition, 14,* 521–533.

Pijnenburg, H. M., & De Bruyn, E. E. J. (1993, October). *The quality of team decision making in residential and ambulatory youth care.* Paper presented at the Third European Congress on Residential Care, Luneburg, Germany.

Potter, R. E., & Beach, L. B. (1994a). Decision making when the acceptable options become unavailable. *Organizational Behavior and Human Decision Processes, 57,* 468–483.

Potter, R. E., & Beach, L. B. (1994b). Imperfect information in pre-choice screening of options. *Organizational Behavior and Human Decision Processes, 59,* 313–329.

Thüring, J., & Jungermann, H. (1986). Constructing and running mental models for inferences about the future. In B. Brehmer, H. Jungermann, P. Lourens, & G. Sevon (Eds.), *New directions in decision research* (pp. 163–174). Amsterdam: Elsevier.

12

DESIGNING MARKETING PLANS AND COMMUNICATION STRATEGIES

Christopher P. Puto
Susan E. Heckler
University of Arizona

Image theory offers considerable potential for assisting marketing strategists and tacticians in developing, executing, and evaluating effective marketing plans. In this chapter, we briefly describe the marketing planning process, paying special attention to the role of marketing communications (i.e., promotion) in the consumer's decision making processes. The impact of various promotional tools is discussed in the context of image theory and its associated stages of decision making: framing, screening, choice, implementation. The chapter concludes with a brief examination of the relationship of image theory to the managerial development of the other strategic marketing variables: product, price, distribution.

MARKETING STRATEGY AND THE DESIGN OF MARKETING COMMUNICATIONS

Marketing is the process of identifying needs; developing solutions to those needs; making the solutions available at the time, place, and cost that are advantageous to both the customer and the organization; and making the customer aware of the solutions. These needs can take many forms. A family may have the need for fun and fulfilling recreational activities, or a person who is preparing for retirement may have the need to maintain his or her

155

current lifestyle. A company may have a need to identify and maintain a source of effective management talent to preserve and improve its competitive position, or that same organization may have a need to produce a product using techniques and materials that do not result in harmful environmental effects. In all of these instances, marketing is the process through which potential solutions are developed and made available to customers, be they individual consumers or organizational entities. In this chapter we focus on the role of image theory as it applies to the decision behavior of individual consumers. However, with modest changes, these concepts can extend directly to organizational buying issues consistent with the philosophy presented in chapter 1—that organizational decisions are "contexts within which individual members' decisions become consolidated" (p. 3).

When developing marketing strategies, the manager must first clearly identify the need in question and develop a thorough description and categorization of the various consumers (grouped into market segments) having this general need. Failure to adequately define the need and accurately group those possessing similar needs leads to ineffective solutions, dissatisfied consumers, and ultimately to failed businesses. It is therefore crucial that each facet of the process be conceived and executed with maximum precision. Consumer needs are rooted in their beliefs and values and their particular goals salient at the time. Consider the preretirement consumer introduced in the previous paragraph. A decision to purchase a lottery ticket may have been the result of seeking a solution to any of several needs: financial independence, excitement, or paying the mortgage or other mounting bills. Similarly, such decisions as increasing the amount of funds allocated to retirement accounts, or decreasing the level of entertainment expenses being incurred could all be related to the overriding need to prepare for a future lifestyle. Thus, a consumer's needs will expand to include preserving one's financial independence, exploring consumption options, changing one's entire lifestyle or all of these.

From among these needs, the marketing strategist would identify those belonging to a sufficient number of consumers, as to make offering a solution profitable, then would develop products or services that the marketer's organization can offer more effectively (e.g., better performance, lower cost, etc.) than the competition. These solutions then become the marketer's products or services. In this chapter we focus on the development of marketing communications strategies that will inform consumers of the effective solutions and integrate the insights offered through image theory. We first define marketing communications and the various vehicles through which information is disseminated to potential customers, current consumers or both. Next, we briefly summarize traditional views of decision making and discuss the development of communications strategies consistent with the precepts of these established theories of consumer choice. Finally, we contrast this approach with one based on the precepts of image theory.

MARKETING COMMUNICATIONS
AND THE PROMOTION MIX

A typical definition of the communications portion of a marketing strategy is: any communication designed to directly or indirectly facilitate the exchange process or the function of informing, persuading, and motivating consumers' purchasing decisions through communication. In developing a communications strategy, the marketing strategist has a variety of tools at his or her disposal. Perhaps the tool most commonly associated with marketing is *advertising*: any paid, nonpersonal presentation of ideas, goods, or services by an identified sponsor. Consumers know that advertisements are developed by organizations to provide information making it more likely that the consumer will buy the product. As a result, the processing of advertising information often includes an automatic "vigilance" in which the consumer believes the information is most likely positively biased in favor of the selling organization. However, it is important to note that consumers do rely on advertising to gain knowledge that significantly affects their choices. Thus, brand name, primary product and service benefits, and information about how or where to buy the product are often obtained through the processing of advertisements.

A commonly discussed element of the promotional mix is *personal selling*: one-to-one communications designed to move potential customers throughout the entire decision making process. Although personal selling is not typically a major influence in consumers' decisions regarding small dollar items, this aspect of communications does play an important role in the decisions for high dollar purchases such as choice of colleges, new homes, cars, professional services, and so forth.

Sales promotion is composed of yet another set of promotional tools. These are various materials, activities, or both that provide an incentive for consumers to behave in ways that are advantageous to the supplier. For example, coupons that appear in a Sunday newspaper remind consumers of brand names and offer the consumer a discount on any purchase made before a given date. Similarly, two-for-one purchases, sweepstakes entries, rebates, and premiums (gifts given at the time of purchase) are all designed to motivate consumers to act in that which benefit the sponsor. An astute marketing strategist develops promotional programs that utilize each of these tools in a manner that differentiates his or her product or service from that of competitors and assists consumers in identifying how the product or service will best fill their needs. With this introduction to marketing communications strategies and tools, albeit cursory, we now briefly illustrate the difficulties marketing managers encounter when attempting to apply traditional decision theories in developing marketing communications strategies.

TRADITIONAL MODELS OF CONSUMER CHOICE

Conventional wisdom and most theories of decision making (e.g., utility theory and its variants; cf. Raiffa, 1968) posit that consumers are active information processors who seek specific information related to the decision at hand and who then use deliberate strategies, heuristics, or both to evaluate the alternatives and make a decision. Several choice strategies or models have been advanced to describe the details of choice processing or the way evaluative judgments are formed and choices are made. (For a more thorough treatment of this topic in the context of consumer judgment and choice, see Johnson & Puto, 1987). Generally, these models differ in two strategic aspects of processing: whether evaluation proceeds within or across attributes and whether the processing is compensatory or noncompensatory. Within-attribute strategies compare alternatives directly on descriptive attributes, whereas across-attribute strategies posit explicit tradeoffs of attribute information. Thus, a low value on one attribute can be made up or compensated for by a large value on another attribute. In contrast, noncompensatory strategies are characterized by the elimination of choice alternatives that do not meet prespecified cutoffs on evaluative attributes. Such strategies are noncompensatory because attribute values cannot be traded off for others. Irrespective of the specific processing details, all of these strategies focus on the specific decision behaviors of individual consumers. Because advertising and sales promotion are mass media-oriented strategies, the individual decision models are not easily utilized as strategic support tools.

For a marketing strategist to apply one of the traditional theories of the choice process in developing a promotional strategy, the first step would be to investigate and analyze the consumers in the target market to ascertain whether a dominant choice strategy existed (e.g., within- versus across-attribute and compensatory versus noncompensatory). If, as is typically the case, substantial groups of consumers utilize different strategies, this suggests multiple segments, each needing a specially designed promotional program.

Clearly, using traditional decision theory frameworks to develop promotional strategies requires extensive, detailed knowledge of consumers' preference structures and of individual processing styles. This renders the task of designing an effective promotional message quite daunting and may explain why so many promotional campaigns fail to meet the originator's objectives. The traditional decision theory framework may work well in a personal selling environment, in which a one-to-one dialogue permits a professional sales person to discern the needed information in the early stages of the sales interview and then adapt the sales strategy to the buyer's processing style and thereby facilitate the effective exchange of information. The result is satisfaction on both sides of the exchange. However, personal selling is the most expensive form of promotion and may not be an option for many firms nor for a variety of products. In fact, marketing strategies based on processing styles of individual consumers may be quite difficult to implement because each style would represent a distinct market segment. Market segmentation is a cornerstone of effective marketing strategy. However, to be useful for marketing strategy purposes, segments must be identifiable and reachable, large enough to be profitable and, across segments, capable of responding differently to a given marketing program. Segments based on processing style meet this last requirement but fall decidedly short on the first two, rendering this approach ineffective for marketing strategy. In contrast, image theory offers a rich set of strategy options with a broad range of applications for the development of marketing communications. The next section expands our examination of promotional activities by incorporating aspects of image theory and its related decision processes.

IMAGE THEORY
AND MARKETING COMMUNICATIONS

Image theory posits that decisions among multiple options occur in several stages and that these stages are formed as a result of a series of images: value, trajectory, and strategic. The value image represents the identification of a need (i.e., the gap between the decision maker's present state and desired state). The trajectory image represents the decision maker's overall goal with regard to the desired state (i.e., what aspects of the desired state are achievable?). The strategic image sets forth the mechanism through which the trajectory image can be achieved. These three images have an impact on the screening process and the ultimate choice. In particular, the images guide the selection of criteria used in screening alternatives. Both marketing strategy and the attendant promotional plans can be implemented more effectively if image theory is taken into consideration (see Nelson, chapter 13, this volume, for an example of how specifically held values can affect a consumer's decision process). In addition to identifying the images that underlie the selection of decision criteria, image theory also delineates four stages of the decision making process: *framing*, the contextual setting of the decision in which needs and options are identified; *screening*, during which incompatibilities between the various decision goals and product or service attributes are examined; *choice*, in which the best of the remaining options is identified; and *implementation*, during which a consumer must both start the process of acting on his or her decision and overcome any barriers that may arise as the decision is pursued.

Perhaps this process is best clarified by returning to one of our early examples. Consider the individual preparing for retirement: The person must first understand the context or frame within which decisions are made. Is the retirement planning horizon one year, five, or fifteen? Is the current concern the type of investments being purchased, the current state of the home mortgage, or the plans for future housing? Depending on the context, a series of options will present themselves. Through the various images described previously, the consumer will then develop a screening mechanism based on the compatibility or incompatibility of the needs and options. If, for example, the concern is related to types of investments, the consumer's risk aversion may play an important role in the screening process. Once the options have been screened, assuming that more than one alternative exists, a specific choice must be made. Once the choise is made, the consumer must now act to implement that decision—calling an investment counselor on the phone, visiting a bank or other financial institution, and so forth. As the activities begin, other issues may arise that serve as barriers to completing the purchase: The paperwork may be more complex than the consumer expected; time and or dollar costs may exceed the consumer's expectations; or upon reflection, the initial choice may no longer fulfill the consumer's needs. This process, now seen through the eyes of the image theorist, is demonstrably more intricate than would be described through the traditional models discussed earlier. It is through an understanding of these complexities of decision making that more effective promotional programs can be developed.

Let us now return to a discussion of marketing communications and the ways in which strategies can be enhanced by integrating the image theory view. As described earlier, advertising provides the consumer with various types of information: brand names, product characteristics, or instructions for purchase (where, at what cost, etc.). This advertising information is likely to be what consumers will use to screen the various alternatives. The advertiser's goal is to have his or her product or service remain as a viable alternative in the choice set. It is important, therefore, that the advertiser understand the underlying goals of the target segment and provide information that will minimize the likelihood that a product or service will be screened from the initial option set. If, in the investment example, the target segment is risk averse, the stability of the funds (rather than the rate of the return) might be the more important attribute to emphasize.

Note that this approach is quite different from traditional advertising development, which assumes that advertising information is used by consumers to make choices, and, as a result, emphasizes information identified as pertinent choice criteria (the fund with the highest rate of return). In current advertising research, the degree to which advertising information is used in the screening process versus the choice process has not been examined. Many interesting questions await study as image theory is more fully integrated into the development of marketing theory: How do images get formed? Can advertising influence the formation of all three images or only certain ones? Once formed, can advertising change images? What role does advertising play in establishing screening criteria? These are just a few examples of the many fruitful research opportunities in this area.

Having completed the screening process, the consumer must now move to make a choice among the undiscarded alternatives. This choice process may be more successfully influenced through the personal attention of salespeople, who develop individualized messages focused on the criteria of importance to the consumer, and who can demonstrate the competitive advantage of their product or service. Certain sales promotion tools may also be effective at this stage (e.g., activities that allow the consumer to experience a product or service [free samples, one week trial memberships, etc.] may assist the consumer in differentiating the "best" option from those screened as acceptable).

A very interesting aspect of image theory is the recognition that making the choice is not the end of the process. The consumer must still complete a variety of activities to transform the choice into a purchase. Once again, personal selling may be an important communication tool at this stage. A salesperson can instruct consumers as they proceed through the purchase process, and can identify potential barriers that might prevent the consumer from completing the process (and solve the problems before they disrupt the purchase). This role of personal selling is well accepted in the marketing literature; however, it has not been presented within a theoretical framework that differentiates choice and implementation. Once again, many interesting research questions await examination as marketers develop a better understanding of the role of promotional tools in consumption activities framed through image theory.

Sales promotion activities may also enhance opportunities to turn choice into purchase. Providing time limited discounts, coupons, or special deals may entice the consumer to move from a discussion of buying a new car to the dealer for a test drive and finally to the signing of a sales or lease agreement. Adding a premium (gift with purchase) may allow consumers to fulfill more than one set of needs (e.g., obtaining a travel set of cosmetics at the same time that regularly used products are replenished). As in the discussion of advertisement development, the degree to which a marketing strategist can predict the barriers to implementation and develop specific communications messages and activities that address those barriers, the more successful the overall promotional program will be. Very little theoretical research has examined sales promotion efforts. This new identification of sales promotion as a motivation for implementation (the movement from choice to purchase) offers many opportunities for future research efforts. Specifically, is there a taxonomy of barriers to implementation and possibly a corresponding taxonomy of effective sales promotion tools for each barrier?

IMAGE THEORY AND MARKETING STRATEGY

We have thus far focused our image theory discussion on the connection between consumers' decision making behavior and marketing communications strategies. However, an understanding of image theory has the potential for influencing other elements of marketing strategy as well. In particular, product strategies, distribution strategies, and pricing strategies can each be influenced by an understanding of image theory. Let us return one final time to our preretirement consumer and examine how his or her values and beliefs, in conjunction with image theory, can influence marketing strategy development. This treatment is necessarily brief, but it serves to introduce the reader to the vast potential of this topic.

We observed in the first section that consumers' needs are rooted in their beliefs and values and those goals that are salient at the time. Values refer to an individual's enduring principles, that guide and influence behavior. Beliefs refer to an individual's perceptions of facts or specified relationships that are likely to obtain when correlated events occur. Thus, for example, a "value" may be that individuals should preserve their financial resources, and a "belief" may be that individuals who do not act prudently regarding financial asset management will ultimately lose their resources.

In the context of our preretirement consumer, the value that individuals should preserve their financial resources, combined with the offer of an early retirement package at work, creates the value image in this consumer that "I must take steps to preserve my current assets." A belief that individuals who do not act prudently regarding financial asset management will ultimately lose their resources can lead to a trajectory image such as, "I need to retain a financial advisor in order to avoid losing my resources." (Note that other trajectory images are equally imaginable. This is but one example.) This trajectory image can, in turn, produce a strategic image that might resemble the following: "I will develop a list of potential financial advisors, interview them to establish their credentials and their fit with my personality, and then select my financial advisor from among them" (the plan). The tactics could then include a set of specific actions to be undertaken in identifying candidates, questions to ask in the interviews, and criteria to use in determining whether or not to keep a given advisor in the choice set. The forecast might include a set of expectations regarding how an appropriate financial advisor will interact with clients and the likely results of such interactions. Each of these is responsive to and suggestive of appropriate marketing strategies.

The marketing strategist can use an awareness of the value (wealth preservation) to segment the market into groups who are concerned about wealth preservation and those who are not. Carefully studying this need can then guide the marketing strategist to develop specific investment products that preserve capital. Then, understanding how the belief in prudent behavior can lead to the trajectory image of retaining a financial advisor will guide the marketing strategist to develop a distribution strategy in which the investment products that satisfy the wealth preservation need are offered through skilled financial advisors. Furthermore, being aware of the consumer's tactics and forecast as outlined above, the marketing strategist could either use promotional tools to establish the criteria the consumer should use in executing these behaviors or initiate appropriate training for the financial advisors so that they act in a manner consistent with the consumer's forecast. Finally, by understanding the criteria the consumer is likely to use during screening, the marketing strategist can formulate a pricing strategy that facilitates the consumer's perception of benefits received for effort expended and thereby enhance the product's chances of surviving the screening process. As evidenced by the foregoing examples, the opportunities for enhancing the practice of marketing through understanding image theory are almost unbounded. Similarly, for theoretical researchers in marketing, each of the foregoing represents a research proposition awaiting refinement.

SUMMARY AND CONCLUSION

Our goal in this chapter was to introduce the reader to the basic precepts of marketing strategy and illustrate the potential for using image theory to advance our understanding of the consumer decision making process. Because the intersection of these topics represents an area virtually devoid of research, we chose to explicate the opportunities by using a variety of examples. In summary, the overall objective in applying image theory to the formation of marketing communications strategies is to use the individual consumer's beliefs and values to develop a thorough understanding of his or her needs. Then the marketing strategist must instigate the development of goods and services that effectively satisfy those needs better than the currently available set of options. Once these solutions are developed, priced, and ready for distribution, the promotional strategy requires that the consumer's beliefs and values be incorporated into the marketing communications efforts so that the consumer can render an accurate judgment of the product or service's ability to effectively satisfy his or her needs. In each case, image theory represents an effective approach for enhancing consumers' abilities to make effective purchase decisions.

REFERENCES

Johnson, M. D., & Puto, C. P. (1987). A review of consumer judgment and choice in marketing. In M. J. Houston (Ed.), *Review of Marketing* (pp. 236–252). Chicago: American Marketing Association.
Raiffa, H. (1968). *Decision Analysis: Introductory lectures on choices under uncertainty*. Reading, MA: Addison-Wesley.

13

CONSUMER DECISIONS INVOLVING SOCIAL RESPONSIBILITY

Kim A. Nelson
University of Washington, Tacoma

Public concern about the environment has become a mainstream issue that affects consumer behavior in a variety of ways. Some consumers use a company's environmental record to eliminate its products and services from further consideration (e.g., the boycott of Exxon products after the *Exxon Valdez* oil spill in Alaska). These same consumers are also likely to consider a brand's "greenness," its lack of harm to the environment, as a product attribute when evaluating alternatives (e.g., Tide detergent advertisements touting the "enviro-pak" refill that sends less packaging to the landfill). Roper Starch Worldwide has been tracking consumer attitudes and behaviors related to the environment on an annual basis for several years, and their 1993 study reports that 55% of American consumers are classified as True Blue Greens, Greenback Greens, or Sprouts—their terms for different types of environmentally active consumers (Stisser, 1994). They also report increasing trends in consumer behaviors that directly affect their choices (e.g., reading labels to see if contents are environmentally safe, avoiding products from companies with poor environmental records, being willing to pay more for green products, and considering both the purchase and disposal of products or packaging).

Concern for the environment can be considered as one dimension of an individual's social responsibility. The Exxon boycott can then be seen as a reaction to that company's perceived lack of corporate social responsibility in an attempt to reduce the possibility of future environmental disasters.

The selection of green products can be seen as a reflection of an individual's social responsibility to protect the environment for others and future generations. Other examples of social responsibility issues that affect consumer choices are political policies of corporations (e.g., doing business in countries with poor humanitarian records), objection to hiring and firing practices (e.g., sexist or lifestyle biases), corporate philanthropy (e.g., contributions to favored or disfavored causes), travel boycotts based on state laws (e.g., lack of Martin Luther King holiday, passage of antigay legislation), and various political correctness issues. Although social responsibility might not be the most powerful influence in a consumer decision, it is a complex factor that needs to be included in the decision model. When a social responsibility issue is present, the salient characteristics of both the decision and the decision maker can differ from those characteristics present in more typical consumer decision contexts.

Characteristics of the Decision

Many consumer decisions involve the satisfaction of a current need (e.g., deciding what to serve for dinner, selecting a spreadsheet program, replacing worn-out running shoes), and these decisions are relatively discrete, unitary events. In contrast, a decision involving social responsibility has a more salient history and future. That decision is often an incremental step toward some larger goal and can be viewed as a vehicle for change. The decision can also protect an individual's values (e.g., social responsibility) and goals (e.g., protection or improvement of the environment). In addition, the expected decision benefits can be deferred in time, resistant to easy quantification, and relatively abstract. These differentiating characteristics are part of a subset of characteristics cited by Beach (1990) as difficult to incorporate into many traditional decision theories but relatively amenable to image theory.

Another difference from a typical consumer decision is the social responsibility attribute itself. Using environmental concern as the context, product or corporate greenness is an attribute that reflects the social responsibility of both the buyer and seller. Greenness differs from more typical product attributes in several ways: Physical examination provides few cues; knowledge of a product's life cycle (raw materials to disposal) is required; and the benefits of reduced environmental damage are uncertain (in timing and degree). Furthermore, the desired benefit of a cleaner environment does not accrue only to the green consumer. As with the benefits of a social good, all people profit from individual efforts of green consumption regardless of participation.

Characteristics of the Decision Maker

When a social responsibility issue is present, the consumer's set of principles and values that generally underlies and guides behavior becomes even more important. The consumer's belief regarding social responsibility (i.e., the obligation to act in ways that enhance society's overall well being) is an obvious example. Because a consumer does not benefit immediately from buying recycled or recyclable brands, comprehension of the effects of one's behavior on others in society could affect a consumer's decision process. Values more directly related to the social responsibility issue could also alter the decision process and outcome. For example, consumers who value a clean environment more than saving money might select a more expensive green brand rather than a nongreen brand. Although principles and values underlie all behavior, their influence is probably more directly felt in these types of decisions. The impact of a third individual factor, perceived consumer effectiveness (i.e., the belief that one's efforts can make a difference in the solution to a problem), is even more uniquely tied to socially responsible decision making. This evaluation of effectiveness involves projecting the results of a single act or series of similar actions into a relatively uncertain future. This is typically not the case with buying a toaster or a loaf of bread.

Application of Image Theory

Although consumer decisions with social responsibility dimensions could be analyzed using more traditional decision theories, image theory offers a more parsimonious and elegant description of the process. This advantage is derived primarily from image theory's emphasis on the decision maker's principles (values and beliefs) as the primary motivator of the entire process. Its secondary advantage lies in the importance of screening alternatives for violations of the decision maker's strongly held principles. The remainder of this chapter includes a conceptual framework, based on image theory, for consumer decision making that involves a social responsibility issue, an empirical test of that framework, and a discussion of the implications of this approach to consumer decision making.

CONCEPTUAL FRAMEWORK

A description of the conceptual framework for consumer decision making in the presence of a social responsibility issue requires a reconciliation of image theory terminology with a more specific social responsibility context (environmental issues). Fig. 13.1 illustrates the correspondence between the images and the illustrative statements used below. Fig. 13.2 relates the images to the general terms and constructs that correspond to this context (e.g., value image→social responsibility principles and environmental value).

Decision Frame

The frame, or decision context, is the choice among several brands or product substitutes for which greenness is one of the differentiating attributes. Choices between cotton and disposable diapers, between ordinary and rechargeable batteries, or between an electric and solar powered water heater are examples. This small subset of examples demonstrates the wide variety of framing issues: disputes over what is greener (diapers), durable versus nondurable goods, availability or unavailability of recycling potential, or wide price and quality differences. Regardless of the frame's complexity and the decision maker's awareness of these issues, the frame will elicit relevant images to guide decision making for each individual. The images discussed in the examples below are those most likely to be elicited by a green consumer.

Value Image

The value image typically explains *why* a decision is made and is composed of strongly held, relatively general principles and values. A green consumer's principle elicited by this frame could be: "As a member of society,

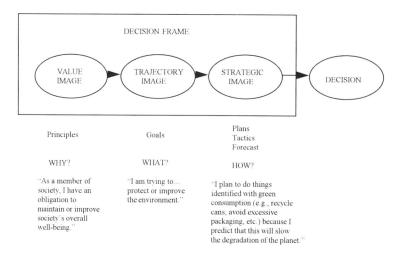

FIG. 13.1. Image theory example.

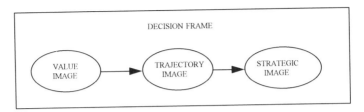

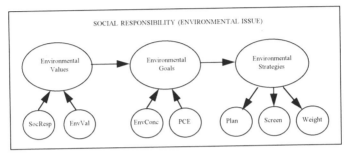

FIG. 13.2. Conceptual framework using image theory.

I have the obligation to maintain or improve society's overall well-being."
As the importance of social responsibility increases, an individual is more
likely to have the ability to identify far-reaching consequences of behavior,
to recognize responsibilities to others in society, and to reconcile conflicting
obligations to satisfy this moral or ethical belief.

A second part of the value image might contain a more domain-specific
statement of social responsibility such as, "Compared to other personal
values, a clean environment is relatively important to me." Although most
of Rokeach's (1973) terminal values centered on the self (e.g., happiness,
an exciting life, a prosperous life), some values involved end-states for
others as well (e.g., equality, a world at peace, family security). Even though
clean environment is not an item in the scale, it could easily fit into the latter
category because a clean environment depends on individual efforts for a
common good.

Trajectory Image

The trajectory image explains what needs to be done to satisfy the value
image. This image is reflected in the statement, "I am trying to protect or
improve the environment." When expressed verbally, trajectory images are
often preceded by, "I am trying to." Because concern implies a desire for
change, environmental concern would be a strong indicator of this relatively

abstract goal to improve the environment. The formation of a specific trajectory image, such as environmental improvement or protection, depends on the strongly held social responsibility principle and the relatively important value regarding a clean environment that comprise the value image.

Perceived consumer effectiveness (PCE), the belief that one's efforts can make a difference in the solution to a problem, has been related to environmental concern (as well as to proenvironmental behaviors) in a variety of ways (Berger & Corbin, 1992; Ellen, Wiener, & Cobb-Walgren, 1991; Schwepker & Cornwell, 1991). Although a complete discussion of these studies is beyond the scope of this chapter (see Nelson, 1994, for a synopsis), the following relationships are posited in this study. PCE directly effects environmental concern, which is the primary element of the trajectory image. Over time, it is reasonable, for the sake of cognitive consistency, to think that concern and PCE would not conflict (Festinger, 1958). For example, high levels of PCE would support continued involvement and more concern, whereas low levels of PCE would emphasize the futility of involvement and reduce concern. Together, environmental concern and PCE would comprise the trajectory image and influence its strength.

Strategic Image

The strategic image contains three contructs that explain the three steps to goal achievement. First, the plan (i.e., a sequence of behaviors seen as a unitary event) might consist of doing the things identified with green consumption in the consumer's mind. Second, the tactics could be the more easily identified tasks that comprise the plan. Some possible tactics are screening alternatives to eliminate those that do not meet a certain level of greenness; weighting the greenness attribute more heavily in comparing alternatives; learning more about the environmental impact of different product categories; and participating in proenvironmental behaviors such as recycling, and consuming less. The first two tactics are directly related to the decision process itself and to the two tests (compatibility and profitability) used in image theory.

Third, the forecast could be reduced harm to the planet or improvement in some aspect of the environment if the plan is carried out. The power of the forecast to provide timely feedback and to alter tactics is not as strong in decisions involving environmental concerns because of the difficulty in relating today's proenvironmental actions to any short-term results. For social responsibility decisions with delayed results, it might be more realistic to capture the impact of the forecast through the more global effects of PCE on the trajectory image. This does not mean that additional knowledge or experience related to outcomes would not affect tactics. A consumer could still drop or add various proenvironmental tactics related to the plan. For example, some consumers returned to disposable diapers when later research showed that they might not be more harmful than cloth diapers to the environment when the entire washing process was included in the impact analysis. Although image theory posits that the forecast is part of the strategic image, it also acknowledges that the forecast is used as a check to see if the plan and tactics (strategic image) will accomplish the goals (trajectory image) that reflect the individual's values (value image). Due to the dynamic nature of the forecast, it was not modeled as a separate part of the strategic image in the study.

Image Theory Framework

From the preceding discussion, the following relationships between the theory's images and the indicators can be expressed as follows:

Value Image = Social Responsibility and Environmental Value

Trajectory Image = Environmental Concern and PCE

Strategic Image = Environmental Plan and Tactics

This framework is presented in Fig. 13.2. For the green consumer faced with a decision frame involving an environmental issue, these three images become salient factors in the decision process. A consumer who believes in social responsibility and values a clean environment is more likely to have the improvement and protection of the environment as a goal (assuming adequate PCE). That goal is then manifested in a general plan to improve and protect the environment that is supported by a set of more specific tactics. These tactics can include the previously mentioned decision tactics of screening brands for green violations or a weighting of the greenness attribute more heavily in comparing alternatives.

EMPIRICAL EVIDENCE

This study was designed to test the ability of image theory to account for consumer decision making in a value laden context (Nelson, 1994). To accomplish this task, the framework presented in Fig. 13.2 was tested to evaluate the fit of all images and their component measures. The value, trajectory, and strategic images are actually latent variables, that is, unobservable constructs that can be indirectly estimated from the manifest (observable) variables already identified (Hair, Anderson, Tatham, & Black, 1992). Structural equation modeling is then used to test the relationships between these latent images and their manifest component measures. The following hypothesis summarizes the relationships in the model to be tested:

> The value image, trajectory image and strategic image are related in this sequential order and provide the basis for decision making. In the context of environmental social responsibility, the value image is formed by the social responsibility principle and the consumer's environmental value. The trajectory image is formed by environmental concern and perceived consumer effectiveness. The strategic image is reflected in commitment to the plan as seen in the consumer's pro-environmental behaviors and in decision tactics that include screening with or heavily weighting the social responsibility attribute. (Nelson, 1994, p. 56)

A between-subjects design was used, in which all subjects completed the same survey measures and performed the same consumer preference tasks. The subjects were 117 undergraduate students in introductory marketing courses. Due to the potential for demand bias because an ethical dimension was included, the ordering of measures and tasks was carefully considered so that the emphasis on environmental issues was not foreshadowed until those measures were collected at the end of the session. Each subject completed a set of three decision scenarios (one of which was the social responsibility measure), a Rokeach Terminal Values Inventory (with an embedded environmental value item), and two product preference tasks, followed by the scales for environmental concern, perceived consumer effectiveness, and proenvironmental consumer behaviors (plan).

Value Image

The value image was formed from the consumer's social responsibility beliefs and the relevant value of a clean environment. The social responsibility measure was created to evaluate general social responsibility with items related to (a) the consequences if people ignore common problems, (b) obligations to improve the world for future generations, and (c) the morality of harming a public good. The decision scenario format was derived from the Defining Issues Test (Rest, 1986), a test of cognitive moral development, and the social responsibility scenario was embedded in a set of three other dilemmas from that instrument. The 3-item scale achieved a coefficient alpha of .70 and loaded on a single factor.

Environmental value, the second part of the value image, was created by replacing national security with a clean environment on Rokeach's (1968) scale of terminal values. The clean environment item fits unobtrusively into this well-known scale. Because the importance of a clean environment relative to the remaining set of personal values was the intent of the measure, a standardized z score was calculated from the ratings provided by the subjects. The correlation between the actual rating on the scale and the z score was .81, which indicates that the final measure was not radically different.

Trajectory Image

The trajectory (goal) image was formed from the consumer's environmental concern and the perceived consumer effectiveness. Previous research has indicated that these two constructs are separate factors related to environmental behavior (Ellen et al., 1991). Items from their scale were pretested with other published items (Schwepker & Cornwell, 1991) and some original items to create the two scales used in this study. The two Likert-type, 7-point scales received acceptable coefficient alphas and loaded on different single factors.

Strategic Image

The strategic image was reflected in the environmental plan and two decision tactics. Rather than directly asking a consumer about having a plan to improve the environment, evidence of an existing plan was sought by asking about an individual's level of participation in a variety of proenvironmental behaviors. Commitment to an overall plan to protect and improve the environment was measured by the breadth and frequency of participation. A 10-item, 7-point scale of proenvironmental behaviors (Berger & Corbin, 1992) was used. Although self-reported behavior could include a social desirability effect, a study that compared household energy consumption behaviors with actual usage measures found no systematic inaccuracies in this type of scale (Warriner, McDougall, & Claxton, 1984).

The two measures of tactics were collected in the product preference tasks that consisted of ranking 16 product profiles based on a full factorial selection using 4 attributes. The 4 attributes were price, quality, greenness, and a relatively trivial but typical attribute. A durable product (refrigerator) and a convenience product (glass cleaner) were matched up with relatively simple environmental issues (i.e., ozone-depleting chlorofluorocarbon

(CFC) content for the refrigerator and biodegradability for the glass cleaner). These environmental issues were related to actual advertising claims made by manufacturers, were not particularly controversial, and were stated explicitly so that technical knowledge was not required. The subjects physically arranged the product profiles for one of the products to indicate their preferences and then numbered each one before returning them to the product category envelope and doing the remaining product.

Two measures were derived from these preference tasks that reflect aspects of image theory's compatibility and profitability tests. The screening (compatibility) measure assumes that the consumer would put the alternatives that violate minimum standards on key attributes at the bottom of the list and that those alternatives that pass the screening would be in the top selections. Observation of the preference task during the pretesting as well as discussions with some of the subjects after the testing indicate that some subjects were definitely screening the profiles on a key attribute. Verbal reports described the process as both eliminating alternatives that violate standards and selecting alternatives that surpass minimum standards. But either description could explain the elimination of violations proscribed by image theory.

Screening the alternatives for violation of green standards would be a tactic in a plan to protect or improve the environment. To quantify the degree of screening that used the green attribute, the number of consecutive green profiles starting with the top ranked profile within the first eight rankings was used. This is a stricter test than a mere use of the number of green profiles in the first half (e.g., having a nongreen profile in the fourth spot with the remaining 7 others in the first half being green results in a score of 3 out of 8 [37.5%] rather than 7 out of 8 [87.5%]. If the green attribute were used to eliminate all nongreen profiles, the score would be 8 because all 8 green profiles would be in the top half starting with first the ranking. If the green attribute is unimportant to the subject, the score would be a relatively low number or 0. Although this measure suffers somewhat from being an indirect measure, it is a highly conservative measure that realistically reflects the results of screening.

Another approach for analyzing the decision process in the presence of a social responsibility attribute is to analyze the importance weights placed on the green attribute as revealed by each subject's preferences. Placing more utility in the greenness attribute would also be a tactic in a plan to improve or protect the environment. Conjoint analysis was used to calculate the part-worth utilities applied to the greenness attribute for each subject (Green & Srinivasan, 1990), and this was standardized as a proportion of the summed ranges of all attributes to create the variable (Wright & Rip, 1980). The resulting measure can be used to facilitate comparison of attribute weights between subjects due to this standardization and the use of two levels of each attribute (Wittink, Krishnamurthi, & Nutter, 1982). A higher value means that the subject placed more importance on the greenness attribute in the preferences expressed for various product profiles. This measure most closely resembles the profitability test of image theory, in which acceptable alternatives are then evaluated for the best choice based on the individual's benefit analysis.

Testing the Image Theory Model

Structural equation modeling allows for the simultaneous testing of all interrelationships in a model. The conceptual framework supporting an image theory decision model was tested with latent (unobserved) variables for the three images and manifest (observed) variables for the measured constructs. A program based on partial least squares (PLS; Lohmoeller, 1987), was chosen as the most appropriate algorithm for this type of theory development because it does not require the restrictive assumptions about measurement and distributions that are typically not available in social science research (Barclay, Higgins, & Thompson, in press; Falk & Miller, 1992). Furthermore, the PLS model emphasizes the variance explained (R^2) and the strength of the relationships between constructs rather than just a goodness of fit index. Figure 13.3 displays the latent variables (ovals) and manifest variables (rectangles) of the model. In this study, the measured

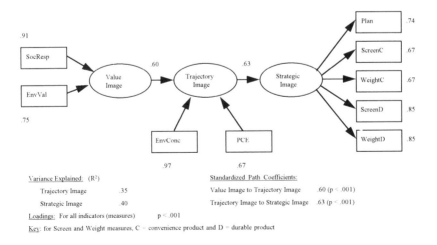

FIG. 13.3. Structural model of image theory using latent variables.

variables of social responsibility and the environmental value are formative indicators of the value image. The value image precedes the trajectory image formed by environmental concern and perceived consumer effectiveness. The goal of the trajectory image requires a strategic image, the third latent variable, that is reflected in the plan and the tactics for this decision context.

Results

A brief summary of the image theory model test results is presented with the schematic diagram in Fig. 13.3. Analysis of the measurement model, which tests the hypothesized pairings between the images (latent variables) and their respective indicators (manifest variables), provided acceptable levels of reliability and validity. More detailed interpretations of the various tests are presented in Nelson (1994). Having an acceptable measurement model allowed for analysis of the structural model with its dependence relationships between images.

The structural model was analyzed on several dimensions to verify that the hypothesized relationship pattern is the most efficient and to discover how much variance the model explains. Using standards discussed in Falk and Miller (1992), the model demonstrated what is usually termed *acceptable fit*, (i.e., the hypothesized links between the images and their indicators described the data better than other possible connections). More simply stated, the arrows between the various boxes (indicators) and ovals (images) in this model are drawn in the most efficient configuration. Each individual link between images (path coefficients) and between images and their respective indicators (loadings) was also analyzed to identify any weak relationships. Using a supplemental jackknife procedure (Fornell & Barclay, 1983), all of the hypothesized paths between images and the loadings of measures on those images were significant ($p < .001$). In other words, all of the individual dependence relationships are meaningful in addition to the satisfactory overall fit of the structural model.

The most important measure of the predictive power of a PLS structural model is its R^2 value, or the variance in the latent variables that is explained (Barclay, et al., in press). Considering the parsimony of this model and the multitude of potential factors in most social science research, this model performed very well. The results showed that 35% of the variance in the trajectory image and 40% of the variance in the strategic image were explained by the hypothesized relationships between the images and between the images and their indicators. To summarize these results, the reliability and validity tests, the variance explained (R^2), the fit of the model as indicated by the small residuals, and the statistically significant path coefficients and loadings all indicate that the image theory model fits the data collected on socially responsible consumer choice and that the research hypothesis was supported.

CONCLUSION

The results of the study support image theory as a more parsimonious model of decision making that relies on just three theoretical latent constructs: the value, trajectory, and strategic images. Image theory provides the basis for the way knowledge can be represented and structured for use in decision making, and it is more descriptive of the actual decision process than the complex, maximizing models of conventional decision theory. The study also provided additional, although indirect, support for the use of compatibility and profitability tests in consumer decision making. Simply stated, decision makers adopt plans with appropriate tactics to reach goals that are consistent with strongly held values and principles.

Even though this study focused on environmental issues, the results can be generalized to consumer decisions that involve social responsibility dimensions or some other value laden decision context. Companies that are trying to be socially responsible or that compete with companies perceived to be socially responsible (in their corporate behavior or in their products) will face consumers with varying images related to these issues. To facilitate the use of examples, we retain the environmental focus in discussing the implications of applying image theory to socially responsible consumer choice.

The goal of a socially responsible company would be to convince the consumer that the company's product is compatible with a socially responsible consumer's goals and principles and that it will be the most profitable way to attain a particular goal. Furthermore, managers need to know how to invoke the related images that would be used to screen out socially irresponsible products and to prefer socially responsible products or companies. In other words, managers must invoke the decision frame (i.e., the store of knowledge that the decision maker uses to endow the context with meaning) that supports socially responsible consumer choice. Even though identifying the best image to address in marketing communications is beyond the scope of the study, a variety of possibilities are discussed because the empirical data supports the idea that the three images are interrelated.

Direct appeal to the value image by showing that the product is compatible with general social responsibility principles or the valued clean environment could lead to the desired frame. Demonstrating general corporate
responsibility in the area of environmental issues, presenting the consumption of a product as socially responsible behavior, or connecting the company or product with the vision of a clean environment could all be
successful strategies for eliciting the previously identified value image.
However, care must be taken because a credibility problem could arise when
high-toned appeals to do the right thing are mixed with an obvious sales
pitch.

Direct appeal to the trajectory image would focus on desired goals.
Moving people to act on concerns is a difficult promotional task (Gill,
Crosby, & Taylor, 1986; Vining & Ebreo, 1991), but demonstrating that
the product or behavior can be a means for attaining the goal of a cleaner
environment could elicit the full range of images in support of proenvironmental behavior. Because the goal of a better environment is linked to
concern for the environment and perceived consumer effectiveness (PCE),
care should be taken in emphasizing the size of the problem. Although the
"sick baby" appeal is the most common in social marketing, emphasizing
the gravity of the situation could also make the problem seem overwhelm-
ing (Fine, 1990). If the consumer perceives that individual actions can
make no real difference in solving environmental problems, the trajectory
image can be weakened and decisions will not be based on environmental
factors.

In contrast, a direct attempt to increase PCE might strengthen the
trajectory image because the goal seems attainable. A recent ad for the Tide
detergent "enviro-pak" pictured the solid waste from the use of its reduced
packaging compared to that of typical packaging. By visually showing the
direct impact of this consumption decision, the ad leads a consumer to
imagine more easily his or her attainment of the goal, and the trajectory
image is strengthened.

When socially responsible consumers are concerned but not acting on
their concerns, the problem could also lie in the lack of a coherent plan with
viable tactics. In other words, the strategic image is lacking and ineffectual
in a decision process. In many cases, an environmentally friendly product
gives the consumer a tactic for improving or protecting the environment.
For example, the use of refillable containers depicted in the Tide advertisement is a tactic for reducing landfill waste (even if detergent use adds to
other environmental problems). In this approach, a stronger strategic image
related to environmental issues could develop.

Regardless of the image targeted in marketing communications, the social marketer's goal would be the use of all three interrelated images to frame the decision and an increase in the probability that a proenvironmental choice would result. Because a large segment of the population has been identified as proenvironmental, a social responsibility attribute such as product greenness becomes a competitive advantage. If the social responsibility attribute is used to screen alternatives, other attributes cannot compensate for shortcomings in this area. Despite commonly held beliefs that green products are slightly more expensive and less effective (The Roper Organization, 1990), the price and quality attributes might not enter the decision until those that violate the green screening criterion have been eliminated.

The above strategies for influencing consumer decisions involve manipulating the decision frame for consumers who already are socially responsible and concerned about the environment. Changing an individual's value system is difficult, time consuming, and perhaps not reasonably possible. However, it is possible to increase general public awareness of social responsibilities and existing problems through educational and public relations efforts. As awareness increases, it is possible that knowledge structures will be created so that the individual can develop and use these environmentally related images to make decisions.

In more general terms, the image theory perspective emphasizes the importance of the consumer's values and principles on consumption decisions, whether they are simple or complex. Decision making under image theory demands consistency between the value, trajectory, and strategic images while the cognitive effort is conserved through profitability–compatibility tests and adoption–progress decisions. The ability of image theory to simply, but elegantly, describe the decision making process for complex, value laden decisions involving social responsibility issues is strong evidence of its value in explaining all types of consumer decision making.

REFERENCES

Barclay, D. W., Higgins, C., & Thompson, R. (in press). The partial least squares (PLS) approach to causal modeling: Personal computer adoption and use as an illustration [special issue]. *Technology Studies.*

Beach, L. R. (1990). *Image theory: Decision making in personal and organizational contexts.* Chichester, UK: Wiley.

Berger, I. E., & Corbin, R. M. (1992). Perceived consumer effectiveness and faith in others as moderators of environmentally responsible behaviors. *Journal of Public Policy and Marketing, 11,* 79–89.

Ellen, P. S., Wiener, J. L., & Cobb-Walgren, C. (1991). The role of perceived consumer effectiveness in motivating environmentally conscious behaviors. *Journal of Public Policy and Marketing, 10,* 102–117.

Falk, R. F., & Miller, N. B. (1992). *A primer for soft modeling.* Akron, OH: University of Akron Press.

Festinger, L. (1958). *A theory of cognitive dissonance.* Palo Alto, CA: Stanford University Press.

Fine, S. (1990). *Social marketing.* Boston, MA: Allyn & Bacon.

Fornell, C., & Barclay, D. W. (1983). *Jackknifing: A supplement to Lohmoeller's LVPLS Program.* Unpublished manuscript, University of Michigan at Ann Arbor.

Gill, J. D., Crosby, L. A., & Taylor, J. R. (1986). Ecological concern, attitudes, and social norms in voting behavior. *Public Opinion Quarterly, 50,* 537–554.

Green, P. E., & Srinivasan, V. (1990). Conjoint analysis in marketing: New developments with implications for research and practice. *Journal of Marketing, 54,* 3–19.

Hair, J. F., Jr., Anderson, R. E., Tatham, R. L., & Black, W. C. (1992). *Multivariate data analysis* (3rd ed.). New York: Macmillan.

Lohmoeller [or Lohmöller], J.-B. (1987). *Latent variables path analysis with partial least squares* (Version 1.8). Berlin, Germany: Free University Berlin.

Nelson, K. A. (1994). *Consumer decision making and image theory: Understanding the socially responsible consumer.* Unpublished doctoral dissertation, University of Arizona, Tucson.

Rest, J. R. (1986). *Moral development: Advances in research and theory.* New York: Praeger.

Rokeach, M. (1968). *Beliefs, attitudes and values.* San Francisco, CA: Jossey-Bass.

Rokeach, M. (1973). *The nature of human values.* New York: The Free Press.

The Roper Organization. (1990). *The environment: Public attitudes and individual behavior.* New York: Author.

Schwepker, C. H., Jr., & Cornwell, T. B. (1991). An examination of ecologically concerned consumers and their intention to purchase ecologically packaged products. *Journal of Public Policy & Marketing, 10,* 77–101.

Stisser, P. (1994, March). A deeper shade of green. *American Demographics, 16,* 24–29.

Vining, J., & Ebreo, A. (1990). What makes a recycler?: A comparison of recyclers and nonrecyclers. *Environment and Behavior, 22,* 55–73.

Warriner, G. K., McDougall, G. H. G., & Claxton, J. D. (1984). Any data or none at all?: Living with inaccuracies in self report of residential energy consumption. *Environment and Behavior, 16,* 503–526.

Wittink, D. R., Krishnamurthi, L., & Nutter, J. B. (1982). Comparing derived importance weights across attributes. *Journal of Consumer Research, 8,* 471–474.

Wright, P., & Rip, P. D. (1980). Product class advertising effects on first-time buyers' decision strategies. *Journal of Consumer Research, 7,* 176–188.

14

IMAGE COMPATIBILITY AND FRAMING

Kenneth J. Dunegan
Cleveland State University

A few years ago, tennis star Andre Agassi was featured in a national advertising campaign for a well-known camera company. In most of the ads, the flamboyant Agassi sports shoulder-length hair, stubble on his chin, and blatantly unorthodox tennis apparel. After flawlessly executing a variety of extraordinary tennis shots, he turns to the camera and defiantly proclaims, "*Image* [a pause for effect] is everything."

Although one could argue whether Agassi's proclamation is literally true, there can be little doubt that images do play a significant role in practically every aspect of our daily lives. Indeed, the desire to achieve or maintain a certain image influences decisions about everything from the cars we drive, to the politicians we support (this could be a null set), to the clothes we wear and the beverages we drink. In fact, it is precisely because images are such a conspicuous and integral part of decision making that the descriptive decision model outlined in image theory (Beach, 1990; Beach & Mitchell, 1990) has so much appeal. However, because the theory is relatively new, empirical research has been limited and tends to focus on screening and profitability tests (Beach, 1993). Although these studies, and others in the same vein, are an important and necessary step in confirming image theory's basic structure, they tend to overshadow one issue about the theory that is most promising—its ability to integrate with existing models of decision making and enrich their capacity for explaining and predicting behaviors.

Drawing on this ability for integration, the current chapter explores image theory as a vehicle for expanding our understanding about one of decision making's most notorious biasing agents—framing. More specifically, the chapter discusses how perceptions of image compatibility can help explain why framing has an effect by showing at how it systematically influences not only decision outcomes but, more importantly how it also alters the process of selecting a course of action.

SOME BACKGROUND ON FRAMING

For purposes of this chapter, *framing* refers to the manner in which information is presented. A classic example is the half-full versus half-empty glass. In either case, the glass contains the same volume of liquid, and a totally rational decision maker should be ambivalent when choosing between them. However, evidence clearly indicates that this is not the case.

In the years since Kahneman and Tversky (1979) first introduced the concept of framing as a biasing agent of decision processes, a host of studies have shown that people are decidedly not ambivalent to the way information is presented. In fact, framing effects have been reported in research dealing with everything from public health policies (Vaughn & Seifert, 1992) to cult indoctrination techniques (Pfeifer, 1992), from purchasing decisions (Grewal, Gotlieb, & Marmorstein, 1994) to preferences toward ground beef (Levin & Gaeth, 1988), and from medical treatments (McNeil, Pauker, Sox, & Tversky, 1982) to fair taxes (Kinsey, Grasmick, & Smith, 1991).

Despite this formidable body of research, the majority of studies conducted to date are fairly narrow in focus. Most look almost exclusively at framing's relationship to decision outcomes. Typically, this is accomplished by separating study participants into two groups, exposing them to information framed in either a positive (e.g., glass half full) or negative (e.g., glass half empty) way, then making between-group comparisons of the courses of action chosen by members of each group. A simplified illustration of this design is shown in Fig. 14.1.

Although there is nothing inherently wrong with this design, it provides little information to help explain why a decision maker may have chosen one course of action over another. Indeed, studies adopting this traditional approach provide very limited knowledge about how framing may be affecting cognitive processes thought to precede and guide a decision maker in selecting from among alternative actions. Even so, this limitation has not been a particular problem until fairly recently.

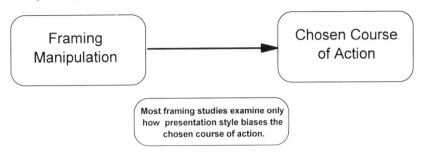

FIG. 14.1. Traditional model for studying framing effects.

As framing research continues to progress, however, and as more studies examine its biasing effects, problems with the traditional design are becoming more apparent. Notwithstanding the extensive list of experiments documenting its influence, there is a growing number of cases in which framing manipulations have apparently not had an effect, or in which the effect has not been consistent with what Kahneman and Tversky's theory (1979, 1984) would predict (e.g., Fagley & Miller, 1990; Miller & Fagley, 1991; Schneider, 1992; Schneider & Lopes, 1986; Sitkin & Pablo, 1992; Takemura, 1994). Because the traditional approach looks only at framing's relationship with decision outcomes, there is little available information that might help explain why these inconsistencies have occurred. As a result, several researchers recently called for studies to expand our limited and somewhat myopic understanding of the framing phenomenon (Miller & Fagley, 1991; Schoorman, Mayer, Douglas, & Hetrick, 1994). Enter image theory.

IMAGE THEORY TO THE RESCUE—WELL, SORT OF

The fact that research on framing is beginning to turn up inconsistent findings does not mean the phenomenon is in danger of being forsaken—at least not yet. Still, it is evident that a more comprehensive picture of framing's influence is needed, and it is precisely in this kind of situation that the descriptive properties of image theory may prove to be especially useful.

In a series of laboratory experiments, my colleagues and I have been incorporating image theory concepts as a way of expanding the traditional framing model. More specifically, we have been looking at image compatibility as an intervening variable between framing and selecting a course of action. For the most part, these experiments used what Beach and Mitchell (1990) called *progress decisions* (i.e., decisions dealing with projects that are already underway).

In decisions of this type, image compatibility refers to a person's subjective assessment of the progress being made toward future goals and the objectives based on relative success or failure of current plans and tactics. The degree of compatibility reflects the congruency between the strategic image (i.e., the image of how well current tactics are performing) and the trajectory image (i.e., the image of future goals). By comparing these two images, the decision maker attempts to answer the question, "Am I going to make it to where I want to go if I keep doing what I'm doing?"

The reason image compatibility is potentially so important, at least according to the theory (Beach, 1990; Beach & Mitchell, 1990), is that it is a catalyst for subsequent actions. To the extent that image compatibility is high, the decision maker is likely to maintain the status quo (Silver & Mitchell, 1990) and continue the endeavor. In contrast, if image compatibility is low, the decision maker will be motivated to revise or reject the current tactics, change the future objectives, or both (Beach, Mitchell, Paluchowski, & van Zee, 1992).

Therefore, determining whether framing manipulations affect perceptions of image compatibility could help explain why a decision maker might choose one course of action over another. In that regard, placing image compatibility as an intervening variable in the traditional framing model makes sense. However, other aspects of the decision event could also prove useful in explaining why framing effects occur, perhaps to a greater degree than does image compatibility. For example, selecting a course of action is often preceded by a process of information assimilation and evaluation (O'Reilly, 1983). Perceptions emerging from this process are collectively referred to as the *problem space* (Payne, 1980). These perceptions deserve research attention because they give meaning to the decision context and define the structure within which alternative courses of action are evaluated (Dery, 1983; Fazio, 1990; Hogarth, 1975). Thus, the extent to which framing influences factors in the problem space (e.g., perceived risk, control or decision importance) could also prove to be of value in explaining differences in a decision maker's chosen course of action.

According to this reasoning, it seemed that a logical and defensible way of expanding the traditional framing model would be to add problem space and image compatibility perceptions as intervening variables. This addition is depicted in Fig. 14.2.

Early results from several laboratory experiments testing this expanded model have been supportive and show a significant increase in predictive capabilities over the more traditional approach (e.g., Dunegan, 1993; Dunegan, 1995). Basically, we found that manipulating the frame used to

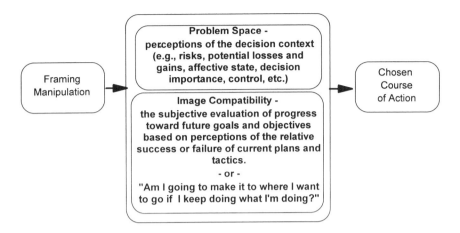

FIG. 14.2. An expanded model for studying framing effects

present objectively equivalent information did indeed alter a decision maker's perceptions of both the problem space and image compatibility. As one might expect, information framed in a negative way resulted in perceptions of the decision context that were significantly more negative. Likewise, strategic and trajectory images were perceived to be significantly less compatible when negative framing techniques were used (Dunegan, 1993; Dunegan & Matthews, 1995). Therefore, results from these preliminary experiments suggest that framing affects the course of action a decision maker chooses by systematically distorting problem space and image compatibility perceptions.

However, in the interest of maintaining parsimonious models, we also wanted to determine if perceptions of image compatibility made any unique contribution toward explaining variance in decision outcomes. In other words, we wondered whether image compatibility would account for variance over and above that explained by items in the problem space. It did. In evaluating data from several experiments, we used hierarchical regression analyses to test the expanded model and control the order of variable entry. Results indicated that even if image compatibility was forced to be the last variable added, it accounted for significant and unique variance in our dependent measures (Dunegan, 1995; Dunegan & Matthews, 1995).

For example, in one study we asked masters-level business students to role play general managers charged with making a resource allocation decisions (Dunegan, Duchon, & Ashmos, 1995). As part of the background information, participants were told that one of their project team leaders, Chris Leamon, had just asked for an additional $100,000 for a project started several months earlier. Half were told, "You are considering Chris' request. Currently you have $500,000 remaining in your budget that is unallocated. These funds must last the rest of the fiscal year and a full three months remain. You know that 33% of the other project leaders have outperformed Chris, and you also know that of the projects undertaken by this project team, 20 of the last 50 have been unsuccessful." The remaining participants were provided with the same information, but it was framed in a more positive way. They were told: "You are considering Chris' request. Currently you have $500,000 remaining in your budget that is unallocated. Although these funds must last the rest of the fiscal year, only three months remain. You know that Chris has outperformed two thirds of all the other project leaders, and you also know that of the projects undertaken by this project team, 30 of the last 50 have been successful."

From an objective standpoint, everyone was provided with the same information about the team's performance history. However, for one group the information was framed in terms of the team's previous failures. For the other group, the same information was framed in terms of previous successes. The task for participants in both groups was to decide how much of the requested $100,000, if any, they would allocate.

Perceptions of the problem space were measured with questions tapping a number of items, including affective reactions (e.g., how things were going, level of dissatisfaction), perceptions of risk, control over the project's outcome, and the relative importance of minimizing losses versus maximizing gains. Image compatibility was assessed by questionnaire items comparing what we called the current and target images (i.e., the strategic and trajectory images, respectively). Participants in the study were asked to "mentally conjure up two images of this project, a current image (reflecting conditions as they are now) and a target image (picturing the way you would eventually want them to be)." We then posed a series of four questions: How close is the current image to the target image? Is your current image of this project moving toward your target image? Given your current image of this project, what is the likelihood your target image will be realized? In terms of ultimate project objectives, how well is the project going? Perceptions of image compatibility were inferred from the combined responses to these four questions.

As expected, based on previous studies, framing the project team's performance history in a positive or negative way significantly affected decisions about additional funding, $t = 5.08$, $p < .001$, with means of $89.6K and $63.2K for the positive and negative conditions, respectively. Consistent with the extended model, framing was also found to affect overall perceptions of the problem space, multivariate analysis of variance, Wilks' Lambda = 0.77, $F = 5.21$, $p < .001$. Further, a regression analysis indicated that even without image compatibility in the model, the group of five problem space items accounted for 24% of funding variance, $F = 5.55$, $p < .001$.

To determine whether image compatibility could improve on this, the same regression model was then rerun with image compatibility entered as the last item. In other words, the model regressed funding decisions on the group of five problem space items, allowing them the first opportunity to account for any shared variance. Image compatibility was added last and given only the opportunity to account for the statistical equivalent of leftovers. The results indicate two very important things. First, the image compatibility measure continued to make a significant and unique contribution, despite being restricted to the leftovers. Second, with the addition of image compatibility, the overall variance predicted by the regression analysis increased from 24% to 31%. This represented an increase of almost 30% and was significant at the $p < .01$ level.

Therefore, according to these and other similar findings (Dunegan, 1993, 1995), there is empirical justification for extending the traditional framing model to include problem space and image compatibility perceptions. Moreover, these results suggest that an explanation for why framing influences decision outcomes is that it systematically affects perceptions of conditions surrounding the decision event (i.e., the problem space) as well as the evaluation of progress being made toward future objectives (i.e., image compatibility). In doing so, framing distorts the very information that is thought to guide decision makers in choosing from among alternative courses of action. The result, then, is the classic framing effect: one course of action chosen when the glass is half full, a different course of action chosen when the glass is half empty.

However, further analysis of our data and additional experimentation show that image compatibility has still another role to play in the framing process.

IMAGE COMPATIBILITY
AND THE COGNITIVE MARATHON

Decision making is an almost constant part of our daily lives. It begins when the alarm goes off in the morning and continues unabated throughout the day. Granted, many of the decisions may be simple and straightforward (e.g., what to wear, what to eat, what hand gesture to share with the person who just cut you off on the freeway). However, each of these decisions, regardless of how trivial and insignificant, requires some degree of cognitive attention and consumes some portion of our limited (though renewable) stores of mental energy. It is as if we are engaged in a decision making marathon. Although each individual step may seem relatively effortless, we know that the only way of not "hitting the wall" or burning out our synaptic running shoes is to look for ways to conserve. We do this by regulating our cognitive modes.

Briefly, *cognitive modes* refer to different levels of mental processing and are distinguished by the degree to which information is examined, analyzed, and used. Cognitive modes can range from highly controlled to virtually automatic (Fazio, 1990; Kernan & Lord, 1989; Klein, 1989; Lord & Maher, 1990). Controlled processing modes are characterized by a more comprehensive, deliberate, and thorough analysis of information. Conversely, automatic modes are characterized by limited information processing, a reduced attention to detail, and a less comprehensive analysis of incoming cues. Furthermore, controlled processing modes are more cognitively and emotionally demanding, and more difficult to employ (Lord & Maher, 1990). Because of this, people seem to gravitate toward using the automatic modes (Beach & Mitchell, 1990; Fiske & Neuberg, 1990), which, for many decisions, are both effective and efficient.

Automatic modes, however, have a downside. When automatic modes are used, decision makers attend to less information and analyze it in a less thorough manner. Thus, evaluations of incoming data and situational cues are not as easily recalled (Maheswaran & Chaiken, 1991) and are not as readily accessible for future use by the decision maker (Chanowitz & Langer, 1981). As a result, subsequent behaviors may not be as strongly guided by cues from the decision context and may actually appear almost mindless (Langer, 1989).

Of particular interest for this chapter is that different cognitive modes can be activated by properties of the information received (Fazio, 1990; Lord & Maher, 1990). When incoming information is negative (Wofford & Goodwin, 1990) or creates the impression that a goal or objective is being threatened (Lord & Hanges, 1987; Lord & Kernan, 1987), decision makers are more likely to respond with controlled processing. Otherwise, the default is to conserve cognitive resources by using modes that are less demanding (Klein, 1989; Mitchell & Beach, 1990).

Yet, in terms of influencing decision making, *perceptions* of information can be more important than the actual information itself (Stubbart, Meindl, & Porac, 1994). Thus, it is quite possible that the use of significantly different cognitive modes could be triggered by objectively equivalent information merely perceived as positive or negative. As part of our continuing investigation of framing effects, we decided to examine this possibility and in the process uncovered some interesting relationships.

In the first of two experiments we found that if a project team's performance record was presented in a negative way, decisions about allocating additional funds were strongly correlated with perceptions of problem space variables (Dunegan, 1993, Experiment 1). When the information was framed in a positive way, the relationship between funding and the same problem space variables was not significant. In other words, when negative framing was used, characteristics of controlled processing were present in that decisions about funding were guided by, or at least consistent with, perceptions of conditions in the decision context. In contrast, characteristics of automatic processing were found when information was presented in a positive way in that funding decisions and problem space perceptions seemed to be unrelated.

Drawing on image theory's descriptive prowess, a second experiment was conducted to try to explain why this occurred. Like other models of decision making, image theory recognizes that people often employ different cognitive modes (Beach & Mitchell, 1987, 1990). Moreover, the theory posits that perceptions of image compatibility may influence whether a controlled or automatic mode is likely. When strategic and trajectory images are compatible, the decision maker sees no need to change the course of action and falls back on automatic processing. Conversely, when images are not compatible, the theory suggests that decision makers will be motivated to employ a controlled processing mode in an effort to turn the situation around (Beach et al., 1992).

Therefore, as part of the second study, data were also collected on perceptions of image compatibility. Findings replicated those of the first experiment in that a significant relationship was found between problem space and funding when the project team's performance history was framed in a negative manner; a nonsignificant relationship was found when the same performance record was framed in a positive way. In this case, however, perceptions of image compatibility provided a clue as to why.

Consistent with the theory's propositions, higher image compatibility scores were associated with characteristics of automatic processing. Specifically, when strategic and trajectory images were perceived to be compatible, funding allocations were not significantly related to conditions in the problem space. In contrast, lower image compatibility scores were found to be associated with characteristics typical of a controlled decision process.

Under these conditions, perceptions of the problem space and funding levels were significant.

According to these findings, then, the relationship between problem space and image compatibility appeared to be more dynamic than was being captured in the framing model illustrated in Fig. 14.2. Instead of a simple main-effect influence, these data suggested that image compatibility might be acting as a moderator of problem space perceptions. This possibility led us to reconfigure the extended framing model, and adjust the role played by image compatibility to reflect this additional influence. These changes are illustrated in Fig. 14.3.

Although the model in Fig. 14.3 should be viewed as work-in-progress, results from initial tests have been generally supportive. For example, as part of the study by Dunegan et al. (1995) referred to earlier, we tested the proposition that there would be a significant interaction between problem space perceptions and image compatibility in predicting decision outcomes. From results of the two experiments reported in the immediately preceding paragraphs, we predicted that the nature of the interaction would be such that a stronger relationship between problem space and decision outcomes would occur when image compatibility was low. This is precisely what we found.

Furthermore, tests indicated that the interaction terms created by crossing problem space and image compatibility measures increased the predicted variance in funding from 31% to 40%. This change was significant at the $p < .05$ level and represented an increase of almost 30% over the model with main effects only. As a final analysis, we split our sample into two groups based on high and low image compatibility scores. We then regressed funding decisions on the problem space items for each group. Results from the low-compatibility group were significant, $F = 3.53$, $p < .01$, $R^2 = .28$;

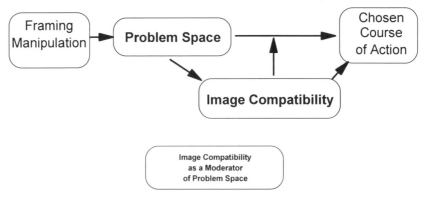

FIG. 14.3. A Moderating Effects Model.

results from the high-compatibility group were not significant, $F = .94$, ns, $R^2 = .10$.

Thus, for a second time, our data indicated a more automatic decision process when image compatibility was high and a more controlled decision process when image compatibility was low. In other words, decisions about funding seemed to be guided by problem space perceptions, but only when strategic and trajectory images were not compatible. When image compatibility was high, decisions about funding appeared to be less deliberate and methodical, and almost independent or cognitively detached from conditions in the problem space.

SO WHAT?

Notwithstanding Agassi's claim to the contrary, image is not everything. Even so, data from these experiments do show that images are an integral part of the decision process. Furthermore, images were found to significantly enhance our understanding of one of decision making's most notorious biasing agents—framing. Collectively, results from our studies show that framing influences the course of action a decision maker selects by systematically altering perceptions of both problem space and image compatibility.

In each of a series of laboratory experiments, objectively equivalent information was presented in a positive (e.g., glass half full) or negative way (e.g., glass half empty). Aside from the framing style used, all information was the same and, according to totally rational models of decision making, should not have had an effect. Yet it did.

When responding to a request for additional funds, our decision makers were systematically biased by whether a project team's performance record was presented in terms of previous successes (positive frame) or previous failures (negative frame). As reported, funding levels were significantly lower when the record was presented as a glass half empty. In and of itself, this is nothing new. Other framing studies have also found this to be the case.

What was missing in previous framing studies, however, and what we were able to provide as a product of our experiments, is an explanation for why this was happening. We consistently found that information framed in a positive way resulted in a more positive perspective of the decision context. We also found that a positive frame resulted in perceptions that current plans and tactics were making significantly greater progress toward future objectives.

Perhaps more important, however, our results indicated that framing's biasing effects on image compatibility were also associated with different modes of cognitive processing. Under conditions of high image compati-bility, characteristics associated with automatic modes were present. More specifically, when image compatibility was high, perceptions of the prob-lem space apparently did not influence decisions about levels of funding.

The opposite condition was found when image compatibility was low. Here, decision makers appeared to utilize a more controlled processing mode in that perceptions of the decision context were strongly correlated with the level of funding granted to the project team.

Of course, the overall importance of these findings will depend on whether future studies can replicate the results and overcome some of the limitations associated with our experiments (i.e., laboratory setting, student subjects, cross-sectional design, the measures themselves, etc.). Even with these shortcomings, however, our results do suggest that the descriptive properties of image theory can be of significant help in expanding our understanding of the decision process. As discussed, in one of our studies we found that adding image compatibility to problem space perceptions increased the predicted variance in funding decisions from 24% to 31%. Adding the interactions between problem space and image compatibility to the model increased predicted variance still further, from 31% to 40%. In all, the addition of image compatibility improved the model's predictive power from 24% to 40%. That represents an increase of almost 67%. Maybe Agassi was not that far off after all.

From a managerial standpoint, our findings could fall into either the "good news" or "bad news" category, depending on how one chooses to look at them. For example, based on these data, it would appear that a manager could easily bias the decision processes of others by intentionally manipulating information in a way that serves his or her interests. On one hand, if those interests would be better served by a controlled and deliberate evaluation of information, then the manager should intentionally frame data in a negative manner. On the other hand, if the manager's interests would be better served by a less deliberate and methodical decision maker, a positive frame should be used.

Unfortunately for the manager, however, he or she is typically not the only source of incoming information. A decision maker might just as easily be influenced by information framed by someone else whose interests run counter to those of the manager. The very real prospects of this happening highlight the importance of a more comprehensive understanding of fram-ing's influence. The manager who is knowledgeable of the role played by image compatibility in framing episodes will be in a much better position to predict when and why the biasing effects will take place. This knowledge could then be applied to circumvent, or at least minimize the undesirable influence attempts by others.

Results from the previously discussed experiments provide an encouraging but admittedly limited perspective on the potential for image theory applications. Although my colleagues and I have chosen to use the theory as a basis for expanding our understanding of framing, there are a host of other areas that also might benefit from image theory's descriptive properties. In the decision making area, for example, image theory could be useful for developing a better understanding of entrapment and escalation of commitment. Opportunity also exists for applying image theory to other types of decisions. We examined decisions dealing with funding allocations. However, it could just as easily be applied to decisions about marketing, political science, finance, human resource management, to name only a few.

As research on image theory continues to move forward, attention must undoubtedly be focused on verifying relationships and propositions coming from the actual model itself. Nevertheless, we argue that one of the theory's distinctive competencies is its ability to improve the predictive capacity of other existing decision models. Researchers should not overlook this capacity, nor should they overlook the myriad opportunities for studies applying image theory's rich descriptive properties in such a manner.

REFERENCES

Beach, L. R. (1990). *Image theory: Decision making in personal and organizational contexts.* Chichester, England: Wiley.

Beach, L. R. (1993). Image theory: Personal and organizational decision. In G. A. Klein, J. Orasanu, R. Calderwood, & C. E. Zsambok (Eds.), *Decision making in action: Models and methods* (pp. 148–157). New York: Ablex.

Beach, L. R., & Mitchell, T. R. (1987). Image theory: Principles, goals, and plans in decision making. *Acta Psychologica, 66,* 201–220.

Beach, L. R., & Mitchell, T. R. (1990). Image theory: A behavioral theory of decision making in organizations. In B. Staw & L. L. Cummings (Eds.), *Research in organizational behavior* (Vol. 12 pp. 1–41). Greenwich, CT: JAI Press.

Beach, L. R., & Mitchell, T. R., Paluchowski, T. F., & van Zee, E. H. (1992). Image theory: Decision framing and decision deliberation. In F. Heller, (Ed.), *Decision making and leadership* (pp. 72–189). Cambridge, UK: Cambridge University Press.

Chanowitz, B., & Langer, E. (1981). Premature cognitive commitment. *Journal of Personality and Social Psychology, 41,* 1051–1063.

Dery, D. (1983). Decision making, problem solving and organizational learning. *Omega, 11,* 321–328.

Dunegan, K. J. (1995). Image theory: Testing the role of image compatibility in progress decisions. *Organizational Behavior and Human Decision Processing, 62,* 79–86.

Dunegan, K. J. (1993). Framing, cognitive modes, and image theory: Toward an understanding of a glass half full. *Journal of Applied Psychology, 78,* 491–503.

Dunegan, K. J., Duchon, D., & Ashmos, D. (1995). Image compatibility and the use of problem space information in resource allocation decisions: Testing a moderating effects model. *Organizational Behavior and Human Decision Processes, 64,* 1, 31–37.

Dunegan, K. J., & Matthews, C. H. (1995). *Testing an expanded model of framing: The role of gender, academic standing, and image compatibility in understanding the effects of a glass half full.* Paper presented at the National Academy of Management Conference, Vancouver, British Columbia.

Fagley, N. S., & Miller, P. M. (1990). The effect of framing on choice: Interactions with risk-taking propensity, cognitive style, and sex. *Personality and Social Psychology Bulletin, 16,* 496–510.

Fazio, R. H. (1990). Multiple processes by which attitudes guide behavior: The mode model as an integrative framework. In M. P. Zanna (Ed.), *Advances in experimental social psychology* (Vol. 23, pp. 75–109) San Diego, CA: Academic Press.

Fiske, S. T., & Neuberg, S. L. (1990). A continuum of impression formation, from category-based to individuating processes: Influences of information and motivation on attention and interpretation. In M. P. Zanna (Ed.), *Advances in experimental social psychology* (Vol. 23, pp. 1–74). San Diego, CA: Academic Press.

Grewal, D., Gotlieb, J., & Marmorstein, H. (1994). The moderating effects of message framing and source credibility on the price-perceived risk relationship. *Journal of Consumer Research, 21,* 145–153.

Hogarth, R. M. (1975). Cognitive processes and the assessment of subjective probability distributions. *Journal of the American Statistical Association, 70,* 271–289.

Kahneman, D., & Tversky, A. (1979). Prospect theory: An analysis of decision under risk. *Econometrica, 47,* 263–291.

Kahneman, D., & Tversky, A. (1984). Choices, values, and frames. *American Psychologist, 39,* 341–350.

Kernan, M. C., & Lord, R. G. (1989). The effects of explicit goals and specific feedback on escalation processes. *Journal of Applied Social Psychology, 19,* 1125–1143.

Kinsey, K. A., Grasmick, H. G., & Smith, K. W. (1991). Framing justice: Taxpayer evaluations of personal tax. *Law & Society Review, 25,* 845–873.

Klein, H. J. (1989). An integrated control theory model of work motivation. *Academy of Management Review, 14,* 150–172.

Langer, E. (1989). *Mindfulness.* Reading, MA: Addison-Wesley.

Levin, I. P., Gaeth, G. J. (1988). How consumers are affected by the framing of attribute information before and after consuming the product. *Journal of Consumer Research, 15,* 374–378.

Lord, R. G., & Hanges, P. J. (1987). A control system model of organizational motivation: Theoretical development and applied applications. *Behavioral Science, 32,* 161–178.

Lord, R. G., & Kernan, M. C. (1987). Scripts as determinants of purposeful behavior in organizations. *Academy of Management Review, 12,* 265–277.

Lord, R. G., & Maher, K. J. (1990). Alternative information-processing models and their implications for theory, research, and practice. *Academy of Management Review, 15,* 9–28.

Maheswaran, D., & Chaiken, S. (1991). Promoting systematic processing in low-motivation settings: Effect of incongruent information on processing and judgment. *Journal of Personality and Social Psychology, 6,* 13–25.

McNeil, B., Pauker, S., Sox, H., & Tversky, A. (1982). On the elicitation of preferences for alternative therapies. *New England Journal of Medicine, 306,* 1259–1262.

Miller, P. M., & Fagley, N. S. (1991). The effects of framing, problem variations, and providing rationale on choice. *Personality and Social Psychology Bulletin, 17,* 517–522.

Mitchell, T. R., & Beach, L. R. (1990). "... Do I love thee? Let me count..." Toward and understanding of the intuitive and automatic decision making. *Organizational Behavior and Human Decision Processing, 47,* 1–20.

O'Reilly, C. A., III. (1983). The use of information in organizational decision making: A model and some propositions. In L. L. Cummings & B. M. Staw (Eds.), *Research in organizational behavior* (Vol. 5, pp. 103–129). Greenwich, CT: JAI Press.

Payne, J. W. (1980). Information processing theory: Some concepts and methods applied to decision research. In T. S. Wallsten (Ed.), *Cognitive processes in choice and decision behavior* (pp. 95–115). Hillsdale, NJ: Lawrence Erlbaum Associates.

Pfeifer, J. E. (1992). The psychological framing of cults: Schematic representations of cult evaluations. *Journal of Applied Social Psychology, 22,* 531–544.

Schneider, S. L. (1992). Framing and conflict: Aspiration level contingency, the status quo, and current theories of risky choice. *Journal of Experimental Psychology: Learning, Memory, and Cognition, 18,* 1040–1057.

Schneider, S. L., & Lopes, L. L. (1986). Reflection in preferences under risk: Who and when may suggest why. *Journal of Experimental Psychology: Human Perception and Performance, 12*, 535–548.

Schoorman, F. D., Mayer, R. C., Douglas, C. A., & Hetrick, C. T. (1994). Escalation of commitment and the framing effect: An empirical investigation. *Journal of Applied Social Psychology, 24*, 509–528.

Silver, W. S., & Mitchell, T. R. (1990). The status quo tendency in decision making. *Organizational Dynamics, 18*, 34–46.

Sitkin, S. B., & Pablo, A. L. (1992). Reconceptualizing the determinants of risk behavior. *Academy of Management Review, 17*, 9–38.

Stubbart, C., Meindl, J. R., & Porac, J. F. (1994). *Advances in managerial cognition and organizational information processing* (Vol. 5). Greenwich, CT: JAI Press.

Takemura, K., 1994. Influence of elaboration on the framing of decision. *Journal of Psychology, 128*, 33–39.

Vaughan, E., & Seifert, M. (1992). Variability in the framing of risk issues. *Journal of Social Issues, 48*, 119–135.

Wofford, J. C., & Goodwin, V. L. (1990). Effects of feedback on cognitive processing and choice of decision style. *Journal of Applied Psychology, 75*, 603–612.

15

IMAGE THEORY AND WORKPLACE DECISIONS: CHALLENGES

Terry Connolly
University of Arizona

The preceding chapters make it abundantly clear that image theory has already had, and continues to have, a significant impact on thinking about decision making processes in organizations. From the most personal decisions of the individual planning a career or choosing a job to the broadest, most significant choices of long-term organizational strategy, image theory has provided both stimulus and framework for a number of novel and interesting studies. The present chapter revisits the theory in hopes of identifying possible areas for further research potential.

We do not confine ourselves to a strict reading of image theory but, rather, use it as the best developed of several somewhat heretical approaches to decision making that have emerged in recent years to challenge the hegemony of the subjective expected utility (SEU) model. These heretical theories differ in various respects but share with image theory a concern with the descriptive inadequacies of the SEU model and, though less clearly, some ideas by which these deficiencies may be overcome. We focus here on image theory partly for its own merits, and partly because it more broadly represents the cluster of heretical theories.

To set the scene for our exploration we first sketch two imaginary but realistic scenarios. In both, events take place that a lay person would describe as decision making but which are surprisingly difficult to formulate in conventional decision theoretical terms. We use these formulation difficulties as a vehicle to compare image theory and its heretical cousins with more conventional approaches. These comparisons, in turn, lead to a sketch of some promising research issues in the image theory framework.

PART 1: THE CHALLENGE
TO CONVENTIONAL DECISION THEORY

Scenario 1: A Decision Tree for a Free Afternoon

You have been attending a professional meeting in a city far from home. The final portion of the program is unexpectedly canceled, and you find yourself with a free afternoon in a city you know and like, with several hours to fill before your flight home. How will you spend your time? A walk seems appealing after several days in lectures. Several favorite old haunts might be fun to visit. You will probably want to stop for refreshment somewhere along the way, and several interesting restaurants come to mind. Moreover, it occurs to you that this might be a good chance to explore a rather unfamiliar part of the city. In short, you face some decisions.

Note first that the problem, though not in the least exotic, is quite complex. It assumes that you wish to act purposively—some possible afternoons would certainly be better than others—although no clear single purpose is specified. There are a variety of places to go to have fun: the art gallery, the museum, a stroll through old town, a teashop, or a view. Not all of these will be reachable in the time available: There are constraints. Some options will complement others (the stroll followed by a rest at tea); others will compete (having tea at one place perhaps precludes coffee immediately afterwards somewhere else). Extensive if incomplete knowledge is assumed of both the environment (the city and its delights) and yourself (your tastes and their likely shifts as the afternoon unfolds, energy lags, hunger increases). You may learn more about both as the afternoon proceeds: Previously unvisited parts of the city may offer new surprises; a new taste may be discovered at a market stand. There are uncertainties and contingencies: Will it rain, will you get lost? There are also important contingencies: One road leads on to another, closing off the road not taken; and one lunch precludes a second while invigorating the traveler for a stroll rather than a stop at a book shop.

I have used this example in conventional decision analysis classes for years and have yet to find a satisfactory decision-tree representation. A typical decision tree treats the traveler's problem as a current choice between alternative paths that are attractive only because of the destinations to which they may or may not lead later. Notice how the complex intertwining of streets, satisfactions, contingencies, and opportunities is simplified and packaged in the abstraction. Time is bifurcated into *now*, the time at which choice is made, and *later*, the time at which outcomes are experienced and evaluated. A road chosen now is treated only as a value-neutral path to a unitary *destination* or *outcome*—perhaps formulated as *spend afternoon in Area A*, *spend afternoon in Area B*, and so on. Any number of issues are treated as exogenous or not treated at all. Why are these and only these options considered? Is the possibility of an earlier flight home considered? Why? Or why not? Is a destination equally liked or disliked regardless of the path by which it is approached? How long is the timeframe within which the afternoon's activities will be evaluated? How does one evaluate a destination when the activities it includes are themselves branched, capricious, opportunistic, unexpected? The questions could go on.

   None of this is intended to be either comprehensive or novel as a critique of conventional decision theory. It is simply an effort to recapture for those of us long steeped in that tradition what a very strange abstraction is at its core. We assume that the root interest of decision theory, orthodox or heterodox, is with how people do, or better could, get around on the ground. The concern is with real roads, really taken or not, that lead to real destinations, satisfactory or not. Conventional decision theory operates at two removes of abstraction from that real world: first the abstraction from territory to map, then the abstraction from map to decision tree. The brilliant achievements of the theory have been won at the level of the tree. It should not surprise us that the two-way path from world to tree and back is sometimes fraught with difficulties. To refer to these simply as issues of "framing" (Tversky & Kahneman, 1981) or "implementation" (Harrison, 1975) seems to understate the conceptual distance that needs to be covered in moving from world to model and back.

Scenario 2: Decision Making in the New Products Division

You have been hired to conduct a major study of the research planning process of a major manufacturer of high-tech consumer products, with special emphasis on the decision processes by which research budgets and priorities are set. Unfortunately, after an extensive round of interviews and study of internal documents, you still have been unable to identify any decision maker, individual or group, who claims responsibility for this decision, or any specific point at which it is made. Instead, you find many actors, each working toward quite local goals. Bench researchers seem primarily interested in pursuing promising research leads and in acquiring state of the art equipment. Their branch chiefs are primarily oriented toward keeping their research teams active, intact, and well supported. Lab chiefs care about maintaining the strongest possible labs and bringing the most recent technological breakthroughs into the corporate product mix. Meanwhile, marketers fight, often successfully, to have funds allocated to development projects identified by their customers, regardless of how interesting or new the required technology might be. It intrigues you that, for all the apparent chaos and fragmentation in the system, the company maintains an excellent record for linking new technology to profitable market opportunities. Somehow, despite the absence of a clear decision maker and a clear decision, good choices are being made in a very difficult arena.

The process you have just encountered is what I referred to elsewhere as a diffuse decision process (Connolly, 1975, 1980). Such processes are diffuse in a number of senses: They involve substantial numbers of people, across many organizational levels, over considerable periods of time, separated from one another by significant distances. As the example suggests, such diffuse processes often make decisions central to the organization's prosperity or even its survival, but we know remarkably little about them (see March, 1978, for an introduction to their many extraordinary properties).

As in the first scenario, it is possible to force the process into a conventional single decision event–single decision maker model, but only at the cost of missing much of the action. It may be descriptively true that efforts are made in some particular system to identify a high-level decision making body responsible for particular decisions, and to bring to that body the information about options and opportunities that would allow wise decisions. It is, however, commonplace for members of such bodies to complain about the lack of discretion the process leaves them, and the extent to which they are controlled by the option packagers and information providers. In an important sense such complaints reflect conceptual error, the implicit belief that if decisions emerge, there must be a decision and a decision maker. No one would be tempted to make the same error on seeing a car roll out of a car plant. It is taken for granted that cars are made by a complex process involving many people and much technology dispersed over space, time, and organizational level; much professional effort is devoted to the design of such car making processes. The theoretical and applied understanding of diffuse organizational decision processes is much less advanced. The first step toward acquiring it would seem to be the acknowledgment that the single decision maker–single decision event model is seriously misleading.

A few years ago Judith Orasanu and I (Orasanu & Connolly, 1993) tried to summarize the key factors that seemed to make naturalistic decisions (a class that includes those made in organizations) difficult to understand through the lens of conventional decision theory. Some of these are especially relevant to the organizational setting.

Ill-Structured Problems. In organizational decisions, significant work may be needed to identify options, or even to recognize that a decision is required. Ill-structured problems have no single right solution, or even a single definition. They are often defined only after they have been solved.

Uncertain, Dynamic Environments. Uncertainty applies not only to the link between action and consequences, as in traditional decision theory. It is also felt about the relevant values to apply, the tradeoffs to be made, and the possibility that the situation might change within the decision time frame. While the commander is thinking about the best way to fight a small fire, it may have become large and quite different. Goals and values shift, creating novel conflicts and tradeoffs.

Time Stress. Important organizational decisions are often made under tight time constraints, whether of the split-second variety of the options trader or of the sort that requires a strategy document by Monday instead of a month from now. In addition to placing decision makers under stress, with the risk of exhaustion and loss of vigilance, time constraints put a premium on decision strategies that do not require extensive deliberation.

Action–Feedback Loops. Decisions in organizations are often taken in the spirit of trying some approach to see how it works. It is thus important to note that subsequent feedback may be only loosely coupled to the original action; that it may be delayed, degraded, or fraudulent; that personnel and priorities may have changed before clear feedback is available; and that other players reconstruct reality to garner credit for successes and dodge blame for failures.

High Stakes. The consequences of decisions made in organizations are frequently of a scope well beyond what most of us do in our private lives. To some people this is invigorating, to others paralyzing, but it is worth noting the obvious: People may well behave differently when real lives and real fortunes are on the line than they do in low-stakes laboratory experiments.

Multiple Players, Multiple Agendas.   As illustrated in the second scenario described earlier, organizational decisions are almost invariably multiperson processes. This may on occasion represent a benign decomposition of the problem, with some players generating information on one option, some on another, and so on. Much more commonly, the players act partially in concert with one another, partly in opposition, and partly in ignorance of one another's activities. Organizational goals and procedures intended to control and integrate this fractionation and conflict are notoriously imperfect instruments for doing so.

We have dwelled on these two examples and the strains they make on conventional decision theory to highlight the challenges taken up by the newer theoretical formulations, image theory in particular. We now turn to an assessment of how well these are meeting the challenges, and how their reach could be further extended.

PART 2: RESPONDING TO THE CHALLENGES

We have traced a broadly familiar litany of issues that conventional decision theory addresses only with difficulty or not at all. To what extent does image theory, either alone or in conjunction with other nontraditional theory, fill the gaps? We argue here for a mixed answer: Even though image theory's contributions to date have been substantial, its potential contributions are much greater.

The majority of image theory research to date has concerned a relatively peripheral cluster of concerns, those associated with the screening of options into a short list of serious candidates. Such screening processes are certainly of real interest, but they do not bear on the central theoretical contrasts with conventional theory. The latter is simply silent on the matter: Options are generally treated as givens or, in some models, as the results of potentially costly searches. Image theory does, of course, make specific predictions as to how screening will proceed—that it will be done by elimination by aspects (EBA) or negative lexicographic filters, ignoring differences on any above-threshold dimension, and that information used in screening will not be reused in later choice. Much evidence consistent with such mechanisms has been generated (see Beach, 1993, for a review). However, such mechanisms, if empirically established, easily could be appropriated by conventional decision theory as a front end—an exogenous, predecision process independent of the central theoretical core.

Image Theory, in our view, offers a far more thoroughgoing challenge to conventional thinking in its central concepts: the images. The core of image theory is a richly interconnected network embedding acts, actions, plans, projections of future outcome streams and other organized sequences of actions with purposes, objectives, principles and values. It is thus highly contextualized. It first addresses the decision maker's understanding of the world, the actions he or she might take, their relationships to one another and to later consequences, and the linkages between these consequences and the decision maker's value structure. For expository and pedagogical reasons this network has generally been presented in terms of the three somewhat distinct images, noted earlier: the *value image,* clustered around principles and purposes, the *strategic image* clustered around actions and their organization, and the *trajectory image,* clustered around the intersection of action and purpose. But the central thrust is to confront head on the fact that actions, purposes, and goals are often richly interconnected. It is perhaps the empirical exception rather than the rule that the three elements are linked in the minimal sense captured in a traditional decision tree. More commonly, we postulate that actions, goals, and purposes are embedded in a rich network of connections built up over time in the mind of the decision maker. The challenge now is to elucidate the organizing principles of this network.

Once again, a comparison with conventional ideas (traditional decision theory; TDT) will help clarify what image theory suggests. At the most basic level the two approaches make different partitions of two crucial matters: What is considered internal, what external to the individual, what is specific to the focal decision, and what is relatively constant and thus relevant to a stream of decisions. TDT treats the decision maker as somehow owning an abstract decision mechanism, resembling an unlabeled decision tree, and the computational skills to analyze it. In making a specific decision, this general-purpose machine is first loaded with content relevant to the decision (option names, values, a selection rule, etc.); then it performs the computations needed to select an action. The output of this process is then back-translated or implemented as a real action in the real world. The content-free, abstract decision engine is internal and changes slowly, as do personal values and preferences. (These may be externally generated, as in agency or organizational decisions.) Action options, contingencies, and consequences are external to the individual.

In contrast, image theory treats the decision maker as owning a context-specific network, slowly assembled over time, connecting values, preferences, goals, actions, plans, and strategies. In making a specific decision, this network is activated by either external stimuli (e.g., loss of status quo, presentation of a new possibility) or internal stimuli (e.g., discrepancy between actual and anticipated outcomes). This activation leads to a search for the closest feasible (most compatible) path through the net, and a new action choice.

Even this oversimplified contrast leads directly to a number of potentially testable empirical propositions.

Typical Number of Options Considered by a Competent Decision Maker. TDT would predict many, image theory few. (Note that the proposition concerns competent decision makers. A narrow search for options could be read as evidence of either an image theory process or an incompetent TDT process. A narrow search with good long-run effectiveness would thus be the crucial evidence.)

Extent of Deliberation, Speed of Decision. TDT would imply relatively extensive deliberation, because large amounts of information need to be processed. IT predicts much less processing, since most of the relevant considerations in matching action to purpose have been previously embedded in the network connections. (Again, the research should address competent performance: Fast, poor decisions would lend support to neither position.)

Cross-Context Transferability of Decision Skills. TDT predicts that individuals capable of skilled decision making in one context are likely to excel similarly in different contexts: They own and operate excellent decision engines. Image theory predicts much less transfer, because the network is specific to a particular context—a given disease group for a physician, a given investment category for a stockbroker.

Reliance on Potentially Flawed Cognitive Processes. Given the enormous recent interest in cognitive biases, illusions, fallacies and the like, it is worth noting that TDT appears heavily reliant on such inference-like processes, whereas image theory is not. The latter may thus offer a more plausible explanation of good performance in real contexts than does TDT.

Implementation Concerns. TDT yields action choice only at the highly abstract, model level, and thus faces potential difficulties in translating this abstract recommendation into action on the ground. Image theory, in contrast, is concerned throughout with recognizable, concrete actions and consequences, so problems of back-translation do not arise as often.

Locus of Subject-Matter Expertise. In TDT, subject-matter expertise is essentially offline, and distinct from decision making expertise. Indeed, the two types of expertise may well reside in different heads, with the decision maker acquiring subject-matter information from advisers or local experts as the need arises. In image theory, subject-matter expertise is central to the decision apparatus itself. It is difficult to imagine an image theory decision maker delegating action selection to another, even to a high priced decision analyst!

Linkage to Central Values and Principles. In TDT, action is linked to the decision maker's central values only indirectly by means of an exogenous process by which values are made manifest as preferences over outcomes. In principle, as long as the decision maker can express preferences at the level of specific outcomes, issues of central, higher-level values need not arise. In contrast, image theory explicitly links these higher-level values into the lower-level objectives, goals, and preferences, opening the possibility for a treatment of values endogenous to the decision process itself.

Articulability of Decision Process and Results. Interestingly, either a TDT or an image theory mode of arriving at a choice can be articulated or defended, although the terms of doing so differ from one to the other. A TDT explanation stresses the comprehensiveness of the analysis, the conformity with canons of rationality, the extent of computations and sensitivity analyses, and the care with which optimal action was selected. An image theory explanation places more stress on the links: between the action chosen and other actions contemplated or already in process and between the action chosen and important goals, values, and objectives.

Selection of Research Subjects and Tasks. TDT, with its implicit assumption of the generic central process, is free to use essentially any convenient subjects and tasks. College students playing low-stakes gambles are a perfectly reasonable and cost-effective choice. Image theory, in contrast, requires tasks and subjects for whom there has been reasonable opportunity to develop the postulated issue-specific network interconnections. This, of course, does not exclude student subjects: students do in fact choose apartments, friends, and areas of study, and may well have developed something more than rudimentary connections among the elements involved. They probably do not, however, routinely gamble with million-dollar stakes at known odds. Their performance in such tasks will thus tell us little of interest to image theory.

As these examples suggest, there is substantial empirical content to the contrast we are drawing between TDT and image theory concepts. (We would claim, indeed, that substantial empirical support favors the image theory over the TDT predictions in many of these issues, but our purpose here is theoretical rather than empirical comparison between the two.) A full development of image theory will, however, require us to take up several more central issues: Just how interconnected and organized is the hypothesized network of values, strategies, and goals in the mind of the competent decision maker? How is this network built up over time? Can alternative network structures yield equivalent performance in terms of successful choices? How broad are subject-matter domains? What elements do they include? Is the three-way division proposed in current versions of image theory empirically supported, or is it merely an expository convenience?

This line of inquiry is not much illuminated by research that takes, say, a value image and reduces it to a simple list. The guiding metaphor, after all, is that of the image. An image of a person's face is more than the items comprising it: an ear, a nose, a mouth, and an eye. To be an image, the elements must be organized, orderly, and interconnected. These organizational issues have been central to psychology at least since Bartlett's work (1932) on the importance of active organization in schemas. In the decision making context these issues have surfaced more recently in several of what we earlier referred to as heretical models. Margolis (1987), for example, built his theory around the role of patterns in cognition and thinking. Pennington and Hastie (1988, 1986) explored the role of narratives—stories and explanations—in organizing complex bodies of information, as in jury decisions. Jungermann (1985, and this volume) made extensive use of scenarios (stories about the future) as organizing devices in decision making, and Lipshitz (1989) found a similar role for argumentation. The issue of network content and organization has, however, been largely neglected in image theory research itself, except for the broad three-image assertion (see Rediker, Mitchell, Beach & Beard, 1993, though, for a step toward exploring the role of more complex cognitive structures in an image theory tradition). One might hope that future research in image theory will be able to capitalize on these various research leads as it builds toward a more complete and satisfactory treatment of these issues of network scope, content, and organization.

There is even some modest help in recent theorizing for the issue of how a given individual comes to have a decision-specific network: the learning issue. Klein (1989) explored situations in which connections between context, goals, and action are so thoroughly learned that skilled, flexible performance is possible with virtually no reflection. (Klein labeled his ideas as *recognition-primed decision making*, rightly emphasizing the perception-like speed with which action is matched to the recognition of a familiar situation. What is less clear is the appropriateness of the decision making label: Most of his examples depict skilled performance in well learned contexts, not deliberate choice in the face of uncertainty.) Noble (1989), similarly, focused on the decision maker's assessment of the requirements of the situation and his or her search for past experience in selecting an appropriate response. Finally, we (Connolly, 1982; Connolly & Wagner, 1988) emphasized the role of incremental, exploratory action (decision cycles) in building up an understanding of action interlocks and consequences and of relevant value and preference connections.

There is, then, no shortage of conceptual and empirical leads that might be pursued toward building a richer core for image theory. As this book attests, image theory has stimulated and organized a considerable body of interesting research already. It offers, in my reading, a framework for further, and perhaps more profound, future work. It brings back to the center of decision research its fundamental issues: How are action, knowledge, and purpose to be coherently organized? What networks of cohesion do competent decision makers actually bring to bear on the process, and how do they acquire these networks? Conventional decision theory offers one view, a work of great beauty and power, but under increasing attack for both descriptive and prescriptive shortcomings. Image theory, in its broader reading, can be seen as offering another view.

I do not wish to leave the reader thinking that the interpretation I propose for image theory is an exercise in decisional metaphysics. The issues I attempt to formulate are concrete, low level, and important. Take the issue of action, for example. In Scenario 1, is the initial choice one of deciding which muscle group to contract, which step to take, which walk to initiate, or which exercise policy to adopt? What connections does the decision maker consider between these actions and other actions facilitated (a saved cab fare) or foregone (a visit to a friend that afternoon)? Actions have networks of implication both vertical (as the step, repeated, constitutes the walk) and horizontal (this walk precluding another). Which, of the many possible connections did the decision maker actually consider?

Similarly, specific, concrete problems arise in thinking about the actor's values, preferences, and tradeoffs. There is, after all, something more to a value structure than a simple listing: People who hold what we see as incompatible values (e.g., pacifism and support for increased defense spending) seem to us inconsistent. We expect values to cluster, or we ask for explanations when they do not. Again, we think of both vertical consistency (views of war in general and of this war in particular) and horizontal consistency (pacifism and defense spending). We expect, both for ourselves and others, that knowing some key values will allow us to infer or construct a range of other values because values, like actions, are structured: They form networks of interconnections. The challenge we pose here for image theory is to elucidate these clusterings and interconnections within the minds of particular decision makers. It seems unlikely that the networks we discover will invariably follow the chaste minimalism specified by SEU theory.

Image theory, though a recent formulation, has succeeded in framing interesting new work and has the potential to be the framework for much more. To read over the chapters in this book is to see a cup a long way from empty. Perhaps this chapter will help to suggest ways in which it might be both filled and expanded.

REFERENCES

Bartlett, F. C. (1932). *Remembering: A study in experimental and social psychology*. Cambridge: Cambridge University Press.

Beach. L. R. (1993). Broadening the definition of decision making: The role of prechoice screening of options. *Psychological Science, 4*, 215–220.

Connolly, T. (1975). Communication nets and uncertainty in R&D planning. *IEEE Transactions on Engineering Management, EM-22*, 50–54.

Connolly, T. (1980). Uncertainty, action and competence: Some alternatives to omniscience in complex problem-solving. In S. Fiddle (Ed.), *Uncertainty: Social and behavioral dimensions* (pp. 69–91). New York: Praeger.

Connolly, T. (1982). On taking action seriously. In G. R. Ungson & D. N. Braunstein (Eds.), *Decision making: An interdisciplinary inquiry* (pp. 42–47). Boston: Kent.

Connolly, T. & Wagner, W. G. (1988). Decision cycles. In R. L. Cardy, S. M. Puffer, & M. M. Newman (Eds.), *Advances in information processing in organizations* (Vol. 3, (pp. 183–205). Greenwich, CT: JAI Press.

Harrison, E. F. (1975). *The managerial decision making process*. Boston: Houghton Mifflin.

Jungermann, H. (1985). Inferential processes in the construction of scenarios. *Journal of Forecasting, 4*, 321–327.

Klein, G. A. (1989). Recognition-primed decisions. In W. B. Rouse (Ed.), *Advances in man-machine systems research* (Vol. 5, pp. 47–92). Greenwich, CT: JAI Press.

Lipshitz, R. (1989). Decision making as argument driven action. Boston: Boston University Center for Applied Social Science.

March, J. G. (1978). Bounded rationality, ambiguity, and the engineering of choice. *Bell Journal of Economics, 9*, 587–608.

Margolis, H. (1987). *Patterns, thinking and cognition*. Chicago: University of Chicago Press.

Noble, D. (1989). *Application of a theory of cognition to situation assessment*. Vienna, VA: Engineering Research Associates.

Orasanu, J., & Connolly, T. (1993). The reinvention of decision making. In G. A. Klein, J. Orasanu, R. Calderwood, & C. E. Zsambok (Eds.), *Decision making in action: Models and methods* (pp. 3–20). Norwood, NJ: Ablex.

Pennington, N., & Hastie, R. (1986). Evidence evaluation in complex decision making. *Journal of Personality and Social Psychology, 51*, 242–258.

Pennington, N., & Hastie, R. (1988). Explanation-based decision making: Effects of memory structure on judgment. *Journal of Experimental Psychology: Learning, Memory and Cognition, 14*, 521–533.

Redicker, K. J., Mitchell, T. R., Beach, L. R., & Beard, D. W. (1993), The effects of strong belief structures on information-processing evaluations and choice. *Journal of Behavioral Decision Making, 6*, 113–132.

Tversky, A., & Kahneman, D. (1981). The framing of decisions and the psychology of choice. *Science, 211*, 453–458.

Author Index

A

Abelson, M. A., 86, *89*
Aldag, R. J., 36, *47*
Allais, M., 22, *30*
American Institute of Certified
      Public Accountants,
      103, 106, 107, *116*
Arachtingi, B. M., 51, *62*
Arnold, H. J., 35, *46*
Arthur Anderson & Co., 102, *116*
Asare, S., 102, 104, 111, *116*
Ash, R. A., 36, *47*
Ashmos, D., 185, 189, *193*
Ashton, A. H., 91, *99*, 101, *116*
Ashton, R., 101, *116*

B

Baker, D. D, 35, *46*
Barclay, D. W., 175, 176, *179*, *180*
Barnard, C. I., 73, *89*
Bartlett, F. C., 206, *208*
Bartol, K. M., 51, *62*
Beach, L. R., 2, 3, 8, 11, 12, 13, 14,
      16, 17, 18, *19*, 23, 28, *30*,
      40, 41, 45, *46*, 51, *62*, 66,
      71, 74, 76, 79, 81, *89*, 91,
      96, 97, *99*, 115, *116*, 118,
      119, 120, *131*, 134, *142*,
      144, 148, 149, *153*, 166,
      179, 181, 183, 184, 188,
      189, *193*, 202, *208*

Beard, D. W., 11, 13 ,16, *20*,
      120, *131*
Behn, R. D., 26, *30*
Bell, D. E., 23, *30*
Belous, R. S., 81, *89*
Bentham, J., 22, *30*
Berger, I. E., 170, 173, *179*
Bettman, J. R., 16, *20*, 28, *31*
Betz, N. E., 51, *62*
Beyer, J. M., 117, 118, *131*
Bissell, B. L., 67, *71*
Bolles, R. N., 57, *62*
Bretz, R. D., Jr., 36, *47*
Bridges, W., 57, 58, *62*
Broeding, L., 63, *71*
Brooks, L., 51, *62*
Brown, D., 51, *62*
Brown, F., 96, *99*
Brumfield, C., 102, *116*

C

Caldwell, D. F., 33, *47*, 129, *131*
Campbell, D. P., 57, *62*
Cappelli, P., 82, *89*
Carroll, S. I., 65, *71*
Chaiken, S., 188, *194*
Chanowitz, B., 188, *193*
Chatman, J., 128, 129, *131*
Christensen-Szalanski, J. J. J., 8, 9,
      18, *19*
Cohen, M. D., 24, *30*

209

Colarelli, S. M., 57, *62*
Colella, A., 34, *47*
Connolly, T., 35, *47*, 140, *142*, 200, 207, *208*
Cooke, R. A., 121, *131*
Cooper, W. H., 140, *142*
Coopers & Lybrand, 102, *116*
Corbin, R. M., 170, 173, *179*
Cornwell, T. B., 170, 173, *180*
Crosby, L. A., 178, *180*
Cyert, R. M., 24, *30*

D

Dalton, D. R., 86, *89*
Dansereau, F., Jr., 64, *71*
Davis, J. H., 3, *19*
De Bruyn, E. E. J., 147, *154*
DeCotiis, T. A., 64, *71*
Deloitte & Touche, 102, *116*
Dennis, A. R., 139, *142*
Dery, D., 184, *193*
Donaldson, G., 25, *30*
Doud, E. Jr., 63, *71*
Douglas, C. A., 183, *195*
Dreher, G. F., 36, *47*
Dubrovski, V., 140, *142*
Duchon, D., 185, 189, *193*
Dunegan, K. J., 184, 185, 187, 189, *193*

E

Ebreo, A., 178, *180*
Edwards, W., 22, 24, *30*
Einhorn, H. J., 148, *154*
Ellen, P. S., 170, 173, *180*
Elliot, R., 102, *116*
Ellsberg, D., 22, *30*
Ernst & Young, 102, *116*

F

Fagley, N. S., 183, *194*
Falk, R. F., 175, 176, *180*
Felix, W. L., 91, 92, 94, 95, 99, 99, 102, *116*
Festinger, L., 170, *180*
Fine, S., 178, *180*
Fiske, S. T., 188, *194*
Fornell, C., 176, *180*
Frayne, C., 60, *62*
Fredrickson, J. R., 91, *99*
Fry, R. E., 64, *71*

G

Galanter, E., 5, *20*
Gallupe, R. B., 140, *142*
George, J. F., 139, *142*
Gill, J. D., 178, *180*
Glueck, W. F., 37, *47*
Goodwin, V. L., 188, *195*
Gore, W. J., 24, *30*
Graen, G., 64, 65, *71*
Grasmick, H. G., 182, *194*
Green, P. E., 174, *180*
Greenhaus, J. H., 50, *62*
Grewal, D., 182, *194*
Griffeth, R. W., 73, 74, 75, 80, 81, 82, *89*
Gutek, B. A., 128, *131*

H

Hachiya, D., 81, *89*
Hackenbrack, K., 104, 111, *116*
Hair, J. F., Jr., 172, *180*
Hand, H., 73, *90*
Hanges, P. J., 188, *194*
Hansen, J. C., 57, *62*
Harren, V. A., 51, 57, *62*

Harrison, E. F., 199, *208*
Hartman, K., 57, *62*
Hastie, R., 148, *154*, 206, *208*
Heller, K. Z., 65, *72*
Herriot, P., 37, *47*
Hetrick, C. T., 183, *195*
Higgins, C., 175, *179*
Hill, K. D., 63, *71*
Hill, R. E., 37, *47*
Hock, S., 102, *116*
Hogarth, R. M., 148, *154*, 184, *194*
Holland, J. L., 50, *62*
Hom, P. W., 73, 74, 75, 80, 81,
    82, *89*
Hulin, C. L., 73, 81, *89*
Huffman, M. D., 18, *19*
Humphreys, P., 2, *19*
Huss, H., 103, *116*

I

Imundo, L. V., 64, *71*
Inskeep, G. C., 65, *72*
Isenberg, D. J., 25, 26, *30*

J

Jacobs, F., 103, *116*
Jacobson, P., 102, *116*
Janis, I. L., 24, *30*
Jerdee, T. H., 65, *71*
Jessup, L. M., 139, *142*
Johnson, E. J., 16, *20*, 28, *31*
Johnson, M. D., 158, *164*
Jonas, H. S., III, 64, *71*
Jungermann, H., 59, *62*, 148, 149,
    154, 206, *208*
Jurgenson, C. E., 45, *47*

K

Kahn, R. L., 64, *71*
Kahneman, D., 1, *20*, 22, 23, *30*,
    31, 96, *99*, 182, 183, *194*,
    199, *208*
Katz, D., 64, *71*
Keisler, S., 140, *142*
Kelley, H. H., 64, *71*
Keon, T. L., 34, 35, *47*
Keren, G. B., 27, 28, 30, *31*
Kernan, M. C., 188, *194*
Kerr, S., 63, *71*
Kida, T., 28, *31*
King, D. C., 67, *71*
Kinney, W. R., 99, *99*
Kinsey, K. A., 182, *194*
Klein, G., 2, *19*, 146, *154*, 188,
    194, 206, *208*
Knechel, R., 102, 104, 111, *116*
KPMG Peat Marwick, 102, *116*
Krackhardt, D. M., 86, *89*
Krishnamurthi, L., 175, *180*

L

Langer, E., 188, *194*
Latack, J. C., 34, 35, 36, *47*
Lee, T. W., 74, 75, 76, 77, 78, 80,
    81, *89*, *90*
Levin, I. P., 182, *194*
Lichtenberg, J. W., 51, *62*
Lichtenstein, S., 28, *31*
Lindblom, C. E., 24, *30*
Lipschitz, R., 21, *30*, 206, *208*
Lohmoeller, J. B., 175, *180*
Loomis, G., 23, *31*
Lopes, L. L., 27, *31*, 183, *195*
Lord, R. G., 188, *194*
Lorsch, J. W., 25, *30*
Lundell, J., 12, 16, *19*, 41, *47*,
    118, 120, *131*

M

Machina, M. J., 23, *31*
Maher, K. J., 188, *194*
Maheswaran, D., 188, *194*
Mahoney, T. A., 65, *71*
Mann, F. C., 64, 65, *71*
Mann, L., 24, *30*
March, J. G., 24, *30*, *31*, 73, 75, 76, 81, *90*, 200, *208*
Margolis, H., 206, *208*
Marmorstein, H., 182, *194*
Matthews, C. H., 185, *194*
Mayer, R. C., 183, *195*
McAllister D., 17, *19*
McNeil, B., 182, *194*
McQuire, T. W., 140, *142*
Meindl, J. R., 188, *195*
Michela, J. L., 64, *71*
Miller, E., 63, *71*
Miller, G. A., 5, *20*
Miller, N. B., 175, 176, *180*
Miller, P. M., 183, *194*
Minami, T., 64, *71*
Minsky, M., 29, *31*
Mitchell, T. R., 2, 3, 8, 11, 12, 13, 16, 18, *20*, 25, *31*, *47*, 51, *62*, 74, 76, 77, 78, 80, 89, *90*, 96, *99*, 118, 120, *131*, 144, *154*, 181, 183, 184, 188, 189, *193*
Mintzberg, H., 24, *31*
Mobley, W. H., 73, 74, 75, 76, 80, 83, *90*
Morgenstern, O., 22, *31*
Morley, D. D., 66, *72*, 118, 120, 129, *132*
Mowday, R. T., 73, 81, 86, *90*
Mudd, S., 119, *131*
Mueller, C. W., 73, *90*

N

Nash, L. L., 118, *131*
Nelson, K. A., 170, 171, 172, 176, *180*
Neuberg, S. L., 188, *194*
Newton, L. A., 64, *72*
Noble, D., 207, *208*
Nunamaker, J. F., 139, *142*
Nutter, J. B., 175, *180*

O

O' Reilly, C. A., III, 33, *47*, 128, 129, *131*, 184, *194*
Okell, B., 102, *116*
Olsen, J. P., 24, *30*
Onachilla, V. J., 65, *72*
Orasanu, J., 201, *208*
Osborn, A. F., 133, 136, *142*
Osborn, D. P., 41, *47*

P

Pablo, A. L., 183, *195*
Paluchowski, T. F., 12, 13, *20*
Pany, K., 101, *116*
Paquette, L., 28, *31*
Pauker, S., 182, *194*
Payne, J. W., 1, 16, *20*, 28, *31*, 184, *194*
Peeters, G., 115, *116*
Peters, L. H., 81, 88, *90*
Peters, T. J., 25, *31*
Pennington, N., 148, *154*, 206, *208*
Pfeffer, J., 88, *90*
Pfeifer, J. E., 182, *194*
Phillips, L. D., 26, *31*
Pickering, J., 102, *116*
Pijnenburg, H. M., 147, *154*
Pitz, G. F., 51, 57, *62*

Pleit-Kupier, A., 28, *31*
Porac, J. F., 188, *195*
Potter, R. E., 12, 13, 14, 15, 16,
    20, 41, *47*, 149, *154*
Power, D. J., 36, *47*
Pratt, J. W., 2, *20*, 22, *31*
Pribram, K. H., 5, *20*
Price, J. L., 73, *90*
Puto, C. P., 158, *164*

Q

Quinn, R. P., 128, *131*

R

Raiffa, H., 14, 16, *20*, 158, *164*
Rediker, K. J., 11, 13, 16, *20*, 118,
    120, *131*, 206, *208*
Rest, J. R., 172, *180*
Richards, G. L., 65, *72*
Rip, P. D., 175, *180*
Rokeach, M., 169, 173, *180*
The Roper Organization, 165, *180*
Rosseau, D. M., 121, *131*
Rothwell, C., 37, *47*
Routhieaux, R. L., 140, *142*
Roznowski, M., 82, *89*
Rynes, S. L., 34, *47*

S

Samuelson, W., 97, *99*
Sathe, V., 118, *131*
Savage, L., 26, *31*
Scarpello, V., 65, 67, *72*
Schandl, C. W., 92, *99*
Schein, E. H., 117, *131*
Schneider, B., 117, *131*
Schneider, S. K., 140, *142*
Schneider, S. L., 183, *195*

Schoorman, F. D., 183, *195*
Schwab, D. P., 34, *47*
Schwepker, C. H., Jr., 170, 173,
    180
Seifert, M., 182, *195*
Sellaro, C. L., 75, *89*
Selznick, P., 25, *31*
Shafer, G., 26, 27, *31*
Shaffer, M., 51, *62*
Shore, L. M., 64, *72*
Sherer, P. D., 82, *89*
Sheridan, J. E., 81, *90*
Shockley-Zalabak, P., 66, *72*, 118,
    120, 129, *132*
Siegel, J., 140, *142*
Silver, W. S., 184, *195*
Simon, H. A., 1, *20*, 24, *31*, 73, 75,
    76, 81, 85, *90*
Sitkin, S. B., 183, *195*
Slovic, P., 27, *31*
Smith, B., 12, 16, *19*, 41, *47*, 118,
    120, *131*
Smith, J. F., 18, *20*
Smith, K. W., 182, *194*
Soelberg, P. O., 34, 36, *47*
Solem, A. R., 65, *72*
Sox, H., 182, *194*
Srinivasan, V., 174, *180*
Srivastva, S., 64, *71*
Staines, G. L., 128, *131*
Staw, B. M., 97, *99*
Steers, R. M., 73, *90*
Stisser, P., 165, *180*
Strom, E., 11, 12, 16, *19*, 41, *47*,
    115, *116*
Stubbart, C., 188, *195*
Stumpf, S. A., 57, *62*
Sugden, R., 23, *31*
Summers, T. P., 64, *71*
Super, D. E., 35, *47*, 50, 52, *62*
Sutton, C. D., 64, *72*
Svenson, O., 2, *19*, *20*, 43, *47*

T

Takemura, K., 183, *195*
Taylor, J. R., 178, *180*
Taylor, M. S., 50, *62*
Telberg, R., 103, *116*
Thompson, R., 175, *179*
Thorngate, W., 28, *31*
Thornton, G. C., III, 64, *72*
Thüring (Thuering), M. J., 59, *62*, 148, 149, *154*
Tom, V. R., 34, 35, 36, *47*
Tudor, W. D., 86, *89*
Tversky, A., 1, *20*, 22, 23, *30*, *31*, 96, *99*, 182, 183, *194*, 199, *208*

V

Valacich, J. S., 139, *142*
van Zee, E. H., 2, 12, 13, *19*, *20*, 41, *47*, 118, *132*
Vandenberg, R. J., 65, 66, *72*
Vari, A., 2, *19*
Vaughn, E., 182, *195*
Vaupel, J.W., 26, *30*
Vines, C. V., 35, *47*
Vining, J., 178, *180*
Vlek, C., 28, *30*
Vogel, D. R., 139, *142*
von Neuman, J., 22, *31*
Vroom, V. H., 34, *47*

W

Wagenaar, W. A., 27, 28, *30*, *31*
Wagner, W. G., 207, *208*
Wallace, W., 105, *116*
Waller, W. S., 18, *20*, 91, 92, 94, 95, *99*
Wanous, J. P., 34, 35, *47*
Warriner, G. K., 173, *180*

Waterman, R. H., 88, *90*
Watts, R., 101, *116*
Weatherly, K. A., 122, *132*
Weick, K. E., 24, *31*
Whittington, R., 101, *116*
Winter, S. J., 128, *131*
Wittink, D. R., 175, *180*
Wright, P., 175, *180*
Wofford, J. C., 188, *195*
Woodman, R. W., 64, *72*

Z

Zeckhauser, R., 97, *99*
Zimmerman, J., 101, *116*

Subject Index

A

Adoption decisions
  goals, 4
  plans, 4
Acceptance analysis, 106
Audit image
  strategic, 93
  trajectory, 93
  value, 93
Automatic decision making, 144

C

Choice, 6, 17–18
Classical decision theory, 21–24, 203
Cognitive modes, 188
Compatibility test, 7, 184
Consumer choice, 158
Control, 26–28
Culture, 118

D

Decision paths, 76–80
Decision tree, 198

E

Error decision, 94
Expectancy Theory, 34
Expected Utility, 1, 9, 197

F

Forecasts, 5, 146, 152
Framing, 6, 55, 168, 182
Generalized Decision Process
    Model (GDP), 36
Group decision making, 134
Group Support Systems (GSS),
    138–141

I

Idea screening, 136
Images
    strategic, 5, 54, 170, 173
    trajectory, 5, 53, 169, 173
    value, 5, 52, 168, 172
Image theory
    informal, 3
    formal, 5
Implementation, 59, 97
Intuitive decision making, 144

M

Marketing communications,
    155, 159
Marketing strategy, 155, 162
Mental models, 148

O

Organizational Culture Survey
    (OCS), 121

P

Plans, 5, 54, 149
Policy, 4, 146
Practice development, 105
Principles, 3
Problem space, 184
Profitability test, 8
Progress decisions, 6

R

Recognition-Primed Decision
    Making (RPD), 206

S

Satisfaction
    job, 68, 128
    organizational, 68
Scenarios, 148
Screening, 6, 11–17, 38–40
Scripted behavior, 81
Shocks to the system, 76, 82
Strategic plan, 119

T

Tactics, 5
Traditional decision theory,
    21–24, 203
Turnover, 74, 85

U

Unfolding model, 74, 76

V

Violations, 11
Vision, 119
Vocational choice, 35